Creativity in the Primary Curriculum

Are you striving to establish a more creative and imaginative classroom? Are you interested in:

- the generosity of creativity;
- creative conjecture;
- being an advocate for creativity;
- welcoming the unexpected;
- the unpredictable and the unconventional;
- taking risks;
- stimulating new or original thinking which is of value?

If so, this completely updated new edition of a classic text will show you how to achieve these ideals.

The book is written in a clear and practical way by leading researchers and practitioners, offering help and advice on the planning and implementation of effective creative teaching and learning, and providing examples of best practice through a rigorous theoretical rationale.

A hallmark of the book is its exploration of creativity through curriculum subjects. It builds on this in its first and last chapters by addressing key cross-curricular themes that thread their way through the book. Throughout there is an emphasis on critical and reflective practice.

New to this edition is:

- the addition of three entirely new chapters on drama, music and geography;
- an update of the introduction to account for advances in creativity research, policy and practice;
- a new final chapter identifying cross-curricular themes;
- greater attention to international dimensions and examples.

In this second edition the authors are drawn from six universities which between them produce some of the best education research internationally, and some of the best teacher education. The authors also come from leading national and international organisations such as the National Gallery in London and the Geographical Association.

Creativity in the Primary Curriculum is a core text for both training and practising primary teachers who wish to maintain high standards when approaching their teaching.

Russell Jones is Senior Lecturer in Childhood Studies, Manchester Metropolitan University.

Dominic Wyse is Professor of Early Childhood and Primary Education, Institute of Education, University of London.

Creativity in the Primary Curriculum

Second edition

Edited by Russell Jones and Dominic Wyse

Routledge
Taylor & Francis Group

LONDON AND NEW YORK

This edition published in 2013
by Routledge
2 Park Square, Milton Park, Abingdon, Oxon OX14 4RN

Simultaneously published in the USA and Canada
by Routledge
711 Third Avenue, New York, NY 10017

Routledge is an imprint of the Taylor & Francis Group, an informa business

First published by David Fulton Publishers 2005

British Library Cataloguing in Publication Data
A catalogue record for this book is available from the British Library

Library of Congress Cataloging in Publication Data
    Creativity in the primary curriculum / edited by Russell Jones and
    Dominic Wyse. -- 2nd ed.
    p. cm.
    1. Creative ability--Study and teaching (Primary) 2. Education,
    Elementary – Activity programs. I. Jones, Russell. II. Wyse, Dominic,
    1964-
    BF408.C7549 2013
    372'.0118--dc23
    2012027499

ISBN: 978-0-415-67546-8 (hbk)
ISBN: 978-0-415-67547-5 (pbk)
ISBN: 978-0-203-80946-4 (ebk)

Typeset in Bembo
by Fakenham Prepress Solutions, Fakenham NR21 8NN

MIX
Paper from
responsible sources
FSC
www.fsc.org FSC® C004839

Printed and bound in Great Britain by
TJ International Ltd, Padstow, Cornwall

Russell would like to dedicate this book to Barrie and Hazel.

Dominic would also like to dedicate it to Walter and Joan Binns.

Contents

Contributors   ix
Acknowledgements   xi

1 **Introduction**   1

   Russell Jones and Dominic Wyse

2 **English**   17

   Russell Jones and Dominic Wyse

3 **Mathematics**   33

   Mamta Naik

4 **Science**   50

   Paul Warwick and Lyn Dawes

5 **Design and Technology**   66

   David Spendlove and Alan Cross

6 **Drama**   83

   Teresa Cremin and Roger McDonald

7 **Geography**   98

   David Lambert and Paula Owens

8 **History**   116

   Paul Bowen

9 Music 130

Pam Burnard and James Biddulph

10 The Visual Arts 149

Alison Mawle

11 Creativity Across the Curriculum 162

Russell Jones and Dominic Wyse

Index 166

Contributors

Natalie Bailey is a classroom teacher at Southfields Primary School in Peterborough.

Paul Bowen is a Senior Lecturer in Primary Education and History in the Faculty of Education at Manchester Metropolitan University.

James Biddulph is Headteacher at Avanti Court Primary School, Redbridge, following successful school leadership as a Deputy in east London and Advanced Skills teacher in Newham.

Pam Burnard is a Reader at the Faculty of Education, University of Cambridge, where she coordinates Masters in Arts, Creativity, Culture and Educational Research.

Teresa Cremin is Professor of Education (Literacy) at the Open University, Fellow of the English Association and Trustee of UKLA, BookTrust and the Poetry Archive.

Alan Cross is a Senior Fellow at the University of Manchester.

Lyn Dawes is a Lecturer in Science and Education at the University of Northampton.

Deborah Gardner is Mathematics Subject Leader and class teacher, Warley Road Primary School, Halifax.

Russell Jones is a Senior Lecturer in Education and Childhood Studies in the Faculty of Education at Manchester Metropolitan University.

David Lambert is a Professor at the Institute of Education (IOE), University of London. He was also Chief Executive of the Geographical Association from 2002 to 2012.

Alison Mawle is Head of Schools, The National Gallery, London.

Roger McDonald is Deputy Headteacher at Saxon Way Primary School and an Associate Tutor, Canterbury Christ Church University.

Paula Owens is an independent consultant and Curriculum Development Leader, Geographical Association.

Mamta Naik is a Senior Lecturer in the Faculty of Education, Manchester Metropolitan University.

Catherine Rizzo is a classroom teacher at Southfields Primary School in Peterborough.

David Spendlove is Director of Secondary PGCE at the University of Manchester.

Paul Warwick is a Lecturer in Science and Education, University of Cambridge.

Dominic Wyse is Professor of Early Childhood and Primary Education at the Institute of Education (IOE), University of London.

Acknowledgements

Dominic and I would like to thank Bruce Roberts, Commissioning Editor at Routledge, alongside Hamish Baxter and Helen Marsden for their support in the production of this book.

David Lambert and Paula Owens wish to thank teachers Jane Mulligan, Jonathan Kersey, Sarah Lewis and Dr Emma Mawdsley for the collaborative work with the Geographical Association that helped to illustrate this chapter.

Paul Warwick and Lyn Dawes are enormously indebted to Catherine Rizzo and Natalie Bailey, teachers at Southfields Primary School in Peterborough. Their work has been a genuine inspiration for us in the writing of this chapter. For information about the 'Thinking Together' project, which looks at ways of encouraging children to engage in exploratory talk, go to: http://thinkingto gether.educ.cam.ac.uk/.

Mamta Naik would like to thank Frank Eade and Shirley Bush for their invaluable advice. Thanks also to Year 5 at Warley Road Primary School in Halifax and your inspirational teacher, Deborah Gardner.

Paul Bowen offers thanks to Stephanie Cooper, Alsager Highfield Community Primary School (Cheshire), Seabridge Primary School (Staffs) St Luke's CE Primary School, (Endon), and the Imperial War Museum North.

Alan Cross would like to thank Sarah Dakin at Hursthead Junior School, Stockport.

Alison Mawle would like to thank the staff and pupils of Grafton School and Rob Watts from Roehampton University.

Russell Jones
Manchester Metropolitan University

Introduction

Russell Jones and Dominic Wyse

'Creativity' is a concept that continues to inspire and motivate beginning teachers and experienced teachers alike but it is also a term which is hard to pin down, to define and to assess. Typical key questions asked by educators are always going to be 'Just what *is* creativity?' and 'Is it possible to *teach* creativity?' It is important that we address these questions and others in order to understand creative processes and to establish some agreed sense of direction for the rest of this book to follow. For example, one of the key starting points we have in dealing with a complex notion like 'creativity' in this context is that we expect it to demonstrate some form of originality. An interesting starting point could be the view that 'Creativity means a person's capacity to produce new or original ideas, insights, restructurings, inventions, or artistic objects, which are accepted by experts as being of scientific, aesthetic, social, or technological value' (Vernon, 1989: 94). Of course, 'originality' itself is a difficult concept because it can never exist in a vacuum. To create something which demonstrates originality necessarily means that there has been some kind of re-examination and re-evaluation of existing knowledge. Let us take the example of Anthony Gormley's sculpture *Angel of the North*. If we accept that this is an example of 'creativity', then it also exists as part of a historical and an artistic set of ideas. There were sculptures made before this one and many were made of metal rather than stone. There were representations of the human form and of angels. Sculptures have been located in public spaces before. Gormley uses casts of his own body regularly to explore the relationship between the human form and its natural surroundings but clearly this particular sculpture demonstrates both creativity and originality. Building on the existing artistic heritage of sculpture, key decisions were made in the creative process. To begin with, it is constructed on a vast scale (20 metres high and 54 metres across), it was not only built of steel, but then located in the industrial north-east of England as both a reminder of manufacturing industries and of the strength of those working communities. The wings of the *Angel* are gently angled forwards as though those communities are being embraced. The form of the sculpture echoes the design and engineering feats of the Tyne Bridge and has been placed by the side of a main road so that it serves several geographical purposes. In more 'poetic' terms, the structure has gathered genuinely iconic status as it stands firm against all weathers, all critics, all detractors and ultimately represents the resilience and strength of the working communities of the north-east. Gormley wrote that 'I wanted to make an object that would be a focus of hope at a painful time of transition for the people of the north-east, abandoned in the gap between the industrial and the information ages' (Gormley, 2012). The point here, clearly, is not that we expect children to build sculptures of this magnitude, but that the roots of originality and creativity are firmly located in childhood; we can bring those same principles of discussion, re-examination and re-evaluation into our classrooms. If we are to understand creativity more deeply and recognise how this connects to classrooms and the work of teachers then we need to look at how research evidence has attempted to clarify the situation.

The modern era for creativity research (according to psychologists) goes back to J. P. Guildford's address to the American Psychological Association in 1949. Guildford began by making a close link between abilities and creative people, something he also described as a series of character traits. He described the neglect of the study of creativity as 'appalling' (Guilford, 1987: 34). Guildford noted the importance of creative talent to industry, science, engineering and government. A key feature of his presentation was that creativity can be expected 'however feeble, of almost all individuals' (p. 36). He argued that up to that point, researchers had emphasised convergent thinking skills and had ignored divergent thinking skills. The use of the word 'creativity' in the title of the presentation and subsequent paper was used to sum up the kind of divergent thinking that he had in mind. In 1957 the Soviets launched the first artificial space satellite and the Americans saw a lack of creativity as one of the reasons for their failure to win the first event in the space race (Cropley, 2001). This had the effect of galvanising the field of creativity research.

Psychological research through the 1970s and 1980s was largely concerned with more detailed attempts to define and ultimately measure creativity. The Torrance tests of creativity were one of the most well known examples of such measurement. Feldman and Benjamin (2006) locate this work in the tradition of psychometric assessment and point out that the frequently cited ideas of 'technological inventiveness' and 'ideational fluency' emerged from this strand of research. The Torrance tests, like so many standardised tests, came under increasing criticism due to the telling argument that creativity was much more complex than even these rigorous tests were showing. As a result, the most recent research has shown some lines of enquiry that are of particular use to educational practitioners.

Csikszentmihályi's early work focused on personality, motivation and the discovery of new problems (Csikszentmihályi, 1990). His research with several hundred artists sought to understand why some produced work that would be judged to be creative, while others did not. As far as personality was concerned, it was found that more creative students had the following features: sensitivity; openness to experiences and impulses; they were self-sufficient and not particularly interested in social norms or acceptance. However, the trait that most consistently distinguished these artists from others was 'a cold and aloof disposition' (*op. cit.* p. 192). Even at this stage, Csikszentmihályi recognised that the fact that these were artists, and not scientists or another group of people, was significant and that these findings probably would not generalise to other groups.

Like other researchers, Csikszentmihályi and his team failed to find any relationship between traditional measures of intelligence and criteria for creative accomplishment. Csikszentmihályi realised that for many creative individuals the *formulation* of a problem is more important than its solution. Thus, he set out to investigate the *discovery orientation* of artists. When presented with visually interesting objects and drawing materials, a group of students were encouraged to do what they wanted, and finish when they had produced a drawing that they liked. The variables used to measure the students' discovery orientation included the number of objects that they touched: the higher the number the more likely that the problem was being approached from a discovery orientation. Another variable was the number of changes the person introduced into the drawing process. Established artists and teachers rated drawing produced by students who had used discovery orientation much higher in terms of originality than other students who had used a more predictable problem-solving approach. In terms of artistic career success some seven years later the correlation was still significant.

Csikszentmihályi's early work through a person-centred approach led ultimately to the view that this was not the full picture. Instead, he proposed that the usual question 'What is creativity?' might have to be replaced by 'Where is creativity?' (Csikszentmihályi, 1990: 200). His well known 'systems perspective' (p. 205) sees creativity as the result of interaction between three subsystems: the person, the field, and the domain. The domain is a system that has a set of rules. This might be a subject like mathematics, or a religion, a game, or a sport. For example, Western classical music is a 'domain' that requires the composition of sound and silence to create pieces of music for the benefit of performers and audiences. The 'field' is part of the social system which has the power to influence the structure of the domain. Music competitions such as the 'Lionel Tertis international viola competition and workshop' are part of the way that the field of classical music has influence. Entry to music colleges and the scholarships that they provide are also part of the influence of the field. The most important function of the field is to maintain the domain as it is, but the field will also act as a gatekeeper to allow changes to the domain to take place. The role of the person is to provide variations in the domain which will be judged by the field. Variations of this kind represent exceptional creativity.

Teaching creativity

There are hundreds of programmes that claim to enhance children's creative development. These range from detailed approaches carried out over quite lengthy periods of time to specific techniques such as SCAMPER which is used to change something that already exists to produce novelty by Substituting, Combining, Adapting, Magnifying, Putting to a different use, Eliminating, and Rearranging/Reversing (Cropley, 2001). Another example is the use of 'brain-storming' which has been extended to include more structured ways of generating ideas such as mind-maps and other visual techniques which use hierarchies of categories. Many of the packages begin their lives in the business sector, such as Edward de Bono's lateral thinking approach. However, In spite of great interest in the area and considerable financial success for some approaches, there is a lack of empirical evidence: 'A clear, unequivocal, and incontestable answer to the question of how creativity can be enhanced is not to be found in the psycho-logical literature' (Nicholson,1999: 407).

Teresa Amabile has made a significant contribution to the creativity research field. Because of her dissatisfaction with standardised creativity tests, she used tests/activities that required the creation of some kind of real world product, for example making paper collages or writing Haikus. These were then judged for creativity and other dimensions by experts, such as studio artists or practising poets who rated the collages. Amabile called this 'consensual assessment' (Amabile, 1990: 65). The conceptual definition of creativity that she used was: 'A product or response will be judged as creative to the extent that (a) it is both a novel and appropriate, useful, correct, or valuable response to the task at hand, and (b) the task is heuristic rather than algorithmic' (p. 66). Amabile made the point that although creativity is often very difficult for judges to define, they can recognise creativity when they see it. They also have considerable agreement about their judgements, particularly with products but less so with creativity in persons or creative processes. She also correctly argued, in our view, that creativity is a continuous rather than discontinuous quality which begins with everyday creativity at one end and ends with Einstein, Mozart and Picasso at the other end. The differences are not the presence of creativity per se but the abilities, cognitive styles, motivational levels and circumstances of the different people concerned.

Working with Amabile, Beth Hennessey's work has built on the work on creativity to link with motivation. Hennessey has shown that intrinsic motivation enhances children's creativity whereas extrinsic motivation, stimulated by an external goal, is a 'killer' of creativity. For example, high-stakes accountability systems have a negative effect on teachers' capacity to engage pupils' intrinsic motivation. However, her research also showed that to a certain extent this negative effect can be mitigated by 'immunisation procedures' (Hennessey, 2010: 343). These procedures involve teachers helping children to understand the value of intrinsic motivation in spite of a range of extrinsic motivators that may be present in classrooms. Hennessey says that this approach only maintained base-line motivation and creativity, not unusually high levels of creativity that are possible in the ideal classroom environment for intrinsic motivation. In a fascinating final section to her chapter, Hennessey advocates the open classroom of the 1970s in America, which was inspired by the British infant classroom model of the 1960s, as the ideal practical realisation of what she and her colleagues have discovered about the optimal classroom conditions for creativity.

Overall, researchers remain optimistic that creativity can be enhanced by the ways that teachers work with pupils and students. A number of factors have been identified that necessitate the need to:

- Reward curiosity and exploration.
- Build motivation, particularly internal motivation.
- Encourage risk-taking.
- Have high expectations/beliefs about creative potential of students: this applies to both teachers' views of their pupils and pupils' own self image.
- Give opportunities for choice and discovery – 'The evidence is fairly compelling, and not surprising, that people are more interested in – more internally motivated to engage in – activities they have chosen for themselves than activities that have been selected for them by others, or in which they are obliged to engage for reasons beyond their control' (Dudek and Côté, 1994; Kohn, 1993).
- Develop students' self-management skills.
- Support domain specific knowledge: pupils need to understand as much as possible about the domain (often the subject area) that they are doing the creative work in.(Nicholson,1999: 409)

This point about opportunities for choice is highly significant and one which the English education system has repeatedly neglected, particularly since 1988.

Creative partnerships

In 1999 the report commissioned by UK government called *All Our Futures: Creativity, Culture and Education* (NACCCE Report, 1999) argued that a national strategy for creative and cultural education was essential to unlock the potential of every young person. One of the most positive developments following the NACCCE report was the national Creative Partnerships (CP) initiative. CP described itself as follows:

> The Creative Partnerships programme brings creative workers such as artists, architects and scientists into schools to work with teachers to inspire young people and help them learn. The programme has worked with over 1 million children, and over 90,000 teachers in more than 8000 projects in England since 2002. Creative Partnerships is England's flagship creative learning programme, designed to develop the skills of children and young people across England, raising their aspirations, achievements and life chances. (Creativity, Culture and Education, 2011: online)

CP's initial commitment to grass-roots control of creative projects was unique in relation to educational initiatives from the New Labour government of 1997 to 2010 which generally featured heavy top-down control. Although the New Labour government failed to implement some of the most important recommendations of the NACCCE report, it did commit significant financial investment in CP.

Two large-scale national evaluations of CP were commissioned. The evaluation addressing the link between attainment and creative partnerships projects found a modest impact at Key Stage 3 and Key Stage 4 but not at Key Stage 2 (Kendall, et al., 2010). However, the measure of attainment was of course the national statutory test scores which are not the most appropriate measure for the impact of initiatives that sought to encourage *creative learning*. The second evaluation looked at the impact of creative partnerships on teachers. Overall, an overwhelmingly positive impact of involvement in CP was found and that teachers felt that CP had particularly benefited their development of skills for leadership and interpersonal work. Perhaps not surprisingly it was also found that those teachers who had higher levels of involvement in CP felt that there had been more impact than those who had less involvement.

Some of the earliest evaluations of CP were the regional ones carried out by David Spendlove and Dominic Wyse in Merseyside and Manchester/Salford from 2003 to 2005 (the main findings of their research reports were summarised in Wyse and Spendlove, 2007). The main academic contribution of the work was to advance understanding of what was a new term in the context of a policy initiative, *creative learning*. It was not clear why creative learning had been selected in preference to creativity as the main idea behind CP. It became apparent from the work that there was uncertainty about the meaning of creative learning for those involved with CP. Hence, one of the outcomes of the research, which included analyses of participants' perceptions and of creativity theory and research, was to offer a working definition of creative learning:

> creative learning is learning which leads to new or original thinking which is accepted by appropriate observers as being of value.

The definition seems to have been helpful as can be seen from David Feldman's and the editors' comments in Craft, Cremin and Burnard (2008). Feldman (2008) made the point that specifying, even in a preliminary way, what the terms *creative* and *learning* mean and how they relate to each other was necessary.

The other key finding of Spendlove and Wyse's work was the idea of barriers to creativity. There was an overriding feeling that creative learning represented something less formal and less restrictive than much practice that was prevalent at the time, but perceptions were that the two most significant barriers to creative practice were the assessment system and the National Curriculum, particularly the national strategies. In the first edition of Jones and Wyse (2004), we highlighted the tension between standards and creativity that were part of England's Department for Education and Skills national strategy *Excellence and Enjoyment* (DfES, 2003). These findings were echoed to a certain extent by the idea of an interaction between *performativity* and creativity policies (Troman, Jeffrey and Raggl, 2007 – Bob Jeffrey and Peter Woods had been researching creative teaching and creative learning from an educational perspective at least since 1996). The idea that there was a tension between curriculum and assessment policy and creativity was not accepted by government. In their response to the Roberts Report, that was commissioned to review creativity in schools, government reiterated their position from the national strategy that 'creativity and standards go hand in hand' (Department for Culture, Media and Sport, 2006: 4). In spite of mutual admiration for CP shown in the Education Select Committee report and the government's response, very regrettably the government funding for CP was cut by the Conservative–Liberal Democrat coalition government from 2011.

Creativity and national curricula

In 2010 the European Commission Institute for Prospective Technological Studies (IPTS) published the final report on its study of creativity and innovation (Cachia, et al., 2010). One of the editors of this book (Dominic) was involved as a collaborator with the IPTS team, contributing to methodological development, critical review of report drafts, analysis of some UK data, and dissemination. The study addressed the role of creativity in primary and secondary education in 27 member states of the European Union. The findings in relation to curricula included the perception that there was in general insufficient encouragement for creativity. This was caused in many cases by a lack of clear definitions and understanding of creativity. Excessive curriculum content was also regarded as a common barrier to creativity. In spite of commitment to curricula frequently stated by teachers, conventional teaching methods such as 'chalk and talk' were an obstacle to creativity. Primary teachers were more likely than secondary teachers to promote creative learning and active learner-centred approaches in class. The process of assessment was recognised as a barrier when the emphasis was on summative assessment, but as an enabler when more versatile assessment processes were used. It was also concluded that revision of curricula to include more creativity required parallel revisions in assessment systems if creativity was to flourish. In relation to the UK, the IPTS study noted that Northern Ireland and Scotland's curriculum texts had the most prominent use of the term 'creativity'.

Creativity featured in the aims for the primary National Curriculum in England from 1999 onwards. The handbook and accompanying website also included creativity in 'Promoting skills across the curriculum' as part of a thinking skills section. At a later date, an extra section called 'Learning across the Curriculum' was added to the online version of the National Curriculum. This section contained extensive requirements and guidance about how creativity could be fostered in the curriculum. In 2010, following a review of the primary curriculum commissioned by the New Labour Government, a new primary curriculum was published online. Creativity was even more frequently referred to in this curriculum, and the context for these references was often a more active form of creativity that required pupils 'to create', 'to develop creativity skills', and 'to develop creativity'. However, in 2011 the new coalition Conservative–Liberal Democrat government announced that there would be yet another review of the National Curriculum. They immediately removed (and archived) the new primary curriculum website, saying that is was no longer government policy. The promoting skills across the curriculum material that had been added to the online version of the National Curriculum was also removed by the coalition government as part of its decision to remove all 'non-statutory' materials from the National Curriculum website.

Wales' Foundation Phase Framework for children age three to seven includes creativity as part of thinking skills in its 'Skills across the curriculum' section. 'Developing thinking' is described as thinking across the curriculum through the processes of planning, developing and reflecting in order that pupils can make sense of their world. It is argued that these processes enable children to think creatively and critically. Uniquely, Wales includes as one of its 'areas of learning' (equivalent to subjects in other countries), 'Creative Development'. This is summarised as follows:

> Children should be continually developing their imagination and creativity across the curriculum. Their natural curiosity and disposition to learn should be stimulated by everyday sensory experiences, both indoors and outdoors. Children should engage in creative, imaginative and expressive activities in art, craft, design, music, dance and movement. Children should explore a wide range of stimuli, develop their ability to communicate and express their creative ideas, and reflect on their work. (Department for Children, Education, Lifelong Learning and Skills, 2008: 10)

In addition, Wales' 'Skills framework for 3 to 19-year-olds' includes the claim that the developing thinking section of the framework is underpinned by creative and critical thinking, although metacognition seems to be the strongest focus.

Northern Ireland also locates creativity in thinking skills in its 'Thinking Skills and Personal Capabilities' section. The context is children being given worthwhile experiences across the curriculum that allow them to develop skills, including being creative. Examples include seeking questions and problems to solve, making new connections, valuing the unexpected, and taking risks.

Unlike the other nations, Scotland does not have a separate section for creativity as part of thinking skills. Instead, creativity is seen as an important theme that is built into the experiences and outcomes across the curriculum areas. Scotland includes a 'Learning across the curriculum' section but creativity is not identified as a separate strand of this as it is in Wales and was in England.

The strongest commitment to creativity as evident from national curricula is seen in Wales' National Curriculum, particularly in its identification of a separate area of learning to complement the inclusion of creativity as part of thinking skills. However, Scotland's inclusion of creativity as a theme that is built into the experiences and outcomes is perhaps the most logical conception because creativity is a process and disposition rather than a subject/area of learning.

Although the inclusion of creativity as part of thinking skills in three of the UK nations is welcome, there is a danger that this categorisation of creativity is somewhat limited. Although creativity is characterised by divergent thinking, this is only one important part of what it means to be creative. However, its inclusion in thinking skills sections in national curricula is often characterised by additional descriptions that indicate a much broader understanding of creativity.

Implications for practice

Before summarising what are the main implications for practice that emerge from this analysis of creativity in the curriculum, we offer the views of a selection of practitioners of a different kind, professional writers. Philip Pullman and David Almond have been fiercely critical of government policy on education, particularly in England. At the time of the National Literacy Strategy, Pullman referred to its guidance on planning for writing as 'Absolutely bonkers' (Pullman, 2001) and on reading as 'half-baked drivel slapped down in front of us, like greasy food on a dirty plate brought to us by a drunken waiter' (Pullman, 2002). Later, he argued:

> There are no rules. Anything that's any good has to be discovered in the process of writing it ... we cannot require everything to take place under the glare of discussion and checking and testing and consultation: some things have to be private and tentative. Teaching at its best can give pupils the confidence to discover this mysterious state and to begin to explore the things that can be discovered there. (Pullman, 2003: 2)

Pullman described the curriculum for young people as 'brutal', suggesting that we are creating a generation of children who hate reading and who 'feel nothing but hostility for literature' (Ward, 2003). Five leading children's authors voiced their concerns personally to the government and left readers in little doubt about their dismay about some teaching practices. Anne Fine felt that there had been 'a real drop in the standard of children's writing – not in grammar, construction or spelling, but in the untestable quality of creativity' (Katbamna, 2003: 3). The *Times Educational Supplement* feature 'My Best Teacher' included Booker prize winner Ben Okri, who used the opportunity to voice his frustration with the education system:

> I think the culture of education is wrong. It is too much like a production line – you're doing this so at the end of the day you'll be doing that ... For the past 10 years I have been trying to find someone to teach me how to swim, and it has led me to thinking that the great problem of teaching is that people have forgotten how to learn. We're not learners any more, we're collectors of facts. People tell me, 'Do it this way, do it that way', and whenever I do, I end up nearly drowning. (Okri, 2000: 7)

Many of the problems identified by these writers chime with findings from curriculum research and scholarship. If we accept that they are real then there are clear implications for teachers who want to make their classrooms more creative places. The chapters that follow each offer insight into the ways in which teachers have continued to construct creative opportunities for children. In each case, the contributor has worked alongside current practitioners to exemplify creative practices in modern classrooms. They offer some very different accounts of work being undertaken to support children's creative enterprises, but there are also commonalities of approach that help us to identify and evaluate exactly what 'creativity' means in the classroom.

So first and foremost, in the context of the primary classroom, creativity is best understood as being about the key components of newness and value. Teachers should engage pupils with classroom activities and learning that encourage them to create ideas and products that exhibit newness and that are valued. Both the teacher and the class are highly appropriate 'judges' of these components. Absolute unanimity about creativity is not what is important here; instead, we are concerned with the *process* of creating, then thinking and discussing what is new and what is of value.

Special creativity programmes are not necessarily needed and the following chapters exemplify the commitment of teachers to some basic creative ideas. One of these is that everyone exhibits creativity to different degrees and in different areas. However, teachers' advocacy of and encouragement of intrinsic motivation, and challenges to the worst features of extrinsic motivation such as high-stakes testing and performance cultures, is vital. We should look to the logic of Scotland's inclusion of creativity as a theme informing the whole curriculum, and to the commitment to creativity evident in the national curricula of Northern Ireland and Wales, and hope that England's review of its National Curriculum will not result in minimising the place of creativity in a country that historically has an internationally renowned reputation for its curricula that celebrate creativity.

Creativity in the Primary Curriculum (second edition)

This edition of *Creativity in the Primary Classroom* sets out to examine ways in which teachers have sought to adopt creative approaches to their work in the classroom from a strong theoretical and research-informed position. There are many differences in these approaches (and of course that is a valuable part of the creative story) but there are also many similarities, and those seeking to engage in more creative classroom practices should be encouraged to discover that whilst these examples originate from classrooms and contexts all over the country, there are some very simple and valuable beginning steps. Having worked with all these authors, we are only too aware that one of these key steps has to be the courage to listen to children's ideas. This is often claimed to be part of healthy classrooms but equally this can be an entirely superficial process. We have all seen instances where teachers 'listen' to groups of children until they get the 'route' or the 'answer' they wanted in the first place; what we see rising from these individual chapters is that listening to children is a fundamental principle in creative pedagogies. It is not merely a case of letting pupils 'do what they want' or 'have their own way'; genuinely listening to children allows many things to happen in the classroom. For example, it demonstrates a classroom ethos of respect between learners and teachers and it offers teachers crucial opportunities to make decisions about pupil progress. Alongside this is a developing awareness of the role and value of talk. Warwick and Dawes offer the notion of 'creative conjecture' which encourages creativity: questions, behaviours, preconceptions, challenges and possibilities are all achieved through productive talk in the classroom. In the 'English' chapter of this book, Wyse and Jones offers clear examples of the value of open-ended talk as part of the process approach to writing, building on real language choices and children's editorial control over their own writing. Talk can never be incidental in creative contexts and both learners and teachers need to understand the different roles and purposes of talk; significantly, children need to learn how to use different kinds of talk for different purposes and teachers need to learn how to *respond* appropriately to talk to encourage creative outcomes.

In this context, all these chapters support a developing notion that children have a right to be heard in classrooms alongside the right to participate in their own learning. This brings with it several key concerns: first, how this sits with the National Curriculum and objectives-driven lesson plans; and second, how 'dangerous' it might be to let children explore and determine their own paths towards learning. There are implications here regarding time allocation, resources, teacher-control, timetabling, cross-curricularity and ownership of the curriculum, and all these issues are explored as each author explains how creativity has been seen in practice in modern classrooms. For example, Warwick and Dawes here discuss '*new* learning' that rises out of lessons which are based on particular objectives but which are not *limited* to those objectives. Similarly, Burnard and Biddulph exemplify structure-free opportunities; a balance of teacher-direction with opportunities for pupils to make real choices about their learning experiences. Collectively, these contributors do not seek to abandon lesson objectives, but rather advocate a new way of thinking about them. They argue for lesson planning that first opens up routes into *other* ways of thinking (that might then generate *other* objectives) and second allows the teacher to realise that a productive and creative shift in lesson objectives does not necessarily mean failure. On the contrary, lessons which have built in the possibility of 'creative conjecture' that leads into new possibility should be seen as successful and spirited teaching.

It is important that we keep an eye on the developing context of these classrooms as education changes in the UK, but that should not let us forget that there are other international contexts where learning and teaching takes place quite differently. Many children in Sweden, for example (where one of the authors works on a regular basis), experience learning and teaching in the context of a Fridaskolan. Here, learning content, target setting, active participation and development of curricular interests are all developed in negotiation with children who are free to participate (or not) in the taught curriculum. Of course the notion of a 'taught curriculum' necessarily needs to change before this becomes a meaningful process for many beginning teachers in the UK, but the example here serves to remind us that there are many approaches to pedagogy and to be creative means that teachers need to think critically about their own relationship with the learning process. Creativity is not a casual 'free-for-all', and as each of the following chapters illustrate, it is a collaborative and exciting process that is deeply embedded in the pedagogical principles that inform learning and teaching.

The curriculum, in this context, does not restrict or bind teachers; it is a document waiting to be brought alive in classrooms by passionate learners and teachers. Listening to children is just a starting point. It does not mean that the teacher becomes passive at all; if anything, the teacher becomes more skilled in the process of listening – understanding not merely pupil interest and motivation but establishing key questions, routes of inquiry, seeking out possibilities to investigate and address misunderstanding, actively supporting questions such as 'but what if …'. The authors here are not suggesting that teachers' planning is simply abandoned if children ask 'interesting questions' – the teacher's skills are paramount in facilitating a process that supports and shapes child-initiated inquiry. That might mean adapting future planning, providing different resources or working groups; it might mean creating space on the curriculum for this to happen, but in each instance that seems to be what happens in the creative classrooms.

We would argue that there is absolute value here in each chapter being *different*; each author establishes a set of creative principles and practices that inform and shape learning and teaching in their own chosen subject areas. We have not sought to establish unanimity or conformity of approach here; rather, we have encouraged each author to identify what creativity means for learners and teachers in each subject context but, in so doing, there are commonalities and pedagogical threads that weave their way through the whole book. There is creative currency in examining the moments where these chapters share ideas and it is worth drawing them together to see *why* they are shared views and experiences.

An interesting starting point is that all authors stress (in different ways) that creativity does not just 'happen' in the classroom; there is a role for the teacher here that needs considerable forethought. Just expecting creativity to happen in the room because there are 'interesting resources' or because the lesson is 'different' to the norm is simply inadequate for every contributor here. The teacher has a role and purpose in this process which is highly complex, relies on considerable skill and planning and, in many cases, professional and pedagogical courage. Each author explains the creative role of the teacher in detail but all seek to establish the value of possibility and unpredictability. Wyse and Jones illustrate the way that unpredictability and the merging of linguistic and artistic outcomes generate new relationships which can be startling or thought-provoking. Similarly, Naik promotes the idea that uncertainty in the classroom should be seen as a 'normal' starting point. Whilst she is writing specifically about mathematics, we would argue that this starting principle is equally applicable across the curriculum. Many beginning teachers feel that this might in some way undermine their authority in the classroom or might indicate a significant lack of subject knowledge, but here every contributor conversely establishes a significantly different rationale, seeing it as an indication of a confident and capable teacher who uses uncertainty as a route into possibility, investigation and creativity.

Cremin and McDonald's chapter on drama establishes commitment and interest as the preconditions for creativity in the classroom. These are qualities that teachers cannot simply 'invent' or 'expect' in their classrooms: it takes professional skill over considerable periods of time to establish a creative ethos in the learning space. Much of this (as Warwick and Dawes discuss in their science chapter) is based on a relationship of trust, and a collective sense that suggestions that are inaccurate or inappropriate or 'wrong' remain intensely valuable because they are part of the creative process. It is only by removing possibilities that are inaccurate or inappropriate or 'wrong' that children begin to realise what is accurate or appropriate or 'right'. Spendlove and Cross establish this as part of 'a curriculum of unknowing' which challenges narrow definitions of conventional teacherly roles. If that process is not part of the ethos in the classroom and not part of a trusted relationship between learners and teachers then creativity is inhibited. As we all argue, this takes time, commitment and considerable professional skill, all demonstrated in the examples of creative teaching in each of the following chapters.

Several contributors mention an 'enriched' curriculum, and Mawle further argues that creativity is 'concerned with the making of new and personal connections'. This, she argues, often begins with an initial 'encounter' followed by a period of exploration during which personal responses are identified and developed. The notion of judgement and of originality here is at least partly made (for Mawle) by pupils themselves, which again raises questions about classroom ethos, power and the creative role of the teacher. Spendlove and Cross also discuss the transformative nature of creative work on the curriculum whereby existing knowledge becomes applied and reusable knowledge in new contexts. This is an important point to make as it again exemplifies one of the key characteristics and outcomes of creative enterprises: the establishment of new knowledge. It is here where teachers have the particular capacity to help shape creative outcomes in the classroom. As we discussed earlier, many theorists (such as Vernon and Csikszentmihályi) discuss the value of 'newness', and part of the skill of the teacher is to know how and when to support a child's developing ideas so that they can move into new and creative contexts.

Issues of 'choice', 'decision-making' and 'open-ended questioning' are regularly discussed by all contributors (as we would expect in any book on creativity in primary classrooms), but Bowen emphasises the need for 'risk-taking'. It is not incidental that he writes about this in the context of studying history, a subject which inexperienced primary teachers might see as one of the least 'risky' subjects on the curriculum. Whereas many history lessons in the past have been (unfairly) characterised as dusty, repetitive, memory-based exercises, Bowen opens up a powerfully different range of opportunities that challenge teachers to present the subject as *not* predetermined at all, encouraging teachers to set up lines of historical inquiry that are genuinely open-ended. He advocates the gathering of data which challenges existing knowledge and encourages pupils to ask *new* and *different* questions about life in the past. The notion of 'risk-taking' stems from the knowledge that the teacher may easily step into places where there is uncertainty and some degree of chaos that may not be easily resolved. Bowen welcomes this as an entirely creative enterprise that supports children's developing notions of rationalisation and probability in the quest for 'answers' that have not been predetermined by the teacher.

In respect of developmental features of creativity in relation to learners, Cremin and McDonald refer to social, moral and personal development in addition to the intellectual progress we might automatically expect as a result of creative work. Much of this is again linked to talk but also in the specific context of collaborative work. To beginning teachers this might seem strange, as they may expect to see creativity as entirely individualistic expressions and yet here, all authors discuss the absolute value of collaborative approaches to creativity. Whereas we have discussed the 'newness' and the 'originality' dimensions we bring to a measurement of creative output, all the contributors here recognise again that this is not something that happens in isolation in the classroom. A teacher who works hard at building a classroom ethos founded on creative inquiry will understand that there are attitudes and behaviours that support that process, and collaborative work involving the sharing of ideas, the discussion of possibilities alongside a sense of trust, purpose and respect all contribute towards a pedagogical climate that encourages and supports creative learning.

Along the way, however, the contributors also discuss the specific value of conflict. This is an interesting word as it initially suggests something negative and undesirable in educational contexts, but it became a valuable part of the way several authors saw creativity in classrooms. The conflicts they discussed were productive conflicts that led to creative places in the classroom. Cremin and McDonald discuss the way that a focus on conflict in drama leads to ambiguity and misunderstandings that then provide exactly the right climate for the creative teacher to make choices about where to lead this enterprise. The same authors also discuss the way that drama can provide opportunities for children to confront conflicting views (often views that they might not hold) and so allows them opportunities to develop socially, morally and personally.

Overall, the following chapters offer a 'call to arms' for those seeking to establish creative learning and teaching. Collectively, they identify and celebrate the work carried out by strong, experienced teachers whilst also offering insight and support for those about to take their first creative steps in the classroom.

Further Reading

Creativity, Culture and Education (2011). *About Creative Partnerships*. Available from http://www.creative-partnerships.com/about/.

Explore the CCE site for examples of creative work in schools.

Hennessey, B. (2010). Intrinsic motivation and creativity in the classroom: Have we come full circle?, in R. Beghetto and J. Kaufman (eds), *Nurturing creativity in the classroom*. Cambridge: Cambridge University Press.

A rich account of Hennessey's long career of research on a key aspect of creativity.

References

Amabile, T. (1990). Within You, Without You: The Social Psychology of Creativity, and Beyond, in M. Runco and R. Albert (eds) *Theories of Creativity*. London: Sage.

Cachia, R., Ferrari, A., Ala-Mutka, K. and Punie, Y. (2010). *Creative Learning and Innovative Teaching. Final Report on the Study on Creativity and Innovation in Education in the EU Member States*. Seville: European Commission. Joint Research Centre. Institute for Prospective Technological Studies (IPTS).

Craft, A., Cremin, T. and Burnard, P. (eds) (2008). *Creative learning 3–11: And how we document it*. Stoke on Trent: Trentham.

Cropley, A. J. (2001). *Creativity in Education and Learning: A guide for teachers and educators*. London: Kogan Page.

Csikszentmihályi, M. (1990). The Domain of Creativity, in M. Runco and R. Albert (eds), *Theories of Creativity*. London: Sage.

Creativity, Culture and Education (2011). *About Creative Partnerships*. Available from http://www.creative-partnerships.com/about/.

Department for Children, Education, Lifelong Learning and Skills (2008). *Framework for Children's Learning for 3 to 7-year-olds in Wales*. Cardiff: Welsh Assembly Government.

Department for Culture Media and Sport (DfCMS) and Department for Education and Skills (DfEE) (2006). *Government response to Paul Roberts' report on nurturing creativity in young people*. London: Department for Culture, Media and Sport (DfCMS)/Department for Education and Skills (DfEE).

Department for Education and Skills (DfES) (2003). *Excellence and Enjoyment: A strategy for primary schools*. Nottingham: DfES Publications.

Feldhusen, J. F. and Goh, B. E. (1995). Assessing and accessing creativity: an integrative review of theory, research, and development. *Creativity Research Journal*, Vol. 8: 231–47.

Feldman, D. H. (2008). Foreword: Documenting creative learning, changing the world, in A. Craft, T. Cremin and P. Burnard (eds), *Creative learning 3–11: And how we document it*. Stoke on Trent: Trentham.

Feldman, D. H. and Benjamin, A. (2006). Creativity and education: An American retrospective. *Cambridge Journal of Education,* 36 (3): 319–36.

Gormley, A. (2012). *Angel of the North* (www.antonygormley.com/sculpture/item-view/id/211#p0).

Guilford, J. P. (1987). Creativity research: Past, present and future, in S. G. Isaksen (ed.), *Frontiers of creativity research*. New York: Bearly Limited.

Hennessey, B. (2010). Intrinsic motivation and creativity in the classroom: Have we come full circle?, in R. Beghetto and J. Kaufman (eds), *Nurturing creativity in the classroom*. Cambridge: Cambridge University Press.

Katbamna, M. (2003). Crisis of Creativity. *Guardian Education*, 30 September 2003.

Kendall, L., Morrison, J., Yeshanew, T. and Sharp, C. (2008). *The longer-term impact of Creative Partnerships on the attainment of young people: Results from 2005 and 2006*. Slough: NFER.

National Advisory Committee on Creative and Cultural Education (NACCCE) (1999). *All Our Futures: Creativity, Culture and Education*. Suffolk: DfEE Publications.

Nicholson, R. S. (1999). Enhancing Creativity, in R. J. Sternberg (ed.), *Handbook of Creativity*. Cambridge: Cambridge University Press.

Okri, B. (2000). My Best Teacher (in discussion with Hilary Wilce). *Times Educational Supplement* (Friday Section), 19 September 2000, p. 7.

Pullman, P. (2001). Pullman Laments the Passing of Teaching as a Creative Force in Society. *Guardian Weekend*, 10 November 2001, p. 54.

Pullman, P. (2002). Pullman reviles Literacy Scheme as Horror Story. *Times Educational Supplement*, 8 February 2002, p. 2.

Pullman, P. (2003). Lost the Plot. *Guardian Education*, 30 September 2003.

Ryhammer, L. and Brolin, C. (1999). Creativity research: historical considerations and main lines of development. *Scandinavian Journal of Educational Research,* Vol. 43 (3): 259–73.

Troman, G., Jeffrey, B. and Raggl, A. (2007). Creativity and performativity policies in primary school cultures. *Journal of Education Policy,* 22 (5): 549–72.

Vernon, P. (1989). The Nature-Nurture Problem in Creativity, in J. Glover, R. Ronning and C. Reynolds (eds), *Handbook of Creativity*. London: Plenum Press.

Ward, L. (2003). Tests are Making Children Hate Books. *Guardian Education*, 30 November 2003.

Wyse, D., and Spendlove, D. (2007). Partners in creativity: Action research and creative partnerships. *Education 3–13,* 35 (2): 181–91.

English

Russell Jones and Dominic Wyse

It is not difficult to argue that English is a creative subject. Imagine your favourite play, say *Romeo and Juliet* for example. Shakespeare's creativity as a writer is continually re-examined and reinterpreted by the creative inspiration of directors, designers and actors. In this case, English shows itself to be a creative subject with aspects of performance art: in America, English is often referred to as a 'language art'. When moulding language, the writer creates the text and the reader responds to the message. In doing this, the reader is invited to construct their own interpretation of the text which in itself is a creative process. It is for this reason that the study of literature is so fascinating because people's views of a text vary so widely. All of these elements and more combine to give English its creative character.

The work of accomplished writers is one source for thinking about creativity in the subject of English. Indeed some of the early modern research on creativity (for example by Mihaly Csikszentmihályi, David Feldman or Howard Gardener) was built on analyses of creative people. Helen Cresswell, a prolific and talented author for both children and adults, describes her way of composing:

> With most of my books I simply write a title and a sentence, and I set off and the road leads to where it finishes. All my books are like journeys or explorations. Behind my desk I used to have this saying by Leo Rosten pinned up on the wall that went 'When you don't know where a road leads, it sure as hell will take you there.' When I first read that, I thought, that's exactly it! That's what happens when I start on my books – I really don't know what's going to happen; it's quite dangerous, in a way. I often put off starting because it seems a bit scary. Yet at the end of the day, I feel that a story has gone where it's meant to have gone. (Carter, 1999: 118)

Philip Pullman, the author of *His Dark Materials* trilogy, reveaed this about stimulus:

> I did *Paradise Lost* at 'A' level, and it's stayed with me all the way through until

I was beginning to think about *Northern Lights* (the first book of the trilogy). But my writing of the book came as a result of a meeting with David Fickling of Scholastic Books. David said he wanted me to do a book for him. I said that what I really wanted to do was *Paradise Lost* for teenagers. So he asked me to develop the idea. Off the top of my head I improvised a kind of fantasia on themes from Book 2 of *Paradise Lost* ... By this time I knew the kind of thing I wanted to do – I knew the length, I knew it was going to be in three volumes and I knew it was going to be big and ambitious and enable me to say things I'd never been able to say in any other form. (Carter, 1999: 188)

Notice here the way another text was the inspiration; the social aspect of being a writer shown through the conversation with a publisher which was also a stimulus; the importance of knowing how long a piece of writing is going to be; and the opportunity to say what you want (within the limits of the law!).

But it is interesting to compare Cresswell and Pullman's approaches with the view of the great Columbian writer Gabriel García Márquez who wrote the astonishing *One Hundred Years of Solitude*.

Interviewer: Do your novels ever take unexpected twists?

García Márquez: That used to happen to me in the beginning. In the first stories I wrote I had a general idea of the mood, but I would let myself be taken by chance. The best advice I was given early on was that it was all right to work that way when I was young because I had a torrent of inspiration. But I was told that if I didn't learn technique, I would be in trouble later on [when] the inspiration had gone and the technique was needed to compensate. If I hadn't learned that in time, I would not now be able to outline a structure in advance. Structure is purely a technical problem, and if you don't learn it early on you'll never learn it. (Gourevitch, 2007)

Just in case you are tempted to assume that this could be interpreted as a need for intense training in the forms of writing, it is important to remember that structure in this context goes way beyond form, and includes thinking such as back-story, researching before writing, the development of living characters, and so on. It is also very important to note that García Márquez had the opportunity to express his torrents of inspiration *before* he felt the need to focus on structure. His experience as a journalist, and hence writing articles, is also likely to have coloured his thinking about structure

Quite apart from Stephen King's popularity as an author of fiction, he also wrote an impressive memoir that includes important practical advice for writers:

If you want to be a writer, you must do two things above all others: read a lot and write a lot.(King, 2000: 164)

You can read anywhere, almost, but when it comes to writing, library carrels, park benches, and rented flats should be courts of last resort – Truman Capote said he did his best work in motel rooms, but he is an exception; most of us do our best in a place of our own. (*op cit.*, p. 177)

In our view, when such insights about the processes of artistic creation are expressed so clearly it is a mark of exceptional people, who have the ability to crystallise aspects of their art or science in a way that speaks clearly to many.

Language and literacy in the curriculum

English, language and literacy have a particularly prominent and important role in the curriculum. English is a 'subject' that crosses all other subject boundaries, it is one that can be the gateway to success in other fields and, most importantly, it is a subject which is highly personal. Language is part of our identity: the words we choose to use, the accent with which we speak, what we choose to read and the 'voices' we use to communicate with wider audiences all tell the wider world things about *us*. To a large extent, we are bound within the language we use and if our language use is criticised then this can be a very personal criticism indeed. If we take this as our starting point in primary settings then it becomes increasingly evident why children need guidance and support when we start asking them to be creative in their language work.

Given the centrality of language work on the curriculum, it is important that those working in educational contexts have a rich and detailed working knowledge about features of English and the contexts for language work. Language acquisition and development, knowledge about language (KAL), the role of talk for learning … this list is not meant to be exhaustive; it is meant to indicate how much the teacher needs to know about language in order to be effective in the classroom. In addition, of course, there is the social context for language work which is of significant importance too. We live in a modern world where bilingualism and multilingualism are common features in a large proportion of classrooms and our starting point needs to be that a bilingual child is, to all intents and purposes, an expert in language use, and multilingualism provides learners and teachers with powerful opportunities to genuinely explore the sounds, the shapes and the meanings of the languages being used.

In a similar way, accent and dialectical variation provide a wonderfully rich starting point for an examination of language use. For example, what do you call a flat, circular slice of potato cooked in batter that you might buy from a fish and chip shop? To many, this would be a simple 'fritter', but in Merseyside or in Yorkshire this might be a 'scallop', in south Wales it may be a 'pattie', in the West Midlands it is sometimes a 'klandyke' and in Crewe it is most definitely a 'smack'. Of course there would be global and historical variations too. We could talk about barmcakes and baps, sofas and settees, backsies and ginnels; a simple discussion at this level with children indicates that we have different ways of describing the world around us and that leads into all kinds of possibility regarding respect for each others' language use and a sense of playful inquiry that we can bring to language study. The dynamic, changing nature of language as it changes over time is equally revealing and interesting; what children see now as 'sick' was, in the 1980s 'bad', it was 'cool' in the 1970s and 'groovy' in the 1960s. Whilst this can be fun, the point here is that whilst we look for 'correctness' in language work we are also interested in diversity and variation and this, primarily, allows children to work with their own language, too.

Once we accept that language is a vital, dynamic and shifting feature of the modern world, we can see that there are clear implications for learning and teaching. In a very real way, all children experience more than one form of language use in their daily lives and could all be seen as expert language users in a multilingual world. Cummins (1979) proposed (as part of his *developmental interdependence hypothesis*) that schools can effectively assist or make things difficult for bilingual learners in the way that language work is presented, if only particular forms of literacy learning are emphasised. His main conclusion was that providing the most appropriate pedagogy stems from focused assessments of bilingual pupils' language and literacy understanding. Research has repeatedly shown that respect and support for home languages dramatically benefits pupils who are learning English as a second (or third!) language, and that teachers who work against the child's home language and insist only on correct use of standard English actually impede the child's progress. Recent work in the field of neuroscience (Kovelman, Baker and Petitto, 2008) showed that bilingual language users have differentiated representations in the brain of their two languages. Interestingly, they also found no evidence to suggest that movement between more than one language might be a source of any persistent language confusion. Reese, et al.'s study (2000) offered further evidence that it was positive engagement with, and experience of, language use that benefited children. So, even if parents were not able to use English, their engagement with stories and books and their interest in language benefited their children in both languages at home and at school.

Engaging with theory at this level indicates that it is the teacher's approach to (and knowledge about) language that can be the most important driving force in a linguistically dynamic classroom. Our starting point would be that we cannot talk about creative approaches to learning and teaching in language unless this kind of pedagogical climate is nurtured. Otherwise, a 'creative' language lesson is little more than a paper exercise that might be marginally more 'fun' to complete. Genuinely creative approaches to language work are absolutely not bolt-on activities; they are part of the very fabric of a successful classroom.

Reading

The essence of creativity in reading begins with the opportunity to discover your own texts to get excited about. There are times when reading is an enjoyable, emotional, stimulating, thought-provoking, escapist, therapeutic (and many other things that are personal to the reader) experience that has no need for analysis.

At other times personal responses (including analysis and critique) are articulated with explicit in-depth knowledge of the text being read and the ability to compare with other texts.

The texts that children choose to read and that teachers select to inspire children are a vital part of language in the curriculum. But also of importance is how we might view the processes or *transactions* that take place when children engage with texts. As Rosenblatt (1985) says, 'we need to see the reading act as an event involving a particular individual and a particular text, happening at a particular time, under particular circumstances, in a particular social and cultural setting, and as part of the ongoing life of the individual and the group' (p. 100). Rosenblatt argued that her notion of the transaction was not the same as the separation of text and reader that is a feature of cognitive views of transaction that include information processing models. For example, psychologists look at what they call reading comprehension in a rather different way to Rosenblatt's transactions, and yet both shed light on the same reading processes.

Irrespective of the preferred way of thinking about reading processes, unless someone is motivated to read then learning to read is less likely to happen. Wigfield and Guthrie (1997) found that children's motivation for reading was correlated with the amount and breadth of their reading. They also found that intrinsic motivation predicted more strongly the amount and breadth than did extrinsic motivation. The implications of these findings for supporting children are first and foremost the importance of encouraging children's motivation, for example by providing texts that are likely to interest them. However, there is of course a dilemma in relation to intrinsic motivation. When does encouragement to read by teachers become extrinsic motivation? This implies a subtle balance between the *requirement* to read and the *encouragement* to read. Text transactions, then, involve cognitive and socio-cultural factors, but what happens over time as reading develops? Stanovich (1986) characterised different amounts of reading experience as the rich getting richer and the poor getting poorer. He showed that there are gains for vocabulary growth and reading skill attributable to increased volume of reading alone – those children who do not experience enough opportunities to read are at a disadvantage.

Writing

Creative writing was an approach to writing popular in the 1960s and 1970s that came about as a reaction to earlier rather formal approaches to the teaching of writing and English. One of the most influential texts from this time was Alec Clegg's book *The Excitement of Writing*. Clegg recognised the extensive use – and potentially damaging effect – of published English schemes and wanted to show examples in his book of children's writing 'taken from schools which are deliberately encouraging each child to draw sensitively on his own store of words and to delight in setting down his own ideas in a way which is personal to him and stimulating to those who read what he has written' (Clegg, 1964: 4).

The creative writing approach involved the teacher providing a stimulus, such as a piece of music or visual art, which was followed by an immediate response. This often resulted in brief personal forms of writing such as a short descriptive sketch or a poem. The positive features of this were the emphasis on creativity and an early attempt to link writing with the arts. However, one of the problems was the fact that all the children still had to complete the teacher-designed task. The use of a stimulus for a group is often very successful, but children need to find the kinds of stimuli that personally motivate them to write.

A key area of debate with regard to writing has been the distinction between the processes of writing and the products and forms of writing. Although Graves' (1975) original research received some criticism (e.g., Smagorinsky, 1987), there are few who doubt the influence his ideas had in practice, particularly in the United States. Graves articulated the *process approach* to writing, the key features of which are: generation of writing topics by pupils; regular writing workshops; 'publishing' in the classroom; teacher–pupil writing conferences; skills teaching in 'mini-lessons' and embedded in one-to-one support for pupils' writing. Wyse's (1988) early research focused on the process approach and showed the ways that teachers integrated some of the ideas of the process approach with other approaches (including more 'structured' teaching). He showed that this integration of teaching approaches was a particular characteristic of the teaching of writing in England at the time.

A challenge to the process approach came from those who felt that the approach was too informal and that teaching of written genres needed to be more systematic. Since that time, clear evidence of the challenges for pupils of what is called 'argumentative' writing has continued to emerge (Andrews et al., 2006; Yeh, 1998). An important consideration for teaching writing is how to strike the appropriate balance between an emphasis on teaching and supporting composition, as opposed to the transcription elements such as spelling, grammar and handwriting.

The importance of processes, environments, ownership, and so on, for writing, combined with individual children's cognitive development, are perhaps implicitly evident in recent empirical work on effective teaching of writing. Research such as that by Graham (2006) has provided experimental trial evidence that the combination of a focus on writing processes, and instruction for writing strategies, is the most effective way to teach writing. As Wyse and Jones (2012) explain, pupil ownership (that is related to motivation) is the other vital aspect of such writing teaching.

Burn and Durran argue that, 'Literacy is transformative and *creative*. It does not simply involve understanding a text – it involves, to different degrees – remaking that text' (2007: 2). They discuss the transformative and creative processes that occur when children engage in tasks involving multiliteracy. Burn and Durran describe the example of teenagers talking about the design of superheroes, drawing on their knowledge of existing 'heroes' such as Harry Potter, the expectations of their audiences and the implications (for example) of replacing the 'Avadakedavra' spell with a flamethrower, and turning him into 'a proper action hero' (p. 2). Examples such as this clearly demonstrate the way that children use their knowledge of character, their appreciation of readership and their sense of genuine 'fun' in handling different forms of media, and this is very valuable and desirable within the context of literacy in the modern classroom.

Writing and choice – two examples from the classroom

Hannah's class were used to cross-curricular stimuli for writing. On one occasion, children had been working with acrylic paint and looking at ways in which they could create moods and feelings using a limited palette of two colours. Acrylic paint had been used on sheets of watercolour paper in a completely abstract manner, allowing different strokes and hues to meet, as though the surface was a sketchbook of ideas about the ways in which these colours could meet.

A week later, these sheets were brought out for another art lesson. The teacher asked each child to select areas of interest from the sheet; areas where the strokes and/or the colour seemed to convey movement or a mood. Pupils were asked to rip out these areas (rather than cut them) and not to worry about the resulting bared white edges. Pupils were then asked to arrange these newly isolated areas into a collage. The teacher was keen to point out that the resulting image did not have to represent anything other than the mood suggested by the individual pieces. Pupils were encouraged to look at ways of reassembling the pieces in ways that would deliberately contradict the original design in order to create a completely different surface.

An extended writing session began with these newly constructed 'mood collages'. Some pupils had built up from the surface of the paper and allowed the collage to take on other dimensions, but most of the results were two-dimensional. The white, ripped parts had been incorporated so that they looked like clouds, or hinted at a landscape. The teacher asked each pupil to draft a written 'mood' response: to construct a four- or six-line response to the image, allowing the two to work together to 'explain' what kind of emotional response was being portrayed. Again, the teacher was keen to encourage responses which were not about 'how I feel right now ...', but more along the lines of writing 'in character', about generating a written account of the mood represented by each collage (see Figures 2.1–2.3).

The importance of poetic writing was a driving force for Hannah, and the use of 'ripped up texts' a very useful strategy for developing poetic and creative language. It is important to acknowledge that this was a strategy that had arisen almost organically within the classroom. The teacher had not set out to follow a predetermined route through to completion. The written work came out of an art lesson, the notion of 'ripping' to create unexpected edges came about from a newly qualified teacher course, but the development into using this process to

FIGURE 2.1 Poem reads: My shadow deforms in the dark, I am lonely and afraid, I pause, still, While clouds cluster, I feel empty and friendless, As I wait and wait for the light.
Colours used: orange and grey.

FIGURE 2.2 Poem reads: My dreams dazzle and dance, My best dreams start, At the darkest part of the night, Shadows shimmer, And scare my soul.
Colours used: grey and black.

FIGURE 2.3 Poem reads: Cystal shining ice, Drops like rain, Splashing in a swaying stream, Music plays silently, As a shimmer of glass crashes, Gently to the ground.
Colours used: blue, turquoise, pink, red and purple.

draw on linguistic responses was entirely creative and a result of the space for interaction between the learners and the teacher, who went on to explain:

> I've been using rip-up techniques to teach poetry. You know, how William Burroughs used to use that whole 'stream of consciousness' approach to writing and then cut it up and reassembled it to create 'new' ways of telling, well I kind of adapted that for my class. We tend to use that as a starting point – children fill up as many pages as they like with initial ideas and then the ripping and reassembling process means that you end up with really interesting combinations of words; words that were never intended to be next to each other suddenly seem to belong to each other, or then set off new trains of thought. We've done this for a while now and they are quite comfortable with it. It's a kind of route into poetry writing I think, for those who feel that poetry isn't for them or that it's just limericks … some have moved on from that now and feel more confident about putting ideas on paper, however tentative they may be. The point is that I wanted them to see this as a starting process, it's not just assemblage, it's a starting point, the words should set off a larger process of writing … It's too easy for children to all respond in an identical way to a given input from me, or for me to just shape what they do so that I end up with 30 versions of a poem I would have liked to have written. What we have today is a set of individual responses, to a high standard, and each one completed. I can't see the point of half finished pieces of work, I think it's counterproductive in the classroom, it feels as though the children's' responses aren't valued.

The second case illustrating writing and choice was experienced directly by Dominic when he was a primary teacher. His first teaching post was in Somers Town, which is an area between Euston and King's Cross stations, at a time well before the regeneration of St Pancras and King's Cross stations and the development of the infrastructure for the Eurostar. Somers Town was seen as an archetype for gritty inner-city reality; indeed, it has featured in several films including one called *Somers Town* by Shane Meadows. Dominic's interest in the teaching of writing had been raised during teacher training at Goldsmith's College. But halfway through his first year of teaching he became concerned about the children's motivation for writing. Having attended one of the excellent sessions provided for new teachers by the Inner London Education Authority, he became aware of the work of Donald Graves and decided to implement this approach with his own class.

The process approach is delivered through writing workshops which take place at least once a week but ideally more frequently. The workshop is a whole-class teaching session where all the children are encouraged to write. The motivation for this comes about mainly through the freedom of choice children are offered over their writing but also through the emphasis on real audiences for the writing. Classroom publishing routines (including bookmaking), which mirror professional ones, are established, with the children's completed texts becoming part of the class reading area. These texts are subject to all the typical interaction surrounding the professionally produced texts. Typically, the main audience for the children's books will be their peers, although the teacher, family and friends, other children in the school, parents, other teachers and other schoolchildren are all potential audiences for the writers. Teaching takes place at the beginning of the session in the form of 'mini-lessons', in 'writing conferences' with individual children throughout, and whole-class sharing time at the end of the session. One of the most important things that offering genuine choices over writing results in is the wide range of genres of writing that relate to the children's natural interests. A snapshot of just one day included: a self-help guide to completing computer games (often called 'cheats'); cathartic writing in the form of a story called 'The New Girl', written by a girl who was herself new to the school; a football fanzine; a book of coded messages written for younger children; a story written in Urdu and English called 'The Magic Coat'; a book called *Catchphrase* stimulated by the popular TV programme of the time; *Chinwag*, a magazine sold in the school; and many, many more. (To see some examples of the range and for a full exploration of the implications of the use of the process approach, see Wyse, 1998.)

When children make real choices about their writing – including topic, form, who to collaborate with, the number of workshops to spend on the writing, layout, whether to publish or not, and so on – they take inspiration from their interests and knowledge. It cannot be emphasised strongly enough how important this is for creativity and for motivation. It is also likely to result in better writing in general (Graham, 2010). Remember also the learning that takes place through publishing texts in the classroom. Primarily this gives the writing a meaningful purpose but it also allows for the generation of a range of writing skills that are firmly contextualised.

The examples offered here demonstrate just how fluid and varied language teaching can be and how much potential there is for teachers who want to be imaginative and creative in their classrooms. It is sometimes the case that teachers are concerned that they have children or even classes who are not particularly creative, but we would dispute this and argue that all children can be encouraged and supported to make creative choices in their language use. At the start of this book we posed the question, 'Can creativity be taught?', and we would argue that we can certainly build creative classroom climates; that we can be imaginative in our language planning; that we can listen to children and support their creative choices. If we do not build classrooms where these characteristics are part of the normal interaction between learners and teachers then creativity is unlikely. What we *can* do is to work to ensure that every possible opportunity for creativity to flourish is present in our professional practice. We can also start with the belief that all children have the potential for creative output. Russell's personal fascination with the works of Neil Gaiman was often his inspiration in this respect. One character in the *Sandman* series says:

> Everybody has a secret world inside of them. All of the people of the world, I mean everybody. No matter how dull and boring they are on the outside, inside them they've all got unimaginable, magnificent, wonderful, stupid,

amazing worlds. Not just one world. Hundreds of them. Thousands maybe. (Gaiman, 1993)

Whilst all subjects on the National Curriculum have the potential for creativity, the potential for creative work in English is enormous. As Gaiman intimates, all children have stories to tell – teachers just need to find ways to help that happen. As a starting point, if children are reluctant to write then they can be encouraged to record their stories rather than write them. If a suitably engaging subject is chosen then every child will have something to say: 'My Favourite Scar', 'The Worst Present I ever Received', 'The Day when Everything Seemed to go Right' for example. These accounts could be downloaded and saved so that all children have access to all stories. From there the possibilities are endless: they could be written down by a helper and presented in book form; they could be illustrated; they could be starting points for musical compositions; they could be used as example text to look at design issues on a computer screen. Once this simple doorway is open and language becomes a commonly shared experience in the classroom and it becomes the focal point for development, then children will be eager to offer new suggestions, new ideas, new possibilities, and the teacher's creative options begin.

Creative touches

Language is the key to learning but creativity is not just about language. Your starting point should be the ethos and environment that you build for pupils. This will not happen immediately but your job is to build environments where inquiry, risk-taking and experimentation can all take place safely in the context of mutual respect and constructive criticism.

- Monitor your own responses to children's ideas – be aware of how many times in a given week children are able to shape a writing task through ideas and strategies that they suggested.
- Find ways to plan for open-ended talk in your language work. Look for opportunities where children can share ideas, offer constructive criticism and collaborate on an agreed outcome. For example, you've just had a field trip and your families are being invited to see the results. What are the best ways you can think of that could inform/amuse/interest/entertain/teach your audience?
- Don't be afraid when things don't work out first time. Instant results in language work are unlikely; think about success over longer periods of time – start by working on attitudes to reading or to writing rather than the outcomes of those events.
- Actively seek out open-ended opportunities for collaborative talk. How would your group find a way to communicate a story with no words at all?

- Be flexible with your feedback. When a child offers you ideas, do you typically mould it towards what you wanted in relation to your objectives or do you seek to discover ways in which *other* objectives might be achieved? Don't feel that moving away from your initial plan means failure – children need to know that their ideas are valuable too.

- Use information technology to its full potential. Create anthologies (which can be printed and sold to finance visiting writers/workshops – we DID this). Create a rolling slideshow of powerful ideas, favourite lines of poetry, new and interesting words, creative questions, and leave them playing in the background. Record children reading their stories and create a talking book that can be downloaded as an mp3.

- Imagine the scenario: you have 30 stories based on the theme 'The scariest recipe I can imagine' or 'The item of clothing I will never wear again', and one child in the class suggests that this collection might make an interesting performance. How might you respond? Who would be the audience? How would you encourage the children to find different and innovative ways to present their account so that there wouldn't be 30 near-identical readings? What would you do to support those who are not ready for 'performance'? How might you make best use of technology? Could the children be arranged in six groups of five to find innovative ways to shape and present their accounts?

- Always seek to have longer-term writing goals that include revisiting and rethinking. Let your planning have the space for children to return to a writing task and complete it over several lessons – don't think that every effective writing task can be achieved in 45 minutes. Understand that there is enormous value in building commitment to a piece of written work and that typically the starting point for this has to come from the child's own interests and motivation.

- Encourage children to identify the skills that make a good 'telling'. Ask them to think about pace, vocabulary, eye-contact, volume, facial expression, changing the mood, and so on.

- Try to find ways to *play* with language. There is a close relationship between creativity and the characteristics and processes of play. What might we mean if something was 'squealistic'? Encourage children to find new words or phrases to describe their everyday experiences. What words might you find for a particularly unappetising meal? What was worse – the lumpitude of the potatoes or the smellocity of the fish?

References

Andrews, R., Torgerson, C. J., Low, G., McGuinn, N. and Robinson, A. (2006). Teaching argumentative non-fiction writing to 7–14 year olds: A systematic review of the evidence of successful practice. Technical Report. *Research Evidence in Education Library*. Retrieved 29 January 2007, from: http://eppi.ioe.ac.uk/cms/.

Beard, G. and Hutchins, H. (2002). *The Adventures of Super Diaper Baby*. London: Scholastic.

British Film Institute (BFI) (2012). http://www.bfi.org.uk/education/teaching/storyshorts2/intro.html.

Burn, A. and Durran, J. (2007). *Media Literacies in schools: practice, production and progression*. London: Paul Chapman

Carter, J. (1999). *Talking Books: Children's authors talk about the craft, creativity and process of writing*. London: Routledge.

Clegg, A. B. (1964). *The Excitement of Writing*. London: Chatto and Windus.

Coles, G. (2003). *Reading The Naked Truth: Literacy, Legislation, and Lies*. Portsmouth, NH: Heinemann.

Cope, B. and Kalantzis, M. (eds) (2000). *Multiliteracies: Literacy Learning and the Design of Social Futures*. London: Routledge.

Cummins, J. (1979). Linguistic Interdependence and the Educational Development of Bilingual Children. *Review of Educational Research*, 49 (2): 222–51.

Gamble, N. and Yates, S. (2002). *Exploring Children's Literature*. London: Paul Chapman.

Gaiman, N. (1993). *The Sandman Vol. 5: A Game of You*. New York: Vertigo.

Gourevitch, P. (ed.) (2007). *The Paris Review Interviews* (Vol. 2). Edinburgh: Canongate.

Graham, S. (2006). Strategy Instruction and the Teaching of Writing: A Meta-Analysis, in S. Graham, C. MacArthur and J. Fitzgerald (eds), *Handbook of Writing Research*. New York: The Guilford Press.

Graham, S. (2010). Facilitating Writing Development, in D. Wyse, R. Andrews and J. Hoffman (eds), *The Routledge International Handbook of English, Language and Literacy Teaching*. London: Routledge, pp. 125–36

Graves, D. H. (1975). An Examination of the Writing Processes of Seven Year Old Children. *Research in the Teaching of English*, 9 (3): 227–41.

Harrison, H. (2002). *Key Stage 3 English: Roots and Research*. London: Department for Education and Skills.

King, S. (2000). *On Writing: A Memoir of the Craft*. London: Hodder and Stoughton.

Kovelman, I., Baker, S. A. and Petitto, L. (2008). Bilingual and Monolingual Brains Compared: A Functional Magnetic Resonance Imaging Investigation of Syntactic Processing and a Possible 'Neural Signature' of Bilingualism. *Journal of Cognitive Neuroscience*, 20 (1): 153–69.

National Reading Panel. (2001). *Home*. Retrieved 7 November 2003 from: http://www.nationalreadingpanel.org/.

Protheroe, R. (1978). When in Doubt, Write a Poem. *English in Education*, Vol. 12 (1): 9–21.

Reese, L., Garnier, H., Gallimore, R. and Goldenberg, C. (2000). Longitudinal Analysis of the Antecedents of Emergent Spanish Literacy and Middle-School English reading Achievement of Spanish-Speaking Students. *American Educational Research Journal*, 37 (3): 622–33.

Rosenblatt, L. (1985). Viewpoints: Transaction versus Interaction: A Terminological Rescue Operation. *Research in the Teaching of English*, 19 (1): 96–107.

Smagorinsky, P. (1987). Graves Revisited: A Look at the Methods and Conclusions of the New Hampshire Study. *Written Communication*, 4 (4): 331–42.

Stanovich, K. (1986). Matthew Effects in Reading: Some Consequences of Individual Differences in the Acquisition of Literacy. *Reading Research Quarterly*, 21 (4): 360–407.

Tolkein, J. R. R. (1955; repr. 2001). *The Lord of the Rings: Part Three Return of the King*. London: Harper Collins.

Van Allsburg, C. (1984). *The Mysteries Of Harris Burdick*. Boston, MA: Houghton Mifflin.

Wigfield, A. and Guthrie, J. (1997). Relations of Children's Motivation for Reading to the Amount and Breadth of Their Reading. *Journal of Educational Psychology*, 89 (3): 420–32.

Wyse, D. (1998). *Primary Writing*. Buckingham: Open University Press.

Wyse, D. and Jones, R. (2012). *Teaching English, Language and Literacy* (3rd edn). London: Routledge.

Yeh, S. (1998). Empowering Education: Teaching Argumentative Writing to Cultural Minority Middle-School Students. *Research in the Teaching of English*, 33 (1): 49–83.

CHAPTER

Mathematics

Mamta Naik

When you're teaching mathematics, I think the really important thing is that when you look round you want the children to be engaged with what they're doing, don't you? ... And the one thing you don't want is the children being that word 'bored'. You don't want them sitting there with absolutely no idea what you're doing and getting absolutely nothing out of it but sitting there because they have to be. Even more so, you don't want children sitting in your classroom worrying or even being frightened.

This is Deborah Gardner, a primary maths specialist teacher, discussing what learning and teaching mathematics in a creative way means to her. Boredom and the worry about 'getting it wrong' have been long-standing mathematical issues. A key finding from a report entitled *Mathematics Counts*, which was focused on the teaching of mathematics within schools, was as follows:

The extent to which the need to undertake even an apparently simple and straightforward piece of mathematics could induce feelings of anxiety, helplessness, fear and even guilt in some of those interviewed was, perhaps, the most striking feature of the study. (Cockroft, 1982: 7)

Similarly, it was highlighted that:

... issues regarding the teaching and learning of mathematics remain, and the United Kingdom is still one of the few advanced nations where it is socially acceptable – fashionable, even – to profess an inability to cope with the subject. (Williams, 2008: 3)

The above quote is taken from another report focusing on the teaching of mathematics within primary schools some 26 years later. Negative attitudes towards the learning of mathematics are also discussed by Boaler (2009), who neatly encapsulates the issue in the title of her book, *The Elephant in the Classroom: Helping Children*

Learn and Love Maths. Here, Boaler discusses this fear and worry about mathematics which almost inevitably features within sections of the teaching profession and those who potentially hope to teach. This 'fear of failure' or 'getting the wrong answer' often exists when initial teacher trainees sit in primary mathematics lectures, or when practising teachers attend mathematics CPD; not wanting to look 'stupid' can genuinely stifle the atmosphere within a lecture or training session. However, the saddest situation of all must be that some teachers lack the confidence to teach mathematics effectively because this fear of failure might be demonstrated in front of their pupils, and so they engage in a safe, risk-averse approach.

This is problematised further by the 'reputation' of the subject as it progresses into adulthood, with mathematics seen by many as a subject to be feared or avoided. As a subject, it is seen 'by most people to be a body of established knowledge and procedures – facts and rules' (Ahmed, 1987: 13), and perhaps this is why many adults and children are not interested in the subject, with the latter often keen to give up its formal study at the earliest possible opportunity. These fears lead to other significant observations, for example: 'Why is it ok to be "no good" at mathematics? Would participants have readily professed to an inability to cope with reading?' (Williams, 2008). So, some of the key questions for this chapter need to be:

- How can creativity be employed to resolve some of the spectres outlined above?
- Does creativity exist within mathematics? If so, what might it look like?
- Does working creatively in mathematics mean working differently? Does it mean doing *more*?
- Do the 'using and applying of mathematics' and 'assessment' documentation have a role in taking a creative approach to mathematics?

Many teachers take great satisfaction and enjoy working in a creative way within the primary curriculum; they see the benefits of, for example, of using a range of drama techniques to support the quality of children's writing within English. Self-expression, the ability to make choices, to evaluate their approach and outcomes, all contribute to a creative approach to learning. However, it is less easy sometimes for teachers to see what the corresponding activities may look like within mathematics. Sometimes this is because certain subjects are seen as 'more creative' than others but:

> creativity is not unique to the arts. It is equally fundamental to advances in the sciences, in mathematics … in all areas of everyday life (NAACE, 1999: 27)

Unfortunately, mathematics is not generally seen as a 'naturally' creative subject and is often perceived to be more difficult to teach creatively than other subjects. Even in schools where the curriculum is organised to reflect a creative or thematic approach, mathematics may still be taught as a discrete subject.

So, is creativity within mathematics a bolt-on, something to add on after the main planning has been carried out? Does it mean more work in order to have a creative approach to learning and teaching in mathematics? Or does having a creative approach align itself closely to working mathematically? Many writers within the mathematics education landscape have captured the essence of what it involves or means to work 'mathematically'. For example, one line of argument is that mathematics is effectively learned only by experimenting, questioning, reflecting, discovering, inventing and discussing (as acknowledged by Ahmed, 1987). Or sometimes the focus is instead on the open nature of working like a mathematician, where ownership is taken by pupils themselves for determining the mathematics needed to solve a problem or task in hand, where there is a purpose, a reason, for carrying out the mathematics. Progression is planned for, based on a clear insight into where the child's understanding is at any specific time in their learning journey within a teacher's classroom (Fosnot and Dolk, 2001; Boaler, 2009). There is no suggestion that this planning or approach is necessarily formal, rigid, inflexible or unconnected and with an emphasis on procedures rather than understanding (typically 'un-creative' characteristics within mathematics). Additionally, in strong mathematical classrooms teachers do not always know the answers or the way in which all the children will get there; they allow themselves to take risks by not fully controlling the learning journey. It is this willingness that can yield the opportunities for children to work like 'mathematicians'.

A range of types of mental activity linked to mathematical thinking are highlighted, focusing on those aspects of mathematics 'which are associated with thinking, reasoning and coming to know a concept' (Watson and Mason, 1998: 7). The notion of questioning one's thinking around a mathematical task/problem/conundrum, or, as teachers, questioning the children's thinking, appears to be a key element of working in a mathematical way.

There is a similar distinction between *learning mathematics*, that is, learning the 'stuff' or content knowledge, and that of *doing mathematics*, where the individual might be producing or developing more of the 'stuff' or content knowledge themselves (Schoenfeld, 1994: 55). However, it is important to note that the skills and knowledge do play an important part in this process. Creativity is absolutely grounded within the notion of opening or freeing up; this is essential:

> … but so too are skills, knowledge and understanding. Being creative in music, or in physics, or dance, or mathematics, involves knowledge and expertise in the skills, materials and forms of understanding that they involve. (NAACE, 1999: 38)

There is a need for pupils to practise skills and to accumulate knowledge in mathematics (Schoenfeld, 1994), but quite often this takes up a disproportionate part of mathematics curriculum time. Deborah agrees that there is a need for this. However, she is also clear in her pedagogical approach:

Every lesson I do, I try to put at least one practical element in. We do lots of talking, lots of group work, have some kind of interaction; I give them an environment that's safe to do that in. Sometimes, I'll get them to write answers on little notes and then put them into a box; that helps them to get over the fear of giving a wrong answer because some children still have that notion.

An interesting analogy has been made between children who spend their time mostly engaging in 'drill' and 'practice' within mathematics, but never actually using and applying mathematical skills and knowledge, and what it must feel like to spend endless hours learning the associated skills and rules for a sport while never actually taking part in any games (Ahmed, 1987; Jones, in Thompson, 2003).

The mathematical qualities associated with problem solving are drawn out when exploring what it means to work in a mathematical way; in particular, 'gathering and ordering information, analysing ... by searching for patterns ... seeking connections, making conjectures, and offering generalities' (Ollerton, in Thompson, 2010: 88). The Realistic Mathematics Education (RME) school of thought, which originated in Holland, sees the relevance of mathematics, something that is real whether in everyday life or which can be imagined as a crucial element of working mathematically. Pupils have the space to explore their approaches and thinking, by themselves and with each other, to use their informal understanding upon which to build more formal procedures. This is generally situated in an initially carefully considered problem (Treffers and Beishuizen, in Thompson, 1999). A clear description of this RME approach is outlined in research articles trialling and then documenting case studies using the approach with secondary-aged pupils (Dickinson and Eade, 2005; Dickinson, Eade, Gough and Hough, 2010).

Working within such contexts requires the ability to negotiate unexpected answers and questions, while in the flow of teaching – described as 'contingency'. This flexibility demands a good level of personal subject knowledge as well as a deep understanding of pedagogical knowledge in order to 'transform' the new knowledge to the learner (Rowland, Turner, Thwaites and Huckstep, 2009).

The need for flexibility also pertains to the importance of taking a holistic view of any mathematics curriculum and to making decisions when planning to teach the subject that reflect a flexibility that allows movement. Effective and creative teachers of mathematics will take a clear overview at the beginning of the year of the whole curriculum to be taught, in order to determine where the natural connections can be made, where areas of the curriculum can be taught in conjunction, through carefully planned activities. This enables relevant and meaningful connections to be made by the children. These connections may be between different areas within mathematics itself; for example, when exploring a number pattern, connecting knowledge of number facts (any operation), factors, multiples, primes, in order to make a generalisation, which can allow the *nth* term to be determined. Connections may also be made between mathematics and other areas of the curriculum such as science or geography. This connectionist approach (Askew, et al., 1997) is viewed as a trait of an effective teacher of numeracy, but can be extended through to wider mathematics. Deborah describes the 'positive tingle' that she gets when children start to make connections for themselves. She also makes links within the mathematics curriculum and between mathematics and other areas as a natural aspect of her pedagogy. The teacher's role can be described as 'to help the child to build up connections between new experiences and previous learning. Learning without making connections is what we would call rote learning' (Haylock and Cockburn, 2008: 9). Deborah notes: 'For example, I look at aboriginal myths and that means looking at symbols and then that's straight into your algebra, and then into why we use Morse code. I try to look at things that come naturally together, trying to make those little links all the time. It gives it context.'

When working mathematically, there is an almost inevitable sense of being drawn to problem-solving perspectives, or of making maths relevant and purposeful for the children being taught. There appears to be a natural relationship with that aspect of the mathematics curriculum which has come to be called 'Using and Applying Mathematics' (UAM). Creativity and solving problems are not necessarily perceived to be the same, as 'Not all problems require creative solutions or original thinking' (NAACE, 1999: 34). What may require such processes to take place, is when children are presented with '... true problematic situations that support and enhance investigation and enquiry' (Fosnot and Dolk, 2001: xv, xix). Furthermore, it is essential that children are given the opportunity to create their own problems to solve. This kind of activity supports children in *mathematising* their world.

Though it is rich in its potential to offer opportunities to work in a mathematical and creative way, the use and application of mathematics is not always embedded within classrooms (Ofsted, 2008; Williams, 2008). However, when brought into the classroom, UAM develops the sense of working mathematically. Teachers are asked to develop an awareness of what holds importance within mathematical work; to encourage and value reasoning (Haylock and Cockburn, 2008). Unfortunately, this is mainly manifested in the solving of word problems, and it seems to have become synonymous with the using and applying of mathematics in mathematics teaching. Such word problems have been described as 'thinly disguised calculations wrapped in words' (Jones, in Thompson, 2003: 87). When UAM happens genuinely in the classroom, there are also fruitful opportunities for confident assessment. Many times teachers lament that a child could, for example, confidently calculate numbers beyond the hundred boundary mentally and yet one day or one week later they appear to have forgotten. When a child has to resolve a problematic situation by 'applying' and 'using' their mathematical knowledge and skills, the teacher *knows* that they can do it.

Whilst debates take place, UAM is generally thought to include such aspects as:

- Making decisions.
- Reasoning and generalising (about numbers and shapes).
- Problems (involving 'real life', money or measures).

(National Curriculum: 1999)

In classrooms where using and applying takes place regularly, children will be (not a comprehensive list): analysing, doing, deciding, planning, creating, interpreting, reasoning, justifying, applying, exploring, conjecturing, posing, questioning, eliminating, enquiring, discarding, probing, connecting, generalising, thinking, choosing, constructing (physical structures and sense), arguing, determining and enjoying. If a child is engaging in aspects of all of the above *over time*, then he will have opportunities to be working in a creative and mathematical way.

A familiar example of where such behaviours might be witnessed is in whole-class projects. This may involve the allocation of fixed budgets to organise and hold a party, for example. This would involve: sourcing and pricing food (budgeting), and representing data about costs and quantities. Decisions regarding what to buy and where from will require communication, reasoning and justi-fication. Safety implications may need to be considered. How many people can be accommodated? What is the area of the classroom or the hall? Similarly, groups may be given a stall at the summer or winter fair with a predetermined budget. From this, they are required to make and sell goods, with the winners being those generating the highest income. Much communication, choice-making and reasoning will be involved in planning and designing products and sourcing materials, and the mathematics involved in determining profit margins is plentiful, with percentages and averages involved amongst other elements. There is nothing contrived here; these very human activities (Treffers and Beishuizen, in Thompson, 1999) promote a natural need to employ the mathematics necessary; there is a purpose and a value to the mathematical processes required to negotiate or solve the 'problematic' situations.

Being creative and working mathematically, particularly in the area of the use and application of mathematics, do not appear to be exclusive of each other. On some levels, there are striking convergences such as:

- Collaborative working and the ability to engage in reasoning.
- Space to engage in following a line of enquiry.
- The need to question and make decisions or choices; and to justify why these have been made.
- Exploring different strategies; relating to prior understanding; judging the value of the strategies being or **not** being employed.
- Having a reason or purpose for doing the activity, including that which can be imagined.
- Using existing prior knowledge to determine next steps.
- Judging the value of that which you have uncovered and how this can be used to support future understanding.

Taking a creative approach can enhance the teaching of mathematics; it is not something to add on as an afterthought but very much present from the first stages of planning. It is embedded into the approach taken by the teacher and the opportunities provided for the children. What might this look like in the classroom? The following is a situated learning experience observed within Deborah Gardner's classroom.

Deborah's starting point in our discussions is that she has no doubt that mathematics can be taught and learnt in a creative way:

> Yes, I think maths can be creative, definitely. Maybe it's because I've come into it (the teaching profession) as an artist … when I just think about how children love pattern, they naturally see and are drawn to patterns, when I watch the children in Art, I am amazed at just how mathematical they are and a lot of it comes from them, it's not always something that I have set up.

Before the start of mathematics sessions in Deborah's classroom, interest levels are high, both for the adults and the children. I wait in the classroom just before the children come in to start their mathematics lesson. No textbook is in sight, and there are no exercise books either at this point in time. What I am struck by is the fact that I personally want to 'get stuck into' this lesson already. There are a number of resources out on the desks just inviting exploration; these include: a tub or basket of Compare bears; a large piece of paper; a piece of foil; and a card explaining an investigation per group. In the room there are also three small tanks of water and some weighing scales. What could this all mean?

The structure of Deborah's mathematics lessons are unsurprisingly varied:

> I don't stick rigidly to a three-part lesson; sometimes I just like to throw it all in the air; sometimes I like to start at the end and then come back. It's about being flexible, too, changing something if its not working. It's about being really well prepared, having different activities, games, etc., ready. Having resources that the children might need to use … and freedom to choose appropriate resources when they are needed.

There is excited chatter as the children enter the room following their assembly. There is much surmising and excited anticipation. The teacher begins by placing each child in a group. When everyone is settled at their table, the mathematical fun begins. Like me, the children are already keen to begin the investigation. The children are in mixed groups of four; they are of mixed ability and one child is assigned as the recorder. This child records all the information arising from the collaborative activity. The children are informed that there are bears who currently live on an island but they face danger and must escape. Their task is to design a boat to take the bears off the island, and this boat will be tested to see if it floats. The most important thing they need to remember is that the bears cannot swim. Deborah is very enthusiastic about the task. She is dramatic in her sharing of the task; no one would doubt whether she was telling the truth or not, and the children engage excitedly with the fiction.

The children are asked to estimate how many bears they think they can save. Weighing scales are available for the children if they wish to use them, but at no point does Deborah inform them that they must be used. She knows that an important part of the children's ability to use and apply their mathematical skills is the ability to choose and use appropriate equipment or tools to enable them to resolve the problem or find the solution. The estimates are collated for each group on a large chart, setting up a scenario for comparison and checking later in the week by the whole class; this information will also serve as the basis for further maths work that can be linked in here, such as fractions, percentages and ratios. Some careful questioning takes place once again. The children are asked to think what might be involved. The questioning is kept very broad and open at this point. Reference to a fair test is made by one child, so links to science are already evident. One young girl continues along these lines by discussing the concepts of floating and sinking and how the children will need to be conscious of these while carrying out the task. She talks about weight, and the implications of the bears being too heavy, while balancing this with the need to save as many bears as possible. Deborah is very keen that mathematics work should be linked closely with that of science, noting that there are many natural connections which should be capitalised on. This is a regular feature of her planning. The questioning continues. Watching the questioning is like watching an art form. No answers are alluded to or given; there is simply probing, a gentle drawing out of information; this involves a move away from traditionally closed questions, to really listening to what the children are saying, and moving on from their responses rather than directing back to the predetermined answer which lies in her head. I notice that Deborah is careful not to give closed feedback such as 'Good', 'Well done', or 'Yes'. Somebody mentions a net and 3D shapes. When responses are not forth-coming, cleverly tailored prompts are used (Watson and Mason, 1998). Deborah simply drops in questions such as:

Why do you think that?
Why not …?
If we know that, what else do we know …?
What do you think about what she has just said?
Do you agree?

She feels strongly about children having wait time when questioned:

Don't give them the answer too quickly either. If they've got something wrong, tell them to try something else, let's not give up. The idea is that we're going to challenge ourselves, we're not going to give in.

These strategies can develop a 'process' for children when approaching the solving of mathematically problematic situations. Having an internal dialogue that questions their approach and the strategies they may employ forms an important part of their creative strategy.

A fundamental ethos within this classroom is that the children are required to explain their thinking and their mathematical reasoning. As the lesson progresses,

I note that children begin to question their own (and others') plans and solutions. Thinking and reasoning are not exclusively verbal; they also take place within written explanations of tasks. Mathematical thinking and reasoning are also represented pictorially which can help children to see some logical, systematic ways of working or even clues to possible solutions.

There has been much discussion and debate before the children set off on the task. This has served to warm up their thinking, to give them ideas, to make them aware of any issues that they need to be aware of when solving this problematic situation. Deborah does intervene at this starting point to ensure that groups work in a fair and truly collaborative way. She has some instructions at the working tables which provide a framework for the children to work within, without taking away the space for them to be creative in their approach. This includes stipulating: which materials can or cannot be used to make the boat; a five-minute discussion time to agree a way forward in terms of designing their boat; estimating the number of bears that can be saved. Taking a creative approach does not necessarily equate to 'letting everything go'; this is the result of subtle choices made by the teacher at the planning stage.

A quick scan of the classroom once the children have started reveals a busy environment; there is lots of talk going on between the teacher and the children and between the children themselves. It is particularly interesting to note the children's mathematical vocabulary; although it is not always accurate, they make a real effort to use appropriate subject-specific vocabulary in context. Where there is interaction with an adult, encouragement to use the appropriate mathematical vocabulary is highly evident. There is also a good deal of movement. This activity involves taking risks for the learner – 'What if the boat sinks?', 'What if we can't save the bears? However, everyone seems willing to take these risks; there isn't an air of worry or dread; quite the opposite: there is a palpable excitement and the children are genuinely eager to get on with the 'work'. There is also a risk for the teacher of working in this way. Deborah confesses that sometimes in the middle of a lesson if someone were to come in, it may seem like chaos, but if you ask the children what they are doing, they are engaged with a purpose, focused and able to explain. Just as importantly, the children do not spend the whole lesson relying upon the teacher to impart information to them.

On the surface, the task appears quite simple. The brilliance of it is in the planning. It is an open investigation; there is no singularly defined way to approach it. The children have the freedom to 'step into' the task in whatever way they wish – and they certainly do. As the lesson progresses and I look around, I am faced with at least four entirely different designs of boats. What is striking about the mathematically 'problematic situation' (Fosnot and Dolk, 2001) in terms of its creativity, is not what the teacher has brought physically to the table but the opportunities that she has brought to the table for the children to work in a creative way. That is, it is not just the teaching that is creative but, more importantly, the learning. The children have enough prior knowledge to initially engage with the task; they have knowledge of 2D and 3D shapes, of nets, of how they can form a 3D shape from 2D shapes. As they progress with the task, they begin to ask questions, of themselves, of each other and of the adult working with them, about capacity, which leads them to explore area, perimeter and mass. Some of the children are comfortable with these concepts and so they push their learning further, now exploring volume. Some may not yet know this concept in such terms, but they are creating some meaning about the space that now exists in the boat they have designed and how this relates to the number, mass and weight of bears that will fit in and float. The children begin to make connections. This truly exemplifies a creative approach. The children have been able to make or create sense of the task using their own present understanding and their ability to apply some sense or informal or pre-formal knowledge (Webb, Boswinkel and Dekker, 2008) to a yet unknown situation. It is this space between the known and the unknown where true creativity can thrive.

The end of the lesson calls for judgement time as the various boats and their occupants are tested in the tanks of water. Not all are successful and a rich discussion exploring possible reasons for this ensues. However, no one is made to feel a failure and all contributions have been valued.

Some considerations for working creatively within the learning and teaching of mathematics

Standing recently within an Early Years Foundation Stage unit, I was struck by the response to the question that I had been asking myself in writing this chapter, 'What does it mean to be creative in mathematics?' It suddenly seemed to have been the obvious place to go to have my question answered. The place exuded a buzz of creativity; children were exploring, demonstrating self-expression, pondering and communicating. They were interested, keen to tell me about the tower they were constructing, comparing with their friends; others were keen that I could see the fair sharing of grapes that they were carrying out so that everyone got the same amount. They engaged in trial and error to see who could put the most items into the smallest box, without any consciousness that failure may result; they made choices to keep or discard. Most importantly, I saw that the children were absorbed in their activity, they had time, they persisted. The children discovered and explored unknown things (to them) and used the knowledge gained a few minutes or hours ago, or even earlier, to help them make sense or create new knowledge of the task facing them. Interestingly, there were also periods of inactivity while they thought about the problem before them.

The realisation was also there that this way of working was intrinsically linked to a rigorous assessment procedure. Any adult working with the children could assess their learning confidently, due to the opportunities that had been created to demonstrate understanding, thought processes and opinions.

Does this change as children become older? Many teachers would say that the children in their maths lessons talk, are active and engage in practical activity; these all contribute to a creative way of working. However, care must be taken to ensure that one does not make the assumption that because practical resources are being used, because children are 'doing' and being 'hands-on', having fun, or because the learning has moved into a different physical space (i.e., outdoor learning), that one is necessarily taking a fully creative approach (Worthington, 2006). These feature within the realm of creativity, in terms of creative contexts, but it is the opportunities to access such tasks in a creative and varied way which further enhance this experience. If pupils are engaged in cutting out a pre-determined set of 2D shapes in order to construct a *given* model of a 3D shape, they are engaging in a practical activity, but how creative is their *approach* to the activity? What of the children who are exploring whether every packet of a given brand of sweets has exactly the same number of each colour in it when they are asked to complete a pre-prepared bar chart on which to represent their data? What *choices* are they being asked to make? Are they given the *flexibility* to make choices if the outcome is predetermined? Can they *ask questions* of others or themselves in order to decide which way to go next, to *experiment*, to *change* tack? Can they *explore* other approaches or explore different outcomes? When these elements are included, pupils are able to be creative in their approach to the task and in their thinking processes. There isn't a requirement for the pupil to work in only one way (often the teacher's way), but rather an option to follow their own line of enquiry, to explore the outcome that they wish to. I am reminded of a conversation with another maths specialist teacher, Diane, who described a situation whereby her school wished to reduce its electricity bill; an electricity consumption counter was fitted which was child-friendly. The children were told that all money saved would be given to the classes in order to buy resources decided by them. Our discussion revolved around Diane allowing the children to explore various energy-saving strategies and collating and representing the data in any way *they chose* in order to determine what energy was being saved and by which means. There was also the opportunity to explore the implications of the resultant data and to seek views on what the money might be spent on; once again, the children choosing their own method of data collection and representation. The potential for working creatively here was enormous.

In order to embrace such opportunities, the ethos within the classroom is a key element in working creatively within mathematics. The teacher has a direct and immediate impact upon this. Enthusiasm for the subject will transfer across to the children. The creation of a creative classroom suggests a movement away from activities that are too tightly structured by the teacher; these are often reliant upon textbooks, worksheets and repetitive exercises, and provide little space within for children's creative inputs. Working in an 'uncreative' atmosphere can lead very quickly to mathematics being seen as dull and stale, which in turn leads to a vicious cycle of negative attitudes towards learning of the subject. This contrasts sharply with the picture in Deborah's classroom of purposeful talk, meaningful activity, movement, and ownership of the approaches to learning.

The ethos of a classroom where creativity thrives in mathematics must also take account of making mistakes. There is a need for pupils to see that it is good to make mistakes and that these are in fact valued (Ryan and Williams, 2007;

Hansen, 2011); that much can be learned about the mathematics under scrutiny and about their approach to the solving of the mathematics in front of them when errors occur. For pupils, it can be truly inspiring to see that it can be the uncertainty, the need to explore further, that truly moves the thought around a problem into a creative sphere. This can be empowering for pupils. The unknown may be explored, or a line of enquiry followed, which may not lead to the 'correct' solution or any solution; therefore the notion of risk-taking within the mathematics classroom is crucial if pupils are to truly develop as creative mathematicians.

In order to incorporate this into mathematics lessons, teachers like Deborah 'create' the opportunity to solve 'unknown' problematic situations together (Piggott, 2007). With shared ownership for solving the mathematical problem or situation, no one person within the classroom holds all the answers or all of the power; this can promote a truly creative approach, as all parties within the classroom can be involved and different 'ways in' to the problem can be tried and evaluated. In this way, everyone can be engaged in a creativity-rich process. How wonderful it is for pupils to see the teacher being puzzled by a problem, to observe her pondering, thinking aloud their reasoning, using the prompt questions that we often supply for pupils to use when enquiring, but within a real context. Whereas a novice teacher might see this as an indication of weakness or even failure, the reality is that it can be a hugely positive experience for pupils. The opportunity to see that the teacher does not know which mathematical way to go may be a real eye-opener for some pupils, helping them begin to understand that this 'uncertain' state of affairs is actually a normal part of the problem-solving process. Seeing the teacher taking these very same risks is to create the security that is required for pupils to be willing to engage in a creative approach themselves.

Children will also gain much from watching how the teacher jots and notes, sometimes providing a logical ordered record of her thinking, sometimes just testing to see if an idea works, and to know that it is fine if it does not. It is also valuable for the pupils to see how the teacher makes connections and links to her and the children's own prior learning, that every bit of information could be the next clue to move on. It is within this sphere of experience that a child will also develop a notion of efficient ways of working, by approaching tasks in different ways, deciding what works for him and building upon this to develop an expedient way of working.

Some teachers get disheartened when trying this approach initially due to the lack of children's resilience when tackling mathematical problems, but the notion of 'stuckness' can also be important. Getting the 'creative juices' flowing is often directly a result of being 'stuck' (Pirsig, 1999; Mason, Burton and Stacey, 1985; Piggott, 2007). When approaching a problem for the first time, one is in a state of conscious incompetence. It can't be solved yet, but similar situations have been encountered and one will move forward from this point. A thought will occur, a connection be made, perhaps in discussion with someone else, feeding off their thinking, or somebody will question someone else's thoughts in a constructive way, or even explain an idea. These are the ways we guide our pupils to 'create' some meaning of the problem for themselves, so that each time, a little more knowledge of strategy, skill or understanding is acquired in order to aid them the next time that they approach a situation which requires solving. The wider the range of strategies developed, the more creative a child can be in their approach to solving the unknown.

To help develop resilience, a carefully considered shared class problem may be introduced at the beginning of the week. Children work through this by choice and share strategies and ideas. Engaging in this can support effective working through similar problems within the mathematics lesson. For example, hopscotch in the playground might be explored – and the numbers changed; the mobile phone keypad might be explored, focusing on the totals of numbers in the rows and columns, the diagonals, the corners. Try it and see what you find. Use the clock-face: there is so much to explore in there and so many links to be made. Get much more creative with exploring the hundred square. What do the children want to find out? Use an old tablecloth or sheet to explore shapes through folding. Which shapes can you make? Which can't you make? Carry out some folds and then ask a question such as, 'From here, can we make a pentagon with only one more fold?'

One effective strategy that teachers use to enable children to work creatively within mathematics and to enable themselves to take risks in a safer space is to work with small groups of children engaged in 'guided reasoning'. This ensures that it is 'consciously' considered when planning for mathematics learning and teaching. Here, the teacher does not actively teach a concept, but provides a situated learning experience for the children to be involved in, where mathematical skills and knowledge will need to be employed in order to resolve the problem or situation. Teachers are sometimes fearful that working in this open, creative way means throwing everything into the air, resulting in inevitable chaos possibly because these are the very situations where one's own subject knowledge is tested. Trainee teachers must take ownership of the development of mathematics subject or content knowledge at their own level and explore deeper pedagogical subject knowledge. Many excellent resources are available to support this aspect of development, and some are listed at the end of the chapter.

Opening up approaches does not have to mean that chaos ensues. In fact, the open, creative-rich activities have often been carefully planned by the teacher in order to enable clear progression in understanding to take place. The teacher knows what the children are capable of in terms of their mathematical understanding, basing this upon careful formative assessment. The learning experience is pitched just a shade above that where the children are currently operating. This allows the teacher to plan for the child's stage of learning, not what is predetermined as 'appropriate' for their age. It is this space between 'What I know now', 'Where I need to get to' and 'How I am going to get there in order to solve this problem' that new thought can be created, possibilities explored and experimentation happen. It is here that 'new' knowledge (for the learner) can be discovered. Once the problem or situation is resolved, the learner can judge the value of that which has been gained by this process, both in terms of the knowledge and the skills that have allowed the discovery to be made. The learner can also self-assess in order to determine his next steps. These correlate closely to those aspects of creativity highlighted earlier (NAAACE, 1999; Craft, et al., 2001). The role of the teacher here is to listen and assess 'how' the pupils undertake the mathematics rather than 'what' the pupils achieve; she will give the space for them to explore and to explain their thinking within the subject, dropping in carefully chosen prompts to move proceedings along only if stalemate is reached.

Potentially, this type of exercise can result in a *virtuous* circle. The more this type of activity takes place, the more the teacher gains knowledge about the mathematical understanding of the children, the more the children can be engaged in creative mathematical work. By working in this way, there are occasions when pupils take responsibility for their own learning and are given the time to do so by the teacher; they gain an understanding that the process of mathematical learning involves making decisions and expressing thought, and is not simply a case of following rules or procedures. There is real potential when working in this guided way for the teacher to trial approaches which foster creativity with a view to scaling up to use with the whole class. The guided session can be the nursery of creativity and its impact can be monitored very closely.

Reflection upon the learning is a key aspect for working creatively within mathematics (Tanner and Jones, 2007). The ability to talk about your findings, to explain decisions and explain your understanding is key to developing a creative approach. In Deborah's classroom, the recorder takes photographs of work in progress and completed work. These are stuck into books and children are encouraged to 'talk' or 'write' about their mathematical experiences. For the teacher, this information gives a firm basis for identifying the child's understanding and where to go next with their learning. For the child, this approach situates them right back in the learning experience where the learning took place. This strategy is also useful for redirecting a child to make connections at a later stage of their learning, thereby building on their prior knowledge.

Here are some sources for ideas which promote the ethos of working creatively within mathematics:

Be a Mathematician (BEAM) – www.beam.co.uk

This website carries a whole host of resources, including the popular 'Talk it, Solve it' series which encourages pupils to develop their reasoning skills. Use these resources to help open up your teaching.

NRICH – nrich.maths.org

Run in conjunction with the University of Cambridge, this website holds thousands of resources to encourage pupils to work like young mathematicians. New resources are added at the beginning of every month. Pupils can complete investigations and send in their solutions. Solutions are available and links to the curriculum identified.

NCETM – www.ncetm.org.uk

This is a network for teachers to share ideas and gain support. Classroom resources are also available on this website.

Deborah Gardner has provided the following list of websites that she uses regularly for inspiration:

- http://www.creative-partnerships.comhttp://www.collaborativelearning.org/
- http://www.collaborativelearning.orghttp://illuminations.nctm.org/
- http://illuminations.nctm.orghttp://nrich.maths.org/
- http://nrich.maths.orghttp://web.me.com/paulscott/info/maths-gallery
- http://web.me.com/paulscott/info/maths-galleryhttp://www.cimt. plymouth.ac.uk/
- http://www.cimt.plymouth.ac.ukhttp://www.nga.gov.kids/
- http://www.nga.gov.kidshttp://www.mathwire,com/
- http://www.mathwire,comhttps://ncetm,org,uk/
- https://ncetm,org,ukhttp://tes.co.uk/
- http://tes.co.ukhttp://www.lancsngfl.ax/u
- http://www.lancsngfl.ax/u

Another possible resource is any mathematical puzzle book. Two favourites of mine are:

Entertaining Mathematical Puzzles by Martin Gardner.
The Big Book of Brain Games. 1000 PlayThinks of Art, Mathematics and Science by Ivan Moscovich.

Creative Touches

- Be generous. To be creative in mathematics as a teacher and as a learner, there needs to be a level of unselfishness. There is little scope for creativity if the teacher's approach is 'my way or the highway'.
- Be flexible, both at the planning stage (a holistic view of curriculum) and within the teaching moment.
- Have the confidence to allow children to follow a line of enquiry where the unknown exists for the teacher as much as the child; encourage risk-taking and view the making of mistakes as positives.

- Give the children opportunities to take ownership of their mathematical learning; to make decisions and choices throughout this process.

- Allow children to pose their own mathematically problematic situations, including ones that have not been considered by the teacher.

- Identify appropriate learning experiences in order to allow for progression. (A range of suitable websites and resources are listed above.)

- Ensure you have sound subject, content and pedagogical knowledge.

References

Ahmed, A. (1987). *Better Mathematics. A Curriculum Development Study*. London, HMSO.

Askew, M., Brown, M., Rhodes, V., Wiliam, D. and Johnson, D. (1997). *Effective Teachers of Numeracy*. London: King's College.

Boaler, J. (2009). *The Elephant in the Classroom: Helping Children Learn and Love Maths*. London: Souvenir Press Ltd.

Butterworth, B. (2000). *The Mathematical Brain*. London: Papermac.

Cockroft, W. H. (1982). *Mathematics Counts, Report of the Committee of Inquiry into the Teaching of Mathematics in Schools*. London: HMSO.

Craft, A., Jeffrey, B. and Liebling, M. (2001). *Creativity in Education*. London: Continuum.

Department for Education and Employment and Qualifications and Curriculum Authority (1999). *The National Curriculum. Handbook for primary teachers in England*. London: Crown Copyright and QCA.

Dickinson, P. and Eade, F. (2005). Trialling Realistic Mathematics Education (RME) in English secondary schools, in D. Hewitt (ed.), *Proceedings of the British Society for Research into Learning Mathematics*, 25 (3).

Dickinson, P., Eade, F., Gough, S. and Hough, S. (2010). Using Realistic Mathematics Education with low to middle attaining pupils in secondary schools, in M. Joubert (ed.) *Proceedings of the British Society for Research into Learning Mathematics*, April.

Fosnot, C. and Dolk, M. (2001). *Young Mathematicians at Work Constructing Number Sense, Addition and Subtraction*. Portsmouth, NH: Heinemann.

Hansen, A. (ed.) (2011). *Children's Errors in Mathematics: Understanding Common Misconceptions in the Primary School*. Exeter: Learning Matters.

Haylock, D. and Cockburn, A. (2008). *Understanding Mathematics for Young Children: A Guide for Foundation Stage and Lower Primary Teachers*. London: SAGE.

Mason, J., Burton, L. and Stacey, K. (1985). *Thinking Mathematically*. Essex: Prentice Hall.

National Advisory Committee on Creativity and Cultural Education (NACCCE) (1999). *All our Futures: Creativity, Culture and Education*. London: DFEE.

Ofsted, (2008). *Mathematics: Understanding the Score*. London: Crown Copyright.

Piggott, J. (2007). Cultivating Creativity. *Mathematics Teaching*, Vol. 202.

Pirsig, R. (1999). *Zen and the Art of Motorcycle Maintenance*. London: Vintage.

Rowland, T., Turner, F., Thwaites, A. and Huckstep, P. (2009). *Developing Primary Mathematics Teaching*. London: SAGE.

Ryan, J. and Williams, J. (2007). *Children's Mathematics 4–15: Learning from Errors and Misconceptions*. Maidenhead: Open University Press.

Schoenfeld, A. (1994). *Mathematical Thinking and Problem Solving*. Oxford: Routledge.

Tanner, H. and Jones, S. (2007). How Interactive is Your Whiteboard? *Mathematics Teaching Incorporating Micromath*, 200 (January).

Thompson, I. (1999). *Issues in teaching numeracy in Primary Schools* (1st edn). Buckingham: OUP.

Thompson, I. (2003). *Enhancing Primary Mathematics Teaching*. Maidenhead: OUP.

Thompson, I. (2010). *Issues in teaching numeracy in Primary Schools* (2nd edn). Maidenhead: OUP.

Watson, A. and Mason, J. (1998). *Questions and Prompts for Mathematical Thinking*. Derby: ATM.

Webb, D. C., Boswinkel, N. and Dekker, T. (2008). Beneath the tip of the iceberg: Using representations to support student understanding. *Mathematics Teaching in the Middle School,* Vol. 14, No 2.

Williams, P. (2008). *Independent Review of Mathematics Teaching in Early Years Settings and Primary Schools – Final Report*. Nottingham: DCSF.

Worthington, M. (2006). Creativity meets Mathematics. *Practical Pre-school* (June).

4

Science

Paul Warwick and Lyn Dawes

Natalie's Year 4 class were excited; they had been given invitations to a 'Forces Science Party'. Looking inside the invitations with their groups, they found some ideas to help to structure and focus their discussions. In the classroom, each group became involved in the party activities – bubble blowing, paper aeroplanes, pass the parcel and 'stretchy and squashy' marshmallows. They raised ideas and questions, discussed them, explored them practically and collected a list of further questions. Finally there was a whole-class party game of pick up and move the jelly cube with the chop sticks – easy! But what if the jelly cube was covered in oil? What if the chopsticks were covered in oil, rather than the jelly cube? At the end of the party, each group had a chance to discuss their findings and ideas with the class, to provide their explanations and share new questions for future work. One child's explanation of how gravity might drag the bubble liquid towards the ground, distorting and eventually bursting the bubble, brought forth a collective 'Wow!'

This is creative teaching of science, stimulating creativity in science learners. It exemplifies how Natalie's classroom operates. We can identify some key aspects of creative teaching from this excerpt:

- an inclusive, stimulating starter which raises interesting questions, creates a sense of wonder and supports the learners as they start to think about their approach to problem solving;
- a motivating and meaningful context for activities;
- chances to make choices and decisions based on discussion with others;
- engaging and relevant enquiry activities, achievable by collaborative working;
- effective planning, with resources and ideas well organised in advance;
- whole-class enquiry and discussion;
- 'what if ...?' questions;
- exploratory talk in which ideas are respected, challenged and negotiated.

This chapter will draw on Natalie's lesson to explore the concept of creativity in the primary science classroom. It will consider how creative teaching and learning are related and how they mirror, to some extent, constructivist and socio-cultural perspectives on the teaching and learning of science; how ideas of context and relevance are integral to a conception of creativity in science education; how a collaborative classroom ethos encourages pupil agency and the expression of creative ideas; and finally how the idea of the 'dialogic classroom' is central to enabling pupils to make creative responses to science exploration and experimentation.

What kind of science learners do we want?

When considering creativity, it is useful to start with learners. In science education we intend that learners will develop 'personal frameworks of understanding' that will become increasingly linked to established science knowledge. We do not expect children to pioneer knowledge new to science in their classrooms; but if science in the primary school is not about children making original scientific discoveries, then what is it about?

Creative and 'authentic' learning is that in which the outcomes for the learner are original and significant for them. Authentic learning occurs when the child's way of seeing the world, or a particular phenomena, has been disturbed, requiring 'a re-representation from one way of seeing things to another, new way of seeing things' (Wegerif, 2010: 54). New learning involves such personal creation of knowledge for children in our science lessons; through it we can see children constructing new meanings, explanations, hypotheses, arguments and procedures. More than this, what we ultimately hope to see is children exhibiting 'flow', that creative state of mind 'in which the person is fully immersed in what he or she is doing, characterized by a feeling of energized focus, full involvement, and success in the process of the activity' (Csikszentmihályi, in Wegerif, 2010: 60).

Enabling children to see things in new ways requires a learning environment in which children are encouraged to use their imagination; to play with ideas like scientists, engaging in 'creative conjecture in the construction of [their] scientific knowledge' (Haigh, 2007: 126; see also Naylor, Keogh and Downing, 2006). This is an environment in which they feel secure in taking risks, both in their thinking and their actions. In Natalie's 'science party' it is clear that the children are engaged in exploring materials and ideas, with guidance but with no initially prescribed outcome; they are encouraged to ask their own questions and to collaborate in looking for solutions, to look for and discuss connections and relationships, and to reflect critically, and collectively, on their experiences. They seem to be demonstrating what might be considered desirable behaviours of creative learners and it will be apparent that there is a strong link between this teacher's pedagogic intentions and the creative responses of her children.

The next section considers the crucial connections between 'creative learning' and 'creative teaching' in primary science.

Creative teaching and creative learning in primary science

It will probably come as no surprise to learn that Natalie doesn't run a 'science party' in every science lesson. But this lesson shows features of the broad approach taken by Natalie and her school colleagues to science teaching and learning. It illustrates the idea that 'a pedagogy that fosters creativity depends on practitioners being creative to provide the ethos for enabling children's creativity' (Craft, 2005: 44). So, if we want creative responses from children then the ways in which we teach should model a range of possible ways of finding out and representing ideas – through enquiry, exploration, experiment, drama, role play or dance. For the child, creative science education is a journey during which there is a chance to interpret and reinterpret natural phenomena. It is also a journey that should involve the creative representation of current understanding through, for example, stories, leaflets, letters, email, diaries, cartoons and texts, depending on the child's audience and their own interests (Feasey, 2005). In order to take children on this journey – and elicit creative responses to experiences from them – the teacher must ask themselves some key questions: 'How can I present this idea to capture the imagination? How might I ensure that the children are motivated and involved with the ideas underlying this area of science? How do I make the children aware of their choices with respect to communicating their understanding?'

It is useful for teachers of science in primary schools to have in mind a list of the essential principles of creative teaching. The 'key aspects of creative teaching' we started with are underpinned by such principles as:

- start with the children's interests, experiences and ideas;
- include group work;
- focus on cooperative learning;
- include exploratory tasks;
- plan for open-ended problems and investigations;
- use practical activities, outdoor and project work;
- ensure that classroom science relates to the children's everyday life.

Each of these involves teachers, in effect, taking risks often through being flexible about how children will achieve understanding (Kind and Kind, 2007).

Working in a large primary school within an area of social deprivation, Natalie and her colleagues – led by Catherine in her inspirational role as science coordinator for the school – certainly see creativity as being founded upon the clear principles that we have outlined above. The first of these, relevance for the children, seems central. In planning, Natalie and her colleagues take objectives from the school's science scheme and then 'look at how we can develop them creatively'. This might mean introducing ideas in a context that is completely familiar to the children as part of their lives. The party theme fits here, and Natalie says of this lesson: 'I really wanted the children to think about how forces connect with everyday life.' Yet ensuring links to everyday contexts isn't the only way in which to make activities relevant to children. In Catherine's classroom her children were presented with a range of genuine challenges related to their topic on electricity. She had created a giant robot (admittedly made from cardboard!) and the problem was how to use electricity to bring the robot slowly to life. Circuit challenges were linked to the need for light, sound and movement on various parts of the robot, providing what turned out to be a hugely motivating stimulus for the children's work over several weeks. Certainly it seems that the higher the relevance of science teaching to children's lives and interests, the greater will be the level of engagement; and a high level of engagement with the work being undertaken increases the likelihood that children will be willing to take the risks that are a necessary part of responding creatively to challenges to their understanding.

Woods (2002) suggests a relationship between the perceived relevance for children of their experiences in science lessons and the degree of control they may have over their own learning. In science, creating an environment for creative responses depends not just on the relevance of the topic but also on whether children can make their own decisions about key aspects of their enquiry, and whether collaboration with others, particularly for practical work, is encouraged. Creativity in the classroom rests on the ethos and practices established in the classroom, and of course 'the stance of the teacher has been demonstrated to play a significant role in this interaction' (Craft, 2008: 242). Natalie and Catherine are well aware of the link between motivation and learning and are able to engage the class without losing sight of their intentions for the children's learning. The following section considers a classroom ethos and associated classroom practices that are likely to promote creative learning in science. After all, as Natalie has said, 'It's about learning, it's not just a magic show.'

A classroom ethos and practices to promote children's creativity

Natalie's teaching is relevant and engaging for her children, but it is more than this; the intention is, in her words, to 'hand the responsibility back to them', providing the 'space' and sense of personal agency children need to think creatively. Central to this approach is a firm commitment to children's personal exploration, investigation and discussion of ideas and materials. Science lessons in Natalie's school are based on particular objectives but are not, in her words, 'limited to the objective'. Relevant, engaging activities are used to enable children to suggest creative questions and ideas that they want to explore further, either through research, discussion or investigation. In order for this to happen, children need to feel secure in expressing their ideas about science concepts and procedures. Natalie is quite clear that in science lessons in her school 'there are no boundaries; no idea is worthless; every idea has value'. From the start of any science lesson there is an emphasis on expressing and sharing ideas that the children take seriously. As Catherine says, 'It's OK to have random ideas … every idea is valued.' In such an environment it seems likely that truly creative responses are more likely. Children who can articulate their thinking and compare it to that of their classmates are in a position where they can genuinely question their own understanding of phenomena.

How is this ethos, which supports creative teaching and learning in science, established? Creative teachers can be observed to:

1   ensure that dialogue is seen as central to learning, by both children and teachers. This includes an emphasis on children discussing their work with their teacher and peers at regular intervals. In addition, there is an awareness that talk supports thinking and learning, so that children can identify what helps them to learn (Harrison and Howard, 2009).

2   discuss with children what creativity and 'a creative response' might actually mean, and how this relates to their development.

Focusing on the second point, the teachers in Natalie's school have employed a particular resource to promote discussions with their classes specifically about the nature of creativity. In discussions about creativity with their classes, both Natalie and Catherine found that most children linked creativity with design technology, though 'one did link it with inventing'. The teachers decided to provide a more concrete basis for their discussions with their children. Using the 'Creativity Wheel' devised by Creative Partnerships in Sunderland, they shared with the children some indicators of creative behaviour (Redmond, 2005):

> I can see more than one way of looking at things
> I don't always believe things just because everyone else does
> I can create things in my mind
> I can find new ways to do things
> I ask questions about things that could happen
> I can think of unusual ways of doing things
> I am able to try out new things
> I am prepared to try things out even if they might not work
> I trust my feelings about things
> I like finding out about new things and new ways of doing things
> I try out lots of different ways to do things and solve problems
> I can compare one thing to another and make connections between different things

Choosing one statement that seemed to relate to their own thinking or their own ideas brought the children into a dialogue about the nature of creative responses in science. As Catherine remarks, 'and once they realised that they were allowed to do that, because there was a purpose – oh, actually, my silly random ideas are creative – that was when the real thinking came in. It changed the whole class ... I have a child in my class who hardly spoke at all and now he's bursting with science ideas. He finds it hard to articulate them … but now if I get my video camera out …'. In using this idea, then, they have encouraged less confident speakers to see that their ideas are valid. Considering the indicator statements after science sessions to evaluate their own development has made a genuine difference to how the children see their role as creative learners in the classroom.

We have discussed the importance of relevant contexts, appropriate activities and children raising creative responses and questions to activities, whilst seeking to identify their own meaningful questions for future investigation. But science in a creative classroom cannot be entirely directed by children's immediate interests. Natalie and Catherine have a clear trajectory for their children's learning in science; teachers will understand that this is not 'discovery learning'. It is clear that 'students will no more discover the methods of scientific enquiry for themselves than they will discover the ways in which conceptual knowledge in science is organised' (Hodson and Hodson, 1998: 119). Teachers need to introduce children to various forms of scientific enquiry, guide their enquiries and challenge their understandings (Goldsworthy, Watson and Wood-Robinson, 2000). They need to balance dialogic enquiry, the creation of an authoritative subject narrative and direct instruction with the range of other tools available in their pedagogic repertoire to maximise children's understanding. But it will be equally clear that, in doing this, teachers also have a responsibility 'to recognise young people's creative capacities; and to provide the particular conditions in which they can be realised' (NAACE, 1999: 11). So any direct teaching of, for example, methods of scientific enquiry, should be within the context of careful questioning by the teacher. Questions should aim to help pupils to think through the processes that might be employed: 'How do you think we could investigate this? What could we do to find out? Do you think we will be able to find out if we do that? What might we need to do next?' and so on.

It is evident that the specific conditions necessary for both a teacher and individual children to work creatively in science are strongly allied to constructivist and socio-cultural perspectives on teaching and learning; it is to these that we now turn.

Creative teachers are constructivist teachers?

From a constructivist perspective, the process of developing ideas involves a personal process of adjustment of pre-existing schemas – in other words, learners can't be given understanding, but instead must construct it; and this means modifying or rejecting existing understandings in favour of 'better' ones. A teaching approach based on a constructivist view of learning might be summarized as follows:

Orientation – arousing children's interest and curiosity;
Elicitation/structuring – helping children to find out and clarify what they think;

Intervention/restructuring – encouraging children to test their ideas: to extend, develop or replace them;

Review – helping children to recognise the significance of what they have found out;

Application – helping children to relate what they have learned to their everyday lives.

(From Ollerenshaw and Ritchie, 1997)

This summary has implications for the role of the teacher. There are strong links between this framework and the features of creative teaching already mentioned. In fact, a constructivist perspective seems to have striking commonality with what Milne refers to as a creative exploration model (chapter 5 in Davies, 2011). Table 4.1 provides a comparison of a creative exploration model with a constructivist model of teaching.

Table 4.1 Comparison of creative and constructivist models

Elements of a creative exploration model	A constructivist model of teaching
Explore – e.g. a problem, artefact, phenomenon Observe – e.g. what is happening, changes, parts/structures	Orientation
Identify evidence – e.g. cause/effect of changes, trends and patterns Create explanations – supported by evidence	Elicitation
Investigate – e.g. test, compare, identify	Intervention/re-structuring
Evaluate – linking this process to ideas/tentative conclusions	Review
Further investigation – as appropriate	
Making connections – with other contexts/similar phenomena	Application

Both of these frameworks for understanding and planning classroom activity suggest that a creative teacher will provide science lessons in which the active involvement of learners is sought and supported. As we suggested earlier, creative teaching is characterised by risk-taking on the part of teacher, since it involves offering children a range of choices at different points, letting them 'decide – with guidance – some different ways to go about answering their scientific questions' (Davies, 2011: 88). It is also characterised by risk-taking by children; risks involve expressing their understanding, asking their questions, sharing their thoughts about how they might work to develop their knowledge and, sometimes, following a previously unexpected route (Roden, 2005). Instead of being unwilling to take risks through fear of failure, we want children to mirror the approach of Thomas Edison (attributed) – 'I have not failed, I have just found ten thousand ways that won't work.'

So, 'a constructivist approach to learning is very close to the notion of creativity – the generating of novel, useful ideas and outcomes through the use of imagination on a spectrum of individual and collaborative activity' (Craft, 2008: 243). In science, teachers and children are engaged in a process of meaning-making where flexibility and responsiveness to one another are essential. Despite its appeal, however, this argument focuses primarily on a cognitive view of learning, and we have already indicated – in particular referring to children sharing ideas – that creative learning may well involve a wider view of learning than can sometimes be implied by a 'pure' constructivist approach. Socio-cultural perspectives on learning are helpful for highlighting the importance of cultural context, social interaction and the use of tools – such as language – for children's learning (Hodson and Hodson, 1998; Säljö, 1999). In this model the basis of learning is children's joint, purposeful activity in particular social and cultural contexts, mediated by the learner's interaction with more expert peers or adults. That is, children take part in activities, talking them through as they unfold. Collaboration is central to creative scientific activity in the classroom and is linked with the development of a creative, dialogic classroom. Children, like other humans, are social beings, with minds organised to know more collectively than can be known individually. Tapping into such collaborative creativity depends on exploratory talk between learners, and between teachers and learners.

'Collaborative creativity' (Craft, 2008: 242) suggests that children are aware that they can use one another's ideas as a classroom resource, sharing the responsibility for their learning during science activities. There is a lot to discuss in science, since '"Talking science" means observing, describing, comparing, classifying, analysing, discussing, hypothesizing, theorising, questioning, challenging, arguing, designing experiments, following procedures, judging, evaluating, deciding, concluding, generalizing, reporting' (Lemke, 1990: ix). Who wouldn't wish to share the responsibility for all of this in discussion with others?

In Natalie's class the children feel free to put forward ideas in pursuing scientific understanding and much of their exploratory and investigative work is carried out collaboratively. Natalie uses several different types of collaborative organisation to suit her teaching purposes. Sometimes she organises mixed ability groups, as in the science party; sometimes group roles are defined – for example, resource manager, designer, feedback – with the children in the group choosing their roles; sometimes there is a focus on 'partnerships rather than group work', with a peer-mentoring structure that reinforces the necessity of children offering their own points of view. At the heart of all the collaborative activity, however, is Catherine's idea that 'the talk, the discussion that's very, very important for learning; listening to one another's ideas'.

Natalie and Catherine's belief that collaboration and talk support active learning means that the 'participation structures' in their classrooms create security for the children expressing and speculating with ideas. Participation structures can be defined as 'the rights and obligations of participants with respect to who can say what, when and to whom' (Cazden, 1986: 437), and of course they vary depending on the values and pedagogic understandings that a teacher brings to the classroom. Natalie believes strongly in the value of more symmetrical participation structures, where the teacher is a guide and organiser for supporting children's appropriation of the scientific tools of thinking. That is, she ensures that children hear scientific vocabulary in a meaningful context; that they can work through an enquiry, communicating their findings and evaluating their ways of working; and that they generally are exposed to the values, attitudes and scientific ways of working we want them to learn. As a result, she creates with children the 'dialogic space' (Wegerif, 2008, 2010) in which questions can legitimately be asked and reasoning is expected, in which they can explore and express their ideas and control, to an extent, the direction and focus of their work. Within this space they feel free to engage in the 'possibility thinking' (Craft, 2000) and 'creative conjecture' that seem so important in creative science learning. Indeed, a genuinely creative approach in science would not be possible where these principles and characteristics of interaction are not in place.

Interestingly, there is evidence that the more children are given the opportunity to talk together in science, the more their feelings of confidence and competence in science activities develop. This is important for achievement; those with more positive attitudes to science have been shown to have higher achievement scores than those with less positive attitudes (Braund, Hall and Holloway, 2007; Martin, Mullis and Foy, 2007). Creativity, rather than being a flash of inspiration, in most cases 'more normally occurs in dialogues and takes the form of lots of little sparks of insight that add up to a significant new view'; in fact, creativity might be seen as 'one fruit of the dialogic relation' (Wegerif, 2010: 54). As suggested earlier, the ultimate aim for the primary science teacher is that children should experience creative flow – total immersion in the idea, activity or problem; and the most common place where flow is experienced is in dialogue with others. Creativity is not just about the individual, it is about how we interact with others (Sawyer, 2007; Wegerif, 2010). This happens in a dialogic space where good ideas are disseminated, problems are solved and agreement is worked towards. And of course all of this can relate to the practical activity which is central to primary science. Indeed, perhaps the most important thinker of all on this subject has said that 'the most significant moment in the course of intellectual development … occurs when speech and practical activity, two previously completely independent lines of development, converge' (Vygotsky, 1978: 24).

So, if talk is so important in developing creative learning in primary science, how do we promote talk in our classrooms in a way that is likely to lead children towards the reasoned argumentation necessary to support creative responses?

Developing talk in the creative science classroom

The first thing a teacher might do in developing a creative classroom is to address children's lack of awareness of the crucial importance of talk for learning. Children need to know that there are different kinds of talk, in the same way that they learn that there are different genres of writing, or types of fiction. They need a clear understanding that talk for learning involves engaging one another in the sort of discussion that will help everyone to do better than each could alone. Individual creativity depends on such shared language use. Creative teaching involves planning to ensure that children can air their thoughts and be given constructive feedback on them (Dawes, 2010, 2011). We have seen Natalie's approach, that is, establishing a classroom ethos that gives children the endorsement to explore their creative ideas; and using the Creativity Wheel to focus their sense of personal creative development. Are there more generic approaches to developing productive classroom talk that would help to provide a framework for children's creative responses in science and in other curriculum areas?

For children to see that talk is important in the classroom, they need to start by considering: what *sort* of talk will help us to learn together? Natalie and Catherine both use 'meta-menus' and 'inference squares', an example of which is provided in Table 4.2, to encourage their children to consider what they are learning, how they are learning it and what language they should use to discuss what they are learning (Simister, 2007). The children's own suggestions about the sort of talk that seems appropriate for sharing ideas might fit with what we, as teachers, can describe as exploratory talk (Mercer and Littleton, 2007). This is talk in which a group openly shares their ideas and knowledge, asking one another questions and elaborating on what they have said, giving reasons, and generally seeking to come to some sort of negotiated resolution (without necessarily arriving at it!).

Table 4.2 Examples of a meta-menu and an inference square

A meta-menu	An inference square
Statements are infinitely adaptable but focus on 'original' discoveries and creative ideas expressed by the children	In groups, and working from a source stimulus, the children address the questions from the centre of the square outwards
What are you currently thinking about? Has any of the lesson so far been about you? What connections have you made? How do you feel about the lesson? How have you got involved in the lesson? What should you do to further your thinking? What breakthroughs have you made? What do you want to know more about?	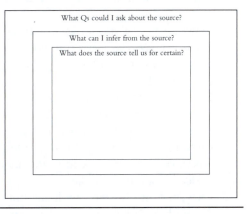

In developing a creative ethos in the social setting of the classroom, children need an explicit awareness of the features of exploratory talk. The talk tools needed to find out what others think, and their reasons for doing so, are not complex; for example, 'What do you think?', 'Why do you think that?' will elicit knowledge, understanding and reasoning. But to ask such probing questions, and to answer them, requires every child in a group to recognise their interdependence. It takes confidence to ask someone what they think; children may feel that their request will be ignored or rejected or that they will receive a dismissive response. In order to ask such questions, a child must know that others are willing to participate in sharing thoughts with the joint aim of creating new understanding.

Thoughts can betray the limits of the child's experience, a lack of ability to articulate things they thought they knew, or everyday misconceptions. To answer the questions, 'What do you think? Why?' transfers knowledge – about the science topic in question, and about ourselves – to others. This can feel rather dangerous; if we all know the same things, how can any of us be distinctive as a person? But shared thinking can usefully show children how similar or different their points of view are. At the same time, shared thinking can be heady and powerful as individual ideas link into new meanings and new ways of thinking.

The importance of talk for creative teaching is that talk stimulates thinking; talk is thinking aloud. Thinking aloud with a group, with a focus on a science question, can help to stimulate what might be termed 'creative reasoning'. The chance to undertake a joint quest for understanding is what makes talking and thinking in science so valuable. Even within the same group, discussing the same stimulus, resources and experiences, each child will create their own ideas. We need children to understand the way the world works from a scientific point of view; discussion of phenomena, investigations, hypotheses and questions is a way to ensure that children develop robust ideas and ways to explain things scientifically, which can be applied in practice. In the following interchange from Natalie's classroom, the investigation featured a starter activity where objects were to be placed into the categories 'solid' and 'liquid'. The children had to engage in creative reasoning when confronted by a bag containing air.

HARRY: Air? Air should go in liquids.

KIRANJOT: Why, it's not a liquid?

OLIVER: No, it's solid.

KIRANJOT: It's solid.

HARRY: No it's air, you can do that to it couldn't you? (*squeezes the bag to show that it moves in the bag like a liquid*)

KIRANJOT: Yeah but you can't drink it or something like that can you?

OLIVER: I drank um air, in my water, you swallow air.

KIRANJOT: You can't swim in it, can you?

HARRY: Yeah, but it's like.

OLIVER: You can swim with alcohol, but you can't swim with air. You can swim with air, you can, you can swim in air because in a swimming pool there's loads of air.

HARRY: The thing is air, it's like water, yeah, but, (*inaudible*) like you could. It's not like a brick, a solid, you couldn't; it's like, if you threw it against the floor (*inaudible*), you can't get it could you? You can trap it, but then it just floats away.

KIRANJOT: How you know it floats?

OLIVER: Um, I think in-between them.

The children placed the air (in its bag) in between their solid and liquid groupings.

In this exploratory exchange we can see tentative ideas expressed aloud; asking for and giving reasons; sharing of information; and the willingness to keep talking in order to come to what is ultimately a good joint decision. From this conversation, Natalie was able to plan for future teaching, and the children were able to say how the discussion had helped them to establish and compare their everyday ideas.

Such creative conversations take place in the context of activities or investigations which the teacher has put in a meaningful context. The following discussions arose from a lesson based on a news story about the oil spill in the Gulf of Mexico in 2010. The children watched the news report and then investigated what happens when you pour oil into water, making careful observations before formulating questions about how scientists could help when there were oil spills. Given a range of equipment and resources (including lab coats and goggles), the children became the scientists who were going to help clean up the oil spill, choosing to investigate which material was the best for removing oil from the surface of the water.

In the observation stage of the investigation, children had noticed that the oil had come together to form a large patch:

EMILY: Wow the oil is coming up to the top in bubbles. It's now joining up.
JACQUIE: It's all joining together now.
JANE: It's about 2mm thick on the surface if you look.
MATT: They are all coming together to join in a big patch.
EMILY: Why does it join up and not stay separate?

As the children devised their investigation they had an interesting debate in which they predicted what would happen to the materials when they put them in the oil/water mix:

MATT: I think the cotton wool would be good for getting lots of the oil because it's really absorbent.
EMILY: Yeah, but it will absorb lots of the water, too, and we don't want water.
MATT: But if we put it carefully on top of the water, it will float so it will only absorb the oil.
EMILY: It will get the oil but then it's going to get heavy and start sinking so it will absorb lots of the water too.

Following this reasoning, the children tested their ideas to discover that the cotton wool was not ideal for clearing up the oil. A further discussion arose about the applications of science at the end of the investigation. After discovering that the polystyrene collected the most oil and least water, the children talked about ways in which this new knowledge could actually be applied to the real world.

EMILY: We could drop large sheets of polystyrene on the sea and lift them.
JACQUIE: How are you going to lift big bits?
JANE: Oh, I know. What about those little curl shapes of polystyrene?

MRS RIZZO: Do you mean like in packaging?

JANE: Yeah, we could get those and spread those out. We could put them in a big net and pull them in.

It is particularly pertinent to re-emphasise here that creative responses to being asked to reason in science are not simply confined to the 'ideas of science'; they are also important in developing an understanding of procedural issues associated with science investigations. In both circumstances, research suggests that children do not just use talk to interact; they can use talk to *interthink*. Interthinking – thinking aloud with peers through exploratory talk – enables children to gain the capacity to create their own understanding (Mercer, 2000; Mercer and Dawes, 2011). Such discussion helps children to see that their knowledge and under-standing are important resources for their classmates; they can help others to create ideas, which is extremely powerful and gratifying. In addition, exploratory talk helps children to 'talk science', that is to hypothesise, predict, and articulate their evaluation of evidence. Creating joint enquiries such as during Natalie's 'science party', and the examples above, depends on individual contributions being negotiated into group outcomes through talk. Pursuing joint understanding of science concepts through discussion can be readily achieved when children are taught how, and why, to conduct exploratory talk.

Some final thoughts

'For children to be partners in the development of their own creativity, they need to develop an understanding of the concept of creativity and appre-ciate that they can take a role in developing and realising their own creative potential' (Feasey, 2005, p. 9).

The teacher is central to classroom creativity. Talking with children about scien-tific ideas, about creativity, and about talk, all help to raise the learner's awareness of the point and purpose of classroom activities. The learner's understanding of their involvement in their own developing thinking, and that of their classmates, is crucial. They need to understand that their ability to think creatively, offering tentative ideas and questions, matters to others. A key task for the science teacher is to establish relevant contexts for enquiry. The teacher also has the responsibility for acting as a model for exploratory talk. But in particular, it is the enthusiasm of the primary science teacher in guiding children's active involvement in thinking creatively, and in engaging children in understanding what it is to be creative in science, that is key to the whole endeavour.

Creative Touches

In summary, there are readily identifiable aspects of creative science lessons that that help children to achieve their creative potential. These match the features of curriculum provision that Ofsted have noted 'support creative learning very successfully'. They include: 'well-organised cross-curricular links that allowed scope for independent enquiry; inclusiveness, ensuring that it was accessible and relevant to all pupils; a focus on experiential learning, with knowledge, understanding and skills developed through first-hand, practical experience and evaluation; well-integrated use of technology' (Ofsted, 2010, p. 10). They link specifically to the 'creative touches' that we believe a teacher needs to incorporate into their planning of primary science lessons if children are to be genuinely engaged in their learning:

- Ensure that the lesson has an inclusive, stimulating starter;
- Provide a motivating and meaningful context for the work that the children are to undertake;
- Provide the children with chances to make choices and decisions;
- Ensure that, wherever possible, the development of science understanding is set within the context of engaging and relevant enquiry activities;
- Linked to the above, create situations where children have the chance to ask, 'What if ...?' questions;
- Provide opportunities for whole-class enquiry and discussion;
- Teach the children to use exploratory talk for learning in their groups.

Acknowledgements

We are enormously indebted to Catherine Rizzo and Natalie Bailey, teachers at Southfields Primary School in Peterborough. Their work has been a genuine inspiration for us in the writing of this chapter and their insights in the editing process were extremely valuable.

For information about the 'Thinking Together' project, which looks at ways of encouraging children to engage in exploratory talk, go to: http:// thinkingtogether.educ.cam.ac.uk/.

References

Braund, M., Hall, A. and Holloway, K. (2007). Talking science in the primary school. *Proceedings of CONASTA and ICASE*. Presented at the World Conference on Science and Technology Education, Perth: Science Teachers Association of Western Australia, pp. 78–84.

Cazden, C. (1986). Classroom Discourse, in M. Wittrock (ed.), *Handbook of Research on Teaching* (3rd edn). New York: Macmillan, pp. 432–63.

Craft, A. (2000). *Creativity Across the Primary Curriculum: framing and developing practice.* London: Routledge.

Craft, A. (2005). *Creativity in Schools: Tensions and Dilemmas.* London: Routledge.

Craft, A. (2008). Studying collaborative creativity: implications for education. *Thinking Skills and Creativity*, 3 (3): 241–5.

Csikszentmihályi, M. (1996). *Creativity: Flow and the psychology of discovery and invention.* New York: Harper Collins.

Davies, D. (2011). *Teaching Science Creatively.* Abingdon: Routledge.

Dawes, L. (2010). *Creating a Speaking and Listening Classroom: Integrating Talk for Learning at Key Stage 2.* London: Routledge.

Dawes, L. (2011). *Talking Points: Discussion Activities in the Primary Classroom.* London: Routledge.

Feasey, R. (2005). *Creative Science: Achieving the WOW Factor with 5–11 Year Olds.* London: David Fulton.

Goldsworthy, A., Watson, R. and Wood-Robinson, V. (2000). *Developing Understanding (AKSIS Project).* Hatfield: Association for Science Education.

Haigh, M. (2007). Can investigative practical work in high school biology foster creativity? *Research in Science Education*, 37 (2): 123–40.

Harrison, C. and Howard, S. (2009). *Inside the primary black box: assessment for learning in primary and early years classrooms.* London: GL Assessment.

Hodson, D. and Hodson, J. (1998). From constructivism to social constructivism: a Vygotskian perspective on teaching and learning science. *School Science Review*, 72 (2): 33–41.

Jeffrey, B. (2006). Creative teaching and learning: towards a common discourse and practice. *Cambridge Journal of Education*, 36 (3): 399–414.

Kind, P. M. and Kind, V. (2007). Creativity in Science Education: Perspectives and Challenges for Developing School Science. *Studies in Science Education*, 43 (1): 1–37.

Lemke, J. L. (1990). *Talking science: Language, learning and values.* Norwood: Ablex Publishing Company.

Martin, M. O., Mullis, I. V. and Foy, P. (2007). *TIMSS 2007 International Science Report: Findings from IEA's Trends in International Mathematics and Science Study at the Fourth and Eighth Grades.* Boston, MA: TIMSS and PERLS Study Centre.

Mercer, N. (2000). *Words and Minds: How We Use Language to Think Together.* London: Routledge.

Mercer, N. and Dawes, L. (2011). Thinking Together. Retrieved from http://thinkingtogether.educ.cam.ac.uk/.

Mercer, N. and Littleton, K. (2007). *Dialogue and the Development of Children's Thinking: A Sociocultural Approach* (1st edn). London: Routledge.

NAACE. (1999). *All our futures: creativity, culture and education.* London: DfEE.

Naylor, S., Keogh, B. and Downing, B. (2006). Argumentation and Primary Science. *Research in Science Education*, 37 (1): 17–39.

Ofsted. (2010). *Learning: creative approaches that raise standards.* Manchester: HMSO/Office for Standards in Education.

Ollerenshaw, C. and Ritchie, R. (1997). *Primary Science: Making It Work* (2nd edn.). London: David Fulton Publishers.

Redmond, C. (2005). The Creativity Wheel. assessing creative development – teacher resource. Creative Partnerships: Arts Council.

Roden, J. (2005). *Primary Science: reflective reader.* Exeter: Learning Matters.

Säljö, R. (1999). Learning as the use of tools: A sociocultural perspective on the human–technology link, in K. Littleton and P. Light (eds), *Learning with computers: analysing productive interaction.* London: Routledge.

Sawyer, K. (2007). *Group Genius: The creative power of collaboration.* New York: Basic Books.

Simister, C. J. (2007). *How to Teach Thinking and Learning Skills: A Practical Programme for the Whole School.* London: Sage Publications Ltd.

Vygotsky, L. S. (1978). *Mind in Society: The Development of Higher Psychological Processes.* Cambridge, MA: Harvard University Press.

Wegerif, R. (2008). Dialogic or dialectic? The significance of ontological assumptions in research on educational dialogue. *British Educational Research Journal,* 34 (3): 347–61.

Wegerif, R. (2010). *Mind Expanding: Teaching and Thinking for Creativity in Primary Education.* Maidenhead: Open University Press.

Woods, P. (2002). Teaching and learning in the new millennium, in C. Day and C. Sugrue (eds), *Developing teaching and teachers: international research perspectives.* London: Falmer, pp. 73–91.

Design and Technology

David Spendlove and Alan Cross

Introduction

The generation of pupils who will be taught by teachers who read this chapter will still be around, hopefully in good health, at the start of the twenty-second century. As such, whilst the ability to see into the future is prone to significant errors, we know that this generation of children are going to face immense challenges to do with population growth, sustainability issues, the emergence of new technologies, the huge ethical dilemmas of new medical advances and the integrating of entertainment and leisure activities that don't yet exist. In addition, our future adults will live and work in different ways and will encounter a whole range of problems that we haven't even considered yet. As a consequence, each of these contexts for change will require significant creative responses to both maintain and develop the quality of life that we hope to have.

Such challenges provide primary Design and Technology (D&T) teachers with a clear rationale, as the subject seeks to engage pupils in interdisciplinary, itinerant and creative activities. The justification for such an approach is that these activities reflect the essential learning dispositions Design and Technology aims to promote in learners, those very dispositions that will be required as we tackle new and emerging challenges. This chapter will therefore explore how Design and Technology promotes creativity in learners and will consider the demands that this places on primary teachers and learners. Using a case study, we will discuss how pupils throughout the primary age range can engage in creative processes and how teachers can support, engage and develop such activities in the primary classroom.

Creative constraints in Design and Technology

It would seem that pupils want to be creative, teachers want pupils to be creative and leaders of industry want pupils to be creative – yet in practice, creativity is often neglected, marginalised and trivialised both in the primary and secondary sectors in Design and Technology in favour of instrumentalist approaches to teaching. To extend this discussion further we want to highlight three key reasons why creativity in Design and Technology may be constrained. By highlighting these inhibitors of creativity, we are hoping that you will see them as opportunities that you can address in your teaching and that it is worth pursuing creativity within Design and Technology despite some of the difficulties you may face. In addition, having identified the constraints we will then look at some ways of moving creativity forward in Design and Technology.

Reason 1: knowing what to teach

A key limiting factor remains that despite Design and Technology having been around for some time (approximately 22 years), it remains a subject that causes much confusion amongst many teachers, parents and pupils. Is it a science or an art, creative or technical, a vocational or an academic subject? The answer of course is 'yes' to all variations and in many ways this is both the greatest strength and greatest weakness of the subject in that it refuses to be tied down as it is 'deliberately interdisciplinary': 'It is a creative, restive, itinerant, non-discipline' (Kimbell and Perry, 2001). To some, the notion of such a mischievous subject epitomises the aims of an imaginative, innovative, liberal and creative approach to contemporary education. However in an age of risk-averse curriculum planners, more interested in 'being' than 'becoming' and measuring 'where you are' rather than 'where you might be', such values can be viewed negatively. Equally, in an age of conspicuous pupil and teacher performance measures, compliance is rewarded more than individualism and the risk averse are rewarded.

Design and Technology is therefore unique in that it deliberately consumes and transforms existing knowledge, from the rest of the curriculum, into applied and reusable knowledge. As such, in many ways it is ideally suited to the 'creative' approach taken by many primary schools to the curriculum, as Design and Technology is creative and technical, disciplined and ill disciplined, theoretical and practical, vocational and academic. For some primary school teachers, such ambiguities can seem a burden, particularly given that their own previous experiences of Design and Technology may have been limited. This is compounded by the difficulty of trying to resolve the perennial debate as to whether teachers should focus upon the 'content' or the 'process' of the subject and which has dominance over the other. In this debate some would argue that the nature of technological content is that it has to be delivered using a 'just in case' model, where information is delivered before you need it, to use as and when required. As such, problem-solving skills are dependent upon considerable domain knowledge (McCormick, 1997) and therefore your ability to solve (or resolve) a technological problem is constrained by the existing knowledge base you have and the understanding you possess.

The alternative to defining content is to have a preference for defining the processes of Design and Technology activities. In working on a process model approach you avoid teaching content 'just in case' it is needed and instead define a range of process steps that enable learners to access information 'just in time' and in 'real time' when needed. As can be anticipated, the debate can be complex, as although these binaries represent extreme positions in the content versus process debate, even with a simplified discussion as above, it can be seen that both sides have merits and that teachers have a difficult task in deciding what to teach. An unfortunate common scenario is therefore where learners experience a hybrid limited content approach (often due to a non-specialist teacher's lack of technical knowledge) and a limited process approach (due to a teacher's lack of understanding of designerly and creative processes). The translation into practice is therefore best achieved where it can be seen that there are limitations and complexities to either approach. For example, in very creative practices, using a content-heavy approach delivered before an activity would be seen as stifling, and the use of contextual and process knowledge may therefore be appropriate. Whereas a highly-technical activity, such as electronics or pneumatics, may require some early content knowledge to enable an activity to be successful. The difficulty comes when all creative activities in technology become seen as content free and likewise when anything technical is seen as creativity free. This is where both the teacher's understanding, personal philosophy and curriculum demands come into play as the teacher has to decide upon the most appropriate pedagogical strategy for their classroom; assuming the teacher appreciates the pedagogical approaches most appropriate to Design and Technology (Cross, 2000). Therefore, although Dewey's constructivist approach of 'learning through doing' is sometimes seen as a process rich and content free approach to Technology education, the reality is the opposite. Learning through doing is both rich in content and process and as a consequence doing (e.g., manufacturing) without learning, and learning without doing represent impoverished forms of technology education which unfortunately are too common and of which there are many poor examples that should be avoided.

Ultimately, determining what should be taught in Design and Technology is often down to the teacher's personal preference (as the content is insufficiently defined or established), but content should be interconnected, progressive, authentic and challenging, raising awareness of issues, values and technical and procedural knowledge.

Reason 2: knowing how to teach

Whilst identifying what to prioritise when teaching Design and Technology is problematic, knowing how to teach to promote creative opportunities provides further demands for primary Design and Technology teachers. Part of the problem related to this is that creativity is often misconceived, difficult to manage, difficult to measure and difficult to conceptualize, particularly if you consider yourself (as a teacher) as not being particularly creative.

Teaching that nurtures and encourages creativity requires a leap of faith; it has to be risky, and the returns from it can be low as well as high. So a teacher who is highly accountable, whose reputation and performance is measured through the perceived success of their pupils, will often, despite all their best intentions, provide their pupils with a benign and impoverished creative experience. Such constraining of creative opportunities in learning experiences can lead to a coercion and collusion of experience (Spendlove, 2010) where students give the appearance of being creative and designerly – yet this is merely an illusion. As such, the modus operandi for creativity within Design and Technology has increasingly become dominated by a limited pedagogical practice model, with pupils offered inadequate creative opportunities. Benson and Lunt (2011) confirm this, with evidence from their study suggesting that although primary school children can be highly motivated by their experience of Design and Technology, they do not always experience teaching approaches which best promote their creativity. The difficulty therefore remains that whilst Design and Technology offers so much, its delivery is often disappointingly poor as the pedagogic strategies employed are often contrived into highly procedural and technicised methods that reduce it to a transmissionist model of redundant skills and processes often modelled upon dated industrial or commercial practices. Indeed, one of the great ironies and misconceptions of Design and Technology is generated when secondary schools demonstrate such redundant processes to primary schools in the hope that the pupil journey into the often mundane practice of the secondary school can be speeded up by adopting such ill-conceived practices in the feeder primary school.

Kimbell et al. (1996) drew attention to this transition paradox when discussing how pupils' progression (and regression) in Design and Technology is limited across the Key Stage 2/3 transition phase. Kimbell describes the best practice in primary school experiences as empowering where the child has ownership of Design and Technology activities and is enabled to make proposals and decisions within a supportive framework where the teacher acts as a consultant and a facilitator. This is contrasted with the same pupils' experiences within the first months of Year 7 (divided by only a six-week summer break) in the secondary school where the experiences of the learner are characterised by the teacher acting as an instructor with the child being given limited ownership and little autonomy in the development of their work. In addition, unlike much of the good practice within the primary curriculum, the work within secondary schools often lacks context or coherence and does not always build upon the valuable contributions that other subjects can make to the processes involved in designing and making. Such an approach loses sight of the essence of Design and Technology and the rationale for its existence within the curriculum.

This narrow view is unfortunate as much of the outstanding practice that has often taken place within the primary curriculum is lost in search of adopting an often-inappropriate model. It is not within the scope of this chapter to fully explore the extent of the reasons – they are in fact already well documented (Barlex, 2003; Kimbell, 2000; Spendlove, 2005) – but one clear reason for failure to engage learners in creative opportunities is both the teacher's and pupil's fear of the unknown. Reproduction of existing privileged knowledge is much easier to conceptualise, manage, measure and be accountable for. Therefore for teachers this means that it is safer to follow the well-worn paths of practice they are familiar with, where they know where they are going and accepting the consequences that pupil autonomy is incrementally being eroded away through being drilled on what is measured, leaving many pupils bereft of initiative and independence.

Reason 3: knowing about knowing

'Traditional' views of teaching would suggest that the teacher is the gatekeeper of all knowledge and shares such privileged knowledge in a reciprocal way, so that those who manage to engage with such knowledge can go on and do the same with other learners. As such, an approach like this maintains the status quo of school and higher education provision, but does little to challenge existing forms of knowledge. Such traditional paradigms are predicated upon a concept of robust knowledge, consistent decision-making and reliable thinking, particularly in the context of designing for other people and improving the quality of life for others through designing better futures.

Our proposal therefore offers the opposite to this and suggests that it is more fruitful to develop creative approaches on the basis of challenging metacognitive processes by identifying cognitive limitations. A 'curriculum of unknowing' recognises that our brains are open to lots of subtle influences that constrain our everyday thinking. For example, if we say 'Don't think about a tarantula', we know you are going to almost certainly start thinking about a spider. Just by planting the idea may also set off a chain reaction of unconscious thinking throughout the day – such as you may even feel slightly uncomfortable, particularly if you don't like spiders (even though you were told not to think of a spider). Such subtle inferences are central to the whole creative, advertising and marketing industry. The difficulty with encouraging creative thinking, however, is that learners are prone to start from the existing norms of everyday occurrences and therefore to break the mould, 'to think outside the box', requires risky thinking, going against what the learner knows and against their instincts and inferences. Shubin (2008) asserts that our limited cognition is the result of a convoluted evolutionary path from life as water-living animals to life on land. As such, far from being large-brained bipedal hominids, the end product of an evolutionary hierarchy, we are vulnerable beings susceptible to physical breakdowns and odd quirks, such as ruptured disks, hernias, hiccups and cancers. Whilst the physical limitations of evolutionary development are increasingly acknowledged, the evolutionary limitations of our cognitive faculties are less prone to interrogation, yet they are far from robust. We generally lack genuine creative thinking skills as we in fact lack autonomy of thought, having been shaped by a whole range of cultural and biological preconditioning which shapes, hinders and constrains our everyday 'creative' thinking.

Therefore, in the same way that we expect to challenge pupil thinking, we also need to challenge what we 'know' as teachers and, as such, question what we value or reject in others' thinking. Such a position challenges the status of teachers as 'knowers' and devalues the enculturation model of knowledge accumulation and validation of such knowing through public examination. 'Unknowing' challenges the status of the school and decision-making through acknowledgement of uncertainty and creative thinking. 'Unknowing' equally represents a diversity of accomplishment and demerits collusion and coercion as the routes to progression, as notions of achievement are less clearly framed.

Some ways forward

Whilst there appears to have been some marginalisation of creative subjects across the curriculum, and whilst it may be argued that some subjects are perceived as more creative than others, it is almost inconceivable that Design and Technology should lack creative opportunities. As indicated previously, Design and Technology also provides the means for transferring knowledge from other subjects into useable and applied knowledge. Fox-Turnbull also highlights the significance of the development of motivation and dialogue in the creative processes of Design and Technology, identifying that when learners 'work together in problem solving situations they do much more than just talk together. They "interthink" by combining shared understandings, combining their intellects in creative ways, and often reaching outcomes that are well above the capability of each individual' (2010: 26). Unfortunately, such opportunities are often lost when the focus becomes increasingly 'outcome' rather than 'process' led, with insufficient focus upon the development of individual creative capability. However, outstanding opportunities for 'high order engagement' as well as establishing an understanding of enterprise and industrial and commercial practice within a flexible and creative setting should be central to providing meaningful learning experiences in Design and Technology.

Opportunities for encouraging creativity in the classroom

Kress (2000) has argued for a curriculum for instability where risk and uncertainty are both welcome. Without both elements, education becomes orientated towards the reproduction of existing practice and defines itself as content with existing practices. Before such opportunities for challenging reproduction are considered further, it is important to explore first the context and conditions, which will enable creative practices to succeed. A critical factor for success is the need for teachers (either as individuals or as part of a team of professionals within a school) to establish a clearly defined, academically supported framework within which children might be encouraged to work towards the development of creative capability. Our own experience has shown that where there is a shared vision and philosophy for the teaching of Design and Technology within a school, children are able to flourish and to frequently exceed the initial expectations of their teachers. The principal reason for this is that in order for creativity to be achieved, there needs to be a measure of uncertainty and a level of risk-taking. Indeed, without engaging with some level of uncertainty there can be no creativity and without risk-taking there can be no innovation. Unfortunately, however, as we have already highlighted, there has been little encouragement for uncertainty within our heavily accountable educational system in recent times, and risk-taking has been discouraged within an educational climate where certainty and predefined measured outcomes are paramount. Therefore, in order to address this, schools and teachers need to offer the security and 'licence' that are provided by a carefully considered, personal or 'corporate' approach to the teaching of creative capability, where uncertainty and risk-taking are accepted components of creative work. To achieve this, we believe there has to be an emotional investment in the three domains of the person, the process and the product in order for creativity to flourish (Spendlove, 2007, 2008). However, without adequate academic underpinning and the establishment of a carefully considered effective philosophy, within which creativity can flourish, the practices offered in this chapter merely become at best a 'quick fix' or, 'hints and tips for teachers', an approach which has previously prevented rather than enabled teachers to effectively respond to the challenge we describe.

Creativity and emotion – the person domain

When we envisage a learner who is capable in the field of Design and Technology there is an expectation for them to be creative, capable of dealing with uncertainty, risk-taking, reflecting upon their own performance, learning in different contexts and interrogating and creating products through engaging with a creative process. When the context of this creative endeavour is an educational one, it can be further argued that the uncertainty and risk-taking are doubled (rather than shared), as the teacher and the learner will be equally uncertain of the outcome of any given creative challenge, therefore requiring a significant emotional investment on both parts. Indeed, it can be argued that creativity can only occur in such circumstances and that uncertainty and risk-taking are essential prerequisites in order for creativity to take place. To exist in such an uncertain state and to be willing to take risks in pursuit of 'authenticity' is both desirable and challenging and as such requires the emotional capacity to be able to do so. By being creative, the creator is expressing a set of values and beliefs about the world. Ultimately, to be creative 'is an expression of the self' (Morgan and Averill, 1992), with such expressions and convictions requiring an emotional capacity, self-efficacy (Bandura, 1997) or 'creative self-efficacy' (Tierney and Farmer, 2002).

To take risks and deal with uncertainty in order to be innovative, however, also requires the management of the emotional discomfort that comes with not always knowing what or how. Henderson (2004) has identified that inventors expressed a profound level of emotional experience as part of their creative process. Shaw (1994) also emphasised that negative emotions are a normal part of the creative process. One theory relating to this level of emotional discomfort is proposed by Runco (1994, 1999), who has identified that creative tensions can exist when one experiences the emotional discomfort of attempting to reconcile a complex problem.

Within the person domain, it can also be argued that emotion and self-esteem are inexorably intertwined within the creative process. As such, full regard has to be considered in facilitating sufficient emotional underpinning that engenders a genuine spirit of uncertainty, risk-taking and creative endeavour within the learner. As a consequence, teachers need to be emotionally 'in tune' with their learners' needs, they need to legitimise risk-taking and be willing to take risks themselves by modelling the very dispositions they wish to encourage.

Creativity and emotion – the process domain

As identified previously in this chapter, a continual debate in Design and Technology, and how to teach the subject in a creative way, relates to engaging pupils in a creative process. It is recognised that learning is a dynamic, complex and multifaceted process in which a vast array of factors have to be considered in position to ensure learning is effective. Whilst acknowledging this within the context of the 'process domain' of learning, attention is drawn to the overarching Vygotskian principles of meaning and sense both being tied to emotional experience and where 'emotion-infused' mental images and 'inner speech' become the learner's focus of attention (Vygotsky, 1971). Within this context, two specific areas of the emotional dimension of learning are considered: first, the emotional climate for the learner; second, the context of emotional engagement within a creative and learning Design and Technology process.

Ahn (2005) suggests that the exemplification of teacher modelling through emotional expression, reaction and regulation, whether intentional or unintentional, teaches the learner the nature of emotions, their expressions and how to regulate negative and positive emotion. Within the creative classroom environment, this would be demonstrated through the teacher's modelling of their emotional capacity to deal with uncertainty and risk, their emotional engagement with the topic and the reinforcement and nurturing of pupils emotional behaviours. This is a powerful prerequisite for facilitating creative approaches within a learning environment, particularly when aligned with the 'person domain'.

Creativity and emotion – the product domain

Previously in this chapter we referred to the need for primary teachers to consider challenging what they value or what they reject in others' thinking, as our notional 'common sense' is typically an unreliable guide (Watts, 2011) to being creative. Yet as teachers and everyday human beings we rely upon our instincts and notional 'common sense' to guide us, often to the exclusion of other forms of thinking. As such, teachers are in a very powerful position in both legitimising and qualifying pupils' creative ideas and 'products' and as a consequence need to be aware of their own influences on pupils' decision-making.

Using the term 'product' in this domain, therefore, deliberately (in one aspect) aligns the 'outputs' of creative and learning processes with such thinking and intentionally associates 'outcomes' with physical responses, systems, services, performances, products and artefacts that may be produced and that may be available for both the creator and others to interface and engage with. In doing this, it is important to acknowledge that the output from a creative process may also not always be a 'physical' product such as those listed and may also be an output that results in new thinking, feelings or the development of a new skill, attitude, concept or knowledge. There is, however, an important tension to acknowledge here, as poor practice within 'education' is often focused, for reasons of expediency, purely on the product stages of the creative process and in doing so bypasses the essential creative (person) and learning (process) elements, resulting in embellished, rather than creative, novel and inspiring, outcomes with limited contextualised learning, emotional engagement or opportunities to engage in risk-taking and uncertainty.

A key feature of engaging with the three 'emotional' domains described is that the creator has a responsibility to bridge the gap between the 'receiver's' emotional needs and the emotional response they generate in others through the outcomes they have created. It is also important that the learner should not only be 'emotionally' aware of the impact of the outcomes (products) and decisions they generate in themselves, but that they should also be 'emotionally critical' and aware of the 'aesthetic emotions' and responses created by the products and decisions that they engage with.

Indeed, often risky creative processes can generate equally risky and creative outcomes, which can be equally emotionally demanding for the creator and the receiver. Such emotions should be engaged with as part of a broader development of emotional literacy (Spendlove, 2009) as well as the creative processes. Where such outcomes result in products, performances, services or outcomes, it is essential to recognise the emotional determinants within the visceral, hedonic, aesthetic, cognitive and personal needs, wants and values of the user, in addition to considering the emotions that such products have the potential to generate in the user. Failure to do so is failure to genuinely engage with the process of design.

Case study: Year 3 Ancient Egypt – tomb traps

Having discussed creativity in theory, we now have the opportunity to examine a case study that illustrates a primary theme, which aimed to link Design and Technology to other curriculum subjects. Within this case study, Design and Technology formed an integral part of a theme based upon the Ancient Egyptians, which included study of the life of the Ancient Egyptians and the exploration by Howard Carter of the ancient pyramids and tombs. The teachers from three classes planned the theme together and the class featured below had just moved from the infant school to the junior school and included a high (higher than national average) proportion of children with special needs. The theme included a visit to Manchester University Museum to see the extensive Ancient Egyptian collection, and an early activity was to write to the museum director to find out more about Ancient Egypt and the collection at the museum. Pupils then went on to recreate Howard Carter's diary and performan a series of short dramas re-enacting his entry to the tomb of Tutankhamun.

The main Design and Technology elements of the theme involved collaborative teamwork, design, use of a range of materials and making and evaluating in a context planned to motivate the whole class. The theme also had a very strong link to English and was also designed to assess pupils' Design and Technology and literacy skills, including their capacity to work with others.

The theme had been initiated with an Ancient Egyptian day where the teachers all dressed as Ancient Egyptians, and the pupils made Anubis masks and wrapped other pupils in bandages. The main Design and Technology activity drew on the well-known fictional character Indiana Jones and required the pupils to design a tunnel within which structures and mechanisms would seek to deter tomb robbers. By way of introduction, a video was played to the class showing part of the Indiana Jones stage show at the MGM theme park, Orlando, Florida (http://www.youtube.com/watch?v=gAs45bKlVVw).

After discussion, each pupil was asked to design three traps, which would kill or deter tomb thieves. The video, group discussions and initial design task caused great excitement amongst the class and resulted in all pupils being engaged in a range of design drawings which including pits, venomous snakes, other creatures, swords, spikes, boulders, arrows, spears, trapdoors, and so on. In all cases, the learners were keen to talk and write about how their trap designs worked and about the consequences for any unwary tomb thieves, with all pupils willing and able to write 20–40 words about each of their designs. In some cases additional adult support was provided, as is routine in the class.

Following the design activity, a number of designs were examined and reviewed collectively by the class. The teacher then explained and modelled (on the interactive whiteboard) the next stage, which was to construct a model of the tunnel containing three selected traps. Each triad of pupils was provided with a cardboard 'tunnel' by the teacher, which was a five-sided box structure around 50 centimetres in length and 12 centimetres high and wide. The pupils having organised themselves into triads, reviewed their plans, selected the best traps and began construction of their designs. Materials provided included adhesives, adhesive tapes, drawing pins, paper fasteners, pipe cleaners, plasticine, match sticks, lolly sticks, string, felt pens, and so on, whilst tools were limited to scissors. Two 40-minute lessons were devoted to the construction, and the results included the completed tunnels and a great deal of insight on the part of the teacher into the creative and Design and Technology capability of the pupils. Interestingly several pupils showed an impressive level of achievement in Design and Technology which had not been referred to in their records and was not predicted based on achievement in other subjects.

Case study: discussion

This theme proved to be highly inclusive in that it engaged all the pupils in the class who readily understood the context and were willing in the limited time available to explore and trial different ideas. The three teachers working together appeared to generate a breadth of ideas from the pupils and this was evidenced in this topic by the diary writing, a museum visit, drama work, use of the MGM stage show, and the tomb trap design. However, could the creativity of the teachers be confused in some way with the creativity of the pupils? Whilst the teachers' planning could increase the opportunity for creativity for the pupils, is it possible that it could have the opposite effect by equally constraining the pupils' creative opportunities in some way? The context, which the pupils understood, sparked imaginative responses, although the MGM stage show may in some cases have limited the diversity of responses by priming the pupil thinking. The powerful images from the video of a pit trap, axes falling and giant balls rolling were all recreated in the pupils' designs and as a consequence may have equally curtailed their creative thinking. This, of course, has to be weighed against the motivational drive created by the Indiana Jones context.

The teachers' pedagogical choices also need to be considered as key factors in both encouraging and inhibiting creativity. For example, the intention in asking each child to design three tomb traps was to encourage a range of responses, but equally why not four or one or some degree of flexibility, as creativity cannot flourish when overly constrained. In a similar way the teachers' decision to provide a ready-made box structure for the model tunnels may also have assisted by releasing time for designing and making, but equally may have constrained more diverse ideas. The children certainly adapted their trap designs as they constructed them, but might they have come up with more creative and diverse ideas if they had started with a wider range of options?

Ultimately, there are a vast number of interrelated pedagogic variables operating in the classroom. The choices teachers make will, as a consequence, heavily influence the creative opportunities that pupils will or will not have. Whilst activities and outcomes can often given the appearance of creativity, this may in fact only be illustrating the teachers' rather than the pupils' creativity.

General discussion of creativity in primary Design and Technology

Primary Design and Technology has often been criticized in the past for poor quality and lack of challenge for pupils (Smithers and Robinson, 1992). There are no doubt numerous instances of primary teachers lacking confidence who resort to formulaic parodies of Design and Technology and sadly we have all seen rows of near identical slippers, photoframes and coats for Joseph. Sometimes giving the appearance of being creative, this work often represents examples where creative opportunities have been bypassed. Creativity throughout primary education is therefore, as exemplified within the case study, affected by a number of variables, including the limited time available for exploring and considering the context from multiple perspectives. Equally, how clear is the primary teaching profession about creativity in subjects such as Design and Technology? We might all too easily provide a wide range of materials and claim that that what follows is creative, as it involves choices and combinations which are new. However, if the extent of creative practice in Design and Technology is about the degree of choice – for example, about the final finish or decoration of a product – we may ultimately be limiting potential pupil development through a somewhat limited or superficial approach.

The choice of an appropriate context in Design and Technology activities appears to be highly influential in enabling creative responses from pupils. Primary pupils benefit from understanding the context they are operating in so that they can learn to understand how people interact with such a context. However, in identifying appropriate contexts to operate in it is essential to consider such features as: clarity about/interaction with a user; a sense of audience for the Design and Technology; novel elements, intriguing elements, new materials, new tools, new ways of working, challenge, and so on. These can include options such as: use of a well-known story; a book format; use of media; team-working; introduction of costing, research, meeting and interrogating the client or user.

The cross-curricular approach taken in the case study above allowed Design and Technology to be linked to other subjects and allowed those links to be empha-sised and made explicit in a natural rather than contrived manner. Hattie (2009) reviewed 30 studies of integrated curricula and found that in the primary years there was a positive effect on pupil achievement. Such positive outcomes may be influenced by the teachers' teaching methods as well as how the curriculum is arranged. However, what we have seen in many case studies are examples of committed, confident teachers taking control of the curriculum and tailoring it and their teaching to suit the pupils and their objectives.

A further feature of the above case study (which impacts on creativity) is the way teachers sought a balance between process and content. The Design and Technology content was clear; the Year 3 children were learning to develop design ideas and working in teams, collaborating, cooperating and developing their ideas. As such, creative opportunities were occurring in different ways and at different times, through the process, the outcomes and in the ideas and language that children developed.

Finally, within this discussion it is important to consider those teachers who may be lacking confidence or who may be ill equipped to utilise uncertainty as a positive feature of the classroom and who might only see uncertainty as a 'certainty' to failure. In such circumstances, this is likely to be extremely limiting as, given the space to develop ideas, primary pupils will rarely disappoint. Many teachers, however, feel that creative activities often mean a relinquishing of their control and as consequence may exhort too much control, debilitating any creative opportunities. Equally, creativity does not mean unfettered freedom and a lack of control. Therefore, it is appropriate for teachers to seek a balance as all teachers need to vary their control as they marshal it along with other teaching variables (Cross, 2000), such as time, resources, pace, and so on. Successful and 'creative' practitioners use their ability to manage pupils, not to impinge upon their creative practices but to create the 'managed' space and freedom for their pupils to develop autonomy and with it the space for creativity.

Concluding remarks

A central theme within this chapter is that it is up to teachers to secure both creative and designerly opportunities, not at the expense of other priorities but as the means of strengthening, contextualising and enriching other aspects of the curriculum. Creativity is embedded into our culture and existence and, as such, we need to nurture, promote and try to understand it. Becoming a 'creative practitioner' requires critical reflection and a commitment to creative practices in your own classroom. As such, creative practitioners are at various times, as within any learning process, a learner themselves. They are also an explorer, a thinker, an information manager, a collaborator, a facilitator, an instigator and a partner in providing a rich learning experience for children. If this is indeed the case then the learner also plays these many roles within the creative learning process and this must be recognised, encouraged and facilitated by the teacher.

To help children to discover and celebrate their creative abilities they must be supported, encouraged and (above all) enabled to interrogate their surroundings and contexts intelligently and emotionally, to imagine and to reimage ranges of alternatives to the existing 'made' environment. We must also recognise that all children have the capability to be creative and to propose changes and to challenge what we might regard as the accepted and the orthodox.

Within creative environments, risk-taking by the teacher and the learner in decision-making must be an accepted part of the creative process. Indeed, as indicated previously, without risk and uncertainty there can be no creativity, for it stands to reason that if the outcomes of a process are preconceived then there is no opportunity for creativity or innovation to take place. It is equally important that we as teachers have confidence in the ability of children to be innovative and creative. For it is frequently the case that the uncommitted mind – a fresh approach, not constrained by existing thinking and practice – can involve fewer inhibitions about challenging accepted ideas and trying out new and different solutions to creative challenges. Failure should also be accepted and seen for what it is – a stage within the creative process. As Churchill is claimed to have said, 'success is going from failure to failure without loss of enthusiasm'. Failure can therefore be turned to advantage and result in a better understanding of a problem if the educational climate is right. The place of playfulness and the ability to work with ideas and to recycle and add value to proposals is important and needs to be recognised and valued as it requires a level of determination and persistence in order to achieve an outcome. It also must be recognised that there are broader educational benefits of such an approach that are of significant value.

Finally, we have said already that teachers must measure the effectiveness of the teaching programmes they develop by determining the extent to which their pupils are capable of working autonomously, being critical, creatively solving problems and innovating. Teaching children to be creative must therefore aim to meet the immediate needs of children who want to express and develop their ideas. Such an approach must build new relationships between teachers and pupils and empower the pupil to question, challenge and take risks, to arrive at new levels of self-awareness and emotional competence. However, if we truly wish our pupils to be creative, critical thinkers, we must also encourage their questioning of our own ideas and ways of thinking. This is perhaps the most challenging aspect of the quest for a more effective and creative approach to the teaching of Design and Technology.

Creative Touches

Suggestions for developing opportunities for creativity in Design and Technology:

- Recognise that D&T applies knowledge from the rest of the curriculum in the development of creative outcomes.
- Choosing the right context is important to ensure that motivating and creative opportunities exist.
- Overly scaffolded teacher activities can give the appearance of creativity but ultimately reduce pupil autonomy and creativity.
- When being creative, pupils should consider and reflect upon their own emotions as a creator and how they manage such emotions.
- It is important for the teacher to consider the needs of the learner working in risky and uncertain creative ways.
- It is necessary that in being creative, the pupil should consider the emotions of the user/receiver of their outcomes.
- Think about how you create trust in the classroom and where/when it is acceptable for failure to occur as part of risk-taking.
- Praise and celebrate pupils who have been ambitious, creative and taken risks.
- Use narratives, key words and language to create an emotionally literate and creative learning environment.
- Good ideas don't have to be neat.
- Creativity does not mean a free-for-all.
- Learning to manage and deal with uncertainty and risk-taking are important life skills.
- Consider the balance between process and content and try to strike the right balance.
- When designing, consider the creative balance between the form and function of a product.

- Remember that learning through doing is a powerful way to learn – but just doing without learning is usually what occurs in D&T.

- Be open to pupils' ideas and challenge your own thinking.

- D&T is a subject that is excellent for developing literacy, numeracy, interaction and critical thinking skills.

- Model personal confidence and acceptance of risk and uncertainty in your own teaching.

- Build a collection of products and ideas that show pupils where creative ideas have been successful.

References

Ahn, Hey Jun (2005). Child care teachers' strategies in children's socialisation of emotion. *Early Child Development and Care*, −175: 1–49.

Amabile, T. M. (1983). *The social psychology of creativity*. New York: Springer-Verlag New York Incorporated.

Amabile, T. M. (1988). A model of creativity and innovation in organizations. *Research in Organizational Behaviour*, Vol. 10: 123–67.

Atkinson, E. S. (1994). Key factors which affect pupils performance in technology project work, in J. S. Smith (ed.), *IDATER 94:30–37*. Loughborough: D&T, Loughborough University.

Atkinson, E. S. (2000). Does the need for high levels of performance curtail the development of creativity in D&T project work? *International Journal of Technology and Design Education*, Vol. 10 (3): 255–81.

Bandura, A. (1997). *Self-efficacy: The exercise of control*. New York: Freeman.

Barlex, D. (2003). Creativity in Crisis, D&T at KS3 and KS4: DATA Research Paper 18. Wellesbourne: DATA.

Benson, C. and Lunt, J. (2011). 'I'm choosing purple not pink': Investigating children's perceptions of their experience of design and technology in relation to creativity! Paper presented at PATT 25: CRIPT8 Perspectives on Learning in Design & Technology Education. Goldmsiths University, July 2011.

Cross, A. (2000). Pedagogy and Curricular Subjects: The Case of D&T as Part of Primary Education, unpublished dissertation, University of Manchester.

Davies, T. (2000). Confidence! Its role in the creative teaching and learning of D&T. *Journal of Technology Education*, Vol. 12 (1): 18–31.

Dewey, J. (1966). *Democracy and Education*. New York: Free Press.

Fox-Turnbull, W. (2010). The Role of Conversation in D&T. *D&T Education: An International Journal*, 15 (1): 24–30.

Hattie, J. A. C. (2009). *Visible learning: A synthesis of 800+ meta-analyses on achievement*. London: Routledge.

Henderson, J. (2004). Product Inventors and Creativity: The Finer Dimensions of Enjoyment. *Creativity research journal*, 2004, Vol. 16, Nos 2 and 3: 293–312.

Hunter, J, P. and Csikszentmihályi, M. (2003). The Positive Psychology of Interested Adolescents. *Journal of Youth and Adolescence*, Vol. 32, No. 1 (February): 27–35.

IBM (2010). *Capitalizing on complexity: Insights from the Global Chief Executive Officer Study*. USA: IBM Global Business Services.

Kimbell, R. (2000). Creativity in Crisis. *The Journal of D&T Education*, 5 (3): 206–11.

Kimbell, R. and Perry, D. (2001). *D&T in the knowledge economy*. London: Engineering Council.

Kimbell, R., Stable, K. and Green, R. (1996). *Understanding Practice in D&T*. Buckingham: Open University.

Kress, G. (2000). A Curriculum for the Future. *Cambridge Journal of Education*, Vol. 30, No. 1: 133–45.

Lave, J. (1988). *Cognition in Practice: Mind, Mathematics and Culture in Everyday Life*. Cambridge: Cambridge University Press.

Macedo, D. (1993). Literacy for stupidification: the pedagogy of big lies. *Harvard Educational Review*, 63 (2): 183–206.

McCormick, R. (1997). Conceptual and Procedural Knowledge, in M. J. DeVries and A. Tamir (eds), *Shaping Concepts of Technology; From Philosophical Perspective to Mental Images*. Dordrecht: Kluwer.

McCormick, R. (2004). Issues of Learning and Knowledge in Technology Education. *International Journal of Technology and Design Education*, 14: 21–44.

Morgan, C. and Averill, J. R. (1992). True feelings, the self, and authenticity: A psychosocial perspective, in D. D. Franks and V. Gecas (eds), *Social perspectives on emotion, Vol. 1*. Greenwich, CT: JAI Press, pp. 95–124.

Runco, M. A. (1994). Creativity and its discontents, in M. P. Shaw and M. A. Runco (eds), *Creativity and affect*. Norwood, NJ: Ablex, pp. 102ff.

Runco, M. A. (1999). Tension, adaptability, and creativity, in S. Russ (ed.), *Affect, creative experience, and psychological adjustment*. Philadelphia, PA: Brunner/Mazel, pp. 165–94.

Shaw, M. P. (1994). Affective components of scientific creativity, in M. P. Shaw and M. A. Runco (eds), *Creativity and affect*. Norwood, NJ: Ablex, pp. 3–43.

Shubin, N. (2008). *Your Inner Fish: A Journey into the 3.5-Billion-Year History of the Human Body*. New York: Pantheon Books.

Smithers, A. and Robinson, P. (1992). *Technology in the National Curriculum: Getting it Right*. London: Engineering Council.

Spendlove, D. (2005). Creativity in education: a review. *D&T Education: An International Journal*, 10 (2): 9–18.

Spendlove, D. (2007). A Conceptualisation of Emotion within Art and Design Education: A Creative, Learning and Product Orientated Triadic Schema. *International Journal of Art and Design Education*, Vol. 26.2: 155–66.

Spendlove, D. (2008). The locating of emotion within a creative, learning and product orientated D&T experience: person, process, product. *International Journal of Technology and Design Education*, 18: 45–57.

Spendlove, D. (2009). *Ideas in Action: Emotional Literacy*. London: Continuum.

Spendlove, D. (2010). The Illusion of Knowing: Towards a Curriculum of Unknowing. Paper presented at the Technological Learning and Thinking Conference. University of British Columbia, Vancouver, 17–19 June.

Tierney, P. and Farmer, S. M. (2002). Creative self-efficacy: Its potential antecedents and relationship to creative performance. *Academy of Management Journal*, 45: 1137–48.

Vygotsky, L.S. (1971). *The Psychology of Art*. Cambridge, MA: MIT Press (not published in lifetime, 1925 dissertation, worked on 1917–22).

Watts, D. J. (2011). *Everything Is Obvious Once You Know The Answer: How Common Sense Fails*. London: Atlantic Books.

6

Drama

Teresa Cremin and Roger McDonald

Introduction

Drama fosters children's creative engagement and enriches their imaginative development. Open-ended and the focus of collaborative exploration, it is also inherently uncertain, ambiguous and frequently full of dramatic tension. In make-believe worlds of their own creation, teachers and children find and solve problems, think laterally, evaluate courses of action, and create new meanings. In reflecting upon this imagined experience and the difficulties encountered, they make creative connections to their own world and learn through reflective engagement.

In this chapter we show that teachers can employ drama, the art form of social encounters, both to teach creatively and to teach for creativity. Furthermore, children learn creatively in and through drama. Initially, we explore the different ways drama is made manifest in primary schools, highlighting in particular the value of improvisational classroom drama in which drama and creativity are indivisibly linked. Then we move to consider some common classroom drama practices in the curriculum, focusing not only on role play areas and text exploration in English, but also on drama as a tool for learning right across the curriculum. We then offer two vignettes from across the curriculum: the first focuses on drama in the context of Personal, Social and Health Education (PSHE); and the second focuses on the theme of sustainability and the environment. We close by arguing that drama is a potent tool for fostering creativity; an indispensable tool in a creative practitioner's repertoire.

Fostering creativity through drama

A wealth of activities exist under the banner of drama within and beyond the boundaries of the primary curriculum. These range from the more formal to the more informal end of a practice continuum (see Figure 6.1 below); from the practiced, prepared and shared with an audience type to the more casual, playful and spontaneous kind. Theatre trips, school productions and assemblies all cluster around the arguably more formal end of the practice continuum and often involve children in watching or being watched as they perform and enact previously prepared scenarios or plays. At the other end of the continuum, children on the playground improvise small scenarios often connected to the world of popular culture and engage in socio-dramatic play in the classroom through table-top role play or when experimenting with resources in art or science; such informal imaginative play is not performed for others. Staff, too, may be involved in performing in plays or assemblies and may also engage in a playful and dramatic manner in the staffroom and in the context of classroom drama.

However, there is no simple dichotomy implied by the more and less watched varieties of drama, and many of these activities, including poetry performances or puppet plays, for example, may commence as improvised group work and conclude with a practised performance, enabling new ideas and interpretations to be generated as part of the process and the product. Additionally, theatre in education groups and opportunities to engage in English Heritage events, for example, can involve both improvisation and performance on the part of those involved. All such activities are likely to trigger children's imaginative involvement, involve an act of pretence and create opportunities for making, sharing and appraising work. In this way children and adults are engaged together in the core processes of generating and evaluating ideas and meanings; they are working creatively.

On the practice continuum of drama, with free play at one end and scripted performance at the other, process drama (Taylor and Warner, 2006) is situated centrally. Such drama, also called story drama (Booth, 1994), classroom drama (Grainger and Cremin, 2001) and structured improvisation (Greenwood, 2009), employs elements of both free flow play and theatre and involves the creation of shared fictitious worlds. It involves children in exploring issues in role and improvising alongside their teacher in role (TIR), building a work in the process. Language is an important part of this symbolic and dramatic play, in which, through the use of TIR and many other drama conventions, alternative ideas and perspectives are voiced. As a multimodal art form, drama draws on more than

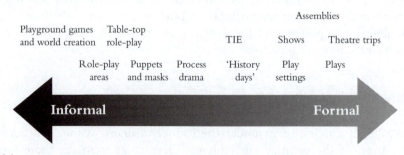

FIGURE 6.1 A practice continuum of drama adapted from Taylor and Warner, 2006

language, though; children and teachers use facial expression, body language, intonation, gesture, mime, movement and space in order to make new meanings and connections.

In process drama, children are involved in working imaginatively to improvise and sustain the different roles that they choose to adopt, offering ideas to develop and shape the unfolding drama and contributing to the problem-solving agenda. In working together, they do not re-enact the known but, working alongside their teacher as a fellow artist (TIR), take risks and explore the unknown. Process drama challenges children to imaginatively make, share and respond to each other's ideas, collaboratively co-authoring new narratives together. These are often linked to known tales, texts of life experience and will draw on knowledge of the area being examined. For example, in a drama based on the Lady of Shallot, the young learners will draw upon their knowledge of the narrative, and in examining the plight of impoverished children in Victorian times, they will draw upon their prior knowledge of the era. In both of these dramas, through role adoption, the creation of contrasts or metaphoric analogies and the development of empathy, they will be prompted to make personal and emotional connections to the issues and themes being examined. Whilst process drama makes use of a range of structures and drama conventions, such as freeze frames, hot seating, ritual, overheard conversations and conscience corridor, for example, it also encompasses considerable spontaneity and playfulness. Thus such drama relies heavily upon the imagination and offers rich opportunities for creative development through the exploration of different possibilities and the adoption of different role perspectives. During such drama, pupils oscillate between engagement and reflection and develop their ability to evaluate the drama, both its content and processes, as well as make connections and find parallels with real world situations.

Many of the key features of creativity are evident in process drama: imaginative play and exploration, curiosity and agency, collaborative engagement and reflection, and innovation and risk-taking. In such drama there is often evidence of children 'possibility thinking' their ways forwards, considering 'what if' questions as they engage in the 'as if world' of their own creation. Craft (2000) asserts that 'possibility thinking' is at the heart of creativity and involves finding ways to cope with problems, trying out possibilities and identifying questions for investigation. It is, research evidence suggests, nurtured by creative pedagogic practice characterised by features such as teachers 'standing back', profiling learner agency and offering time and space for full immersion in imaginatively engaging contexts (Cremin et al., 2006; Craft et al., 2012). These characteristics are all employed in the context of process drama and in addition, the teacher is creatively involved. McWilliam (2008) suggests that teachers who foster creativity are neither the 'sage on the stage' nor the 'guide on the side', but are more actively involved as co-constructors of meaning and are 'meddlers in the middle'. This certainly describes the teacher's role in drama; all practitioners need to be prepared to respond flexibly and seize opportunities through TIR to foster and challenge children's creative learning.

Enriching the curriculum through drama

There are multiple opportunities to employ process drama in the curriculum: in literacy, maths and science, in the humanities and in thematic work. It is a powerful motivating tool; indeed, Ofsted (2002) argue that it is *the* most motivating tool in the curriculum. Providing space and time for children to engage in improvisational drama can help engage children's interest, enrich curriculum provision and foster their creative learning. There are three areas in particular which offer rich scope for drama: role play areas; literacy sessions; and cross-curricular work.

Role play areas

Role play areas are potentially inspiring contexts for creative learning for children from the Early Years Foundation Stage right through to the end of Key Stage 2, though the nature of them and children's attitude towards them will differ across this time. They constitute a place to imagine, play and pretend, using a variety of skills in the process, including reading and writing for different purposes and audiences. Too often, however, such areas are confined to real world places, such as doctors' surgeries, police stations or supermarkets, but fictional or book-based areas, more open-ended fantasy places and imaginative cross-curricular contexts also need to be offered; each makes different demands upon the creativity of the young. For example, Miss Wobble the Waitress's café, Clarice Bean's home, Mr Wonka's Chocolate Factory, Fern's family farm, Hagrid's cottage or the White Witch's palace could be created. Ideas for more generic fantasy areas include undersea kingdoms, castles, rockets, cottages, woods and caves. Creating areas which connect to the rest of the curriculum can also be useful; examples include an Anderson shelter from World War Two, an Egyptian tomb/catacombs, a homeless shelter, the offices of the Red Cross/ Oxfam, a museum, and a corner of the Rainforest. In such areas, children can make use of their prior knowledge as well as stories they know which are set in such contexts, and draw upon different known and imagined characters to create new narratives and events.

Through co-creating such areas and bringing resources to enrich them, children develop their commitment and interest, key preconditions for creativity; they also need to consider collectively the kinds of characters and problems that might surface in these contexts. Critical to the success of such areas, particularly with regard to creativity, is the extent of dramatic tension and problems which arise within them; simply pretending to be people in a café, however well-resourced it is, will not in itself prompt creative problem-solving or possibility thinking. The three core elements of any dramatic scenario – people, place, predicament (Cremin and Grainger, 2001) – need to be planned for explicitly, as without a predicament or a problem to solve at the seaside, the YMCA, or Cape Canaveral, the children's play may remain at the level of imitation, and will not move towards co-creation and innovation.

The teacher's role is important here. TIR is needed in role play areas since although adults sometimes circumvent or direct children's play (in a desire for an identifiable outcome, for example), the TIR can enhance play through creating challenges and introducing tensions and difficulties to which the children feel the need to respond. However, teachers do need to sensitively observe the children's self-initiated play before intervening, 'standing back' in order to consider their play and the direction they are exploring, before seeking to build on this. Through observation and TIR, and listening and talking to children in and out of role, teachers can evaluate and extend the learners' creative engagement. The TIR might, for example, enter the café as a confused customer who has lost her dog, or the chef's mother coming to report that he is ill and unable to prepare for the impending children's party; alternatively, the TIR might arrive as an inspector of some kind seeking to arrange a time for the inspection. In taking such roles, teachers seed and trigger problems to solve, but do not seek to direct the way in which the young learners respond. Additionally significant is ensuring that children are given the space to share their adventures in the role play area with the rest of the class, as later, the problems they solved and the characters they met/ created will be adopted and adapted by other learners.

Some teachers also seek to enrich children's imaginative engagement by introducing toys as characters, with which the children can communicate; this may be a stuffed bear, doll, robot or mannequin, for example, found hiding in the corner of the room, perhaps bearing a message to the class. Alternatively, mysterious evidence of the visitor may be noticed and collected over time (e.g., lettuce leaves and pieces of carrot, prior to a toy rabbit's arrival), until they are revealed and a new friend created. Such characters often become honorary members of the class, may be read to, attend outings, get invited to parties, and enjoy sleepovers and so on. Children may also write to them with the teacher writing back in role as the character. This involves considerable commitment, but is highly engaging and creates rich opportunities for purposeful reading and writing – postcards from trips abroad, birthday cards, get well cards and letters from relatives can all be created. Some such characters have their own diary which they take when invited to stay with members of the class, who care for them and can be invited to report back on their adventures.

Drama in literacy sessions

Creative teachers often use drama in literacy time as part of shared reading or as preparation for shared and independent writing. Through employing one of a range of drama conventions, teachers can enrich children's comprehension as they explore character motivation or behaviour via interior monologues or the unfolding plot or theme in a text via freeze frames or group sculptures. Such activities can help children employ their inference and deduction skills and prompt close interrogation of texts.

In addition, drama provides meaningful contexts for writing, both individually and collaboratively. Through orally rehearsing and refining ideas for writing and through listening to those of others, children often find that writing in drama is less challenging. Teachers can use drama in literacy sessions to focus on a form of writing and, during more extended process drama sessions, can 'seize the moment' to write at a tense and dramatic point. Research evidence suggests that both links have potential, but that the flexibility and intuitive nature of 'seizing the moment to write' tends to foster more voice and verve, and more creative edge in children's writing (Cremin et al., 2006). This is perhaps because, caught up in the emotional moment and engaged in sustained in-role work, the imagined experience resonates through their writing. If drama is used to enrich a particular genre, then careful bridges need to be built between the drama conventions used and the form of writing desired. Whilst several conventions may be used to generate ideas and involve the learners, the final convention needs to link to the chosen genre. In this way, the last improvised scenario acts as a kind of dress rehearsal for their writing. For example, thought tracking a character's views and concerns is well aligned to creating thought bubbles or diary writing.

Drama also contributes towards the generation of oral ideas and possibilities, children's spoken confidence and the naturally creative use of gesture, facial expression, movement and voice. Children think on their feet and negotiate their way forwards in drama, in conversation with one another, asking and answering questions, retelling events and creating new ones. In literacy sessions, fiction and non-fiction texts can be brought to life and examined through hot seating or forum theatre, for example, requiring pupils to find a spoken register and content appropriate to their role and the situation.

In literacy sessions, teachers often seek to use drama to bring a book to life and select moments from the text to expand through drama conventions. Such moments need to focus on conflict, ambiguity, challenge or misunderstanding, as these will help trigger more focused and generative improvisations. Teachers may want to consider:

- What possible 'offstage' scenarios might be occurring that could be fruitfully investigated through drama?
- What possible roles or conventions could be employed at this moment and with what purpose?
- How much needs to be read aloud immediately before the drama to contextualise the action?

Tensions may also be found through examining gaps in the text, for example, unmentioned conversations, nightmares, premonitions, a character's conflicting thoughts on an issue, and earlier problematic events that hint at the challenge to come. Through drama, these 'omissions' can be co-constructed, investigated and packed with meaning before the class return to the text itself.

Integrating drama across the curriculum

Teachers can seize opportunities to integrate drama into subject specific studies and in thematic work – for example, in their examinations of World War Two and the Egyptians – as well as in more generic explorations of the social issues, financial consequences and environmental concerns which orbit around the rainforest or pollution, for example. Alternatively, teachers may work to teach maths more creatively, leaning on drama prompted through literature perhaps to explore issues of size, weight and volume, for example (see Pound and Lee, 2011). They may also engage in creative explorations of both secular and faith tales in order to support spiritual development through inhabiting the lives of others. The opportunity to engage in open exploration and reflection through being as well as doing, and experience feelings of wonder and transcendence, can foster children's spirituality (Grainger and Kendall–Seatter, 2003).

Additionally, process drama allows children to develop personally, socially and morally in secure imaginative contexts and enables them to develop qualities such as empathy, self-control, respect for others' views and the ability to work constructively with their peers. Imaginative situations often put children in a position of confronting ethical principles, examining their personal values and moral codes, and can help them learn to tolerate ambiguity and uncertainty (Grainger, 2003). Heathcote's 'mantle of the expert' approach to the whole curriculum is also a valuable way to build bridges between subjects and demonstrates the potential of drama as a teaching and learning medium across the curriculum (Heathcote and Bolton, 1995). In this kind of process drama work, children adopt roles with expertise, authority, knowledge and specialists' skills. Such expertise may be acquired from classroom research or be bestowed imaginatively by the TIR. Either way, their positioning prompts them to use and widen their skills, knowledge and understanding in a particular area.

As drama opens up a wealth of imagined experiences in a variety of curriculum contexts, it can deepen children's knowledge of the subjects or themes being taught. This occurs, in part, due to the intellectually demanding nature of drama (Cremin, 2009), and in part because it encourages children to experiment with images in their minds, making them visible and voiced as they stretch towards new understandings in different contexts (Airs et al., 2005). New learning also takes place as a result of the choices and decisions made in the drama as they search for new solutions in order to settle an emotional dichotomy or respond to conflict. Whether teaching a subject specific curriculum or a themed approach, teachers can harness this power in a number of ways, as the following examples indicate.

Developing drama through PSHE: an example

Tackling issues of racism, prejudice and bullying forms part of the Personal, Social and Health Education (PSHE) and the Social and Emotional Aspects of Learning (SEAL) curriculum for primary schools. These are emotive issues about which some children will have direct experience; others will have read about this or seen examples in the news and on TV. Many schools also take part in the national anti-bullying campaign, so such drama work could be integrated within that focus.

The following case study describes how drama can be used, together with a powerful literary text, to explore attitudes and feelings, it also seeks to demonstrate the creative learning opportunities which emerged when children, imagining with each other and with their TIR, meet new challenges. The ten year olds involved in the session had experience of working with emotive texts in drama and were engaged in a wider unit of work on difference, diversity and prejudice. In this particular session, drama was used to help them immerse themselves in the text in order to examine the issues, and it culminated in a piece of writing which also enabled them to examine these issues through the voice of one of the characters.

The Green Children by Kevin Crossley-Holland (Oxford, 1997) was chosen to support this work; a thought-provoking picture book, it is about two children who find themselves in a different world to their own where the sky, the buildings and the people are not green as they are in their own world. The class began by examining the front cover and the title and creating a class freeze frame of the cover visual in which the Green Children are seen by a group of other children, arguably from the past, but also from the 'real world' known to the children. The young learners positioned as the Green Children reflected a sense of panic on their faces and anxiety in their postures, the others gathered around cautiously, peering at them, pointing to them, and showing expressions of curiosity, questioning, confusion and interest, as well as a degree of wary uncertainty on the part of some. To develop the freeze frame further and to discover what the characters were thinking, the children, when prompted with a touch on the shoulder by the teacher, voiced their thoughts. These included:

'Ahhh, look they are all green; they're strange.'
'What are they?'
'Where do they come from?'
'Look at them; how weird they are.'
'Don't go near them.'
'Let's get out of here.'
'Be careful – they might be dangerous.'

'Where are we? Who are they? What do they want?'
'How can we get back to our own world?'
'Hold on to me, I don't like it here.'
'Please don't hurt us.'

Almost immediately and without detailed discussion, the young people positioned themselves in the fictional context and were able to voice the projected thoughts of both sets of characters. A degree of tension, fear and distrust could be heard in the tenor of their words. Many expressed their suspicions and none voiced concern for the other party or a willingness to help the Green Children, despite the obvious consternation and fear which they physically conveyed. It could be argued that the first encounter was more concerned with self-protection and preservation than empathy and concern for the plight of those who presented as 'different'.

In order to help the class imagine what the world might be like for the Green Children, the teacher read on and when the inquisitive Green Boy finds a pale marble stone in the forest, the class were invited to imagine that they were there, a Green Child encountering a new multi-coloured world. The teacher suggested that they might find something on the ground, on the branch of a tree or in the air. Various ideas were shared in pairs and the imagined objects drawn. In such a context there were no 'right answers' and all the children pictured and drew possibilities, sharing and developing ideas in interaction with one another. The diverse suggestions included feathers, a ladybird, the blackened remains of a bonfire, a shiny sixpence, twigs, a sheep's skull, leaves and a dead black raven. One child who drew a green caterpillar jotted down: *This could be our dinner, I must take it home – it's making my hands tingle – take it quickly – it's the same colour as us. It's copied us.* Another drew a dried autumnal leaf and jotted down: *What is it? How does it work? Why isn't it green? Why can't it talk?* Their ideas reflected lateral thinking and a degree of repositioning as they made the familiar strange through role adoption and imaginative engagement.

Later in the narrative, after 'supper', the Green siblings try to find their way back home but are unable to do so. Night after night they remain in the new world, but the boy, desperate to return home, grows gradually weaker and eventually he dies in his sister's arms; 'the song went out of him'. The Green girl loses her only connection to her world. This created a new and tangible emotional problem for the class and needed sensitivity and the professional judgement of the teacher to help them consider her situation. One group formed a circle around a chair which depicted the dead boy and in role as the Green girl, members of the circle stepped forward to touch the chair and voice their feelings. These encompassed: personal hopes for the future and for the boy's soul; concerns and worries about their parents' loss; and regrets and self-recrimination for having brought her brother into this new world. Another group decided to make use of the convention 'role on the wall' and each wrote a last message to their brother on a sticky pad which they then ceremoniously placed on an outline of him drawn on a large sheet of lining paper. Yet another group examined the thoughts and feelings of the villagers, which varied from empathy to concerns about disease.

In the narrative as the Green girl's relationship with her new family grows, she seems to be accepted and, although she misses her home country, she begins to learn the words and customs of her hosts. She is invited by a young man, Guy, to attend the fair which he explains is like a market – a carnival. Arriving there, however, she finds that people stop and stare at her, pointing, teasing and mocking her because she is different. This pivotal moment was recreated in the classroom. Children took on various roles such as market sellers, entertainers and customers and soon the classroom buzzed with laughter and movement. However, when the classroom door opened, silence fell and all activity ceased as the children focused their attention on the Green girl, the TIR. In role, the teacher walked around the market; some remained silent, others voiced their thoughts, mumbling and muttering to one another about this 'strange creature'. The TIR responded naturally, sought to offer a personal view, and tried to share and show a common sense of humanity. At various points the action was frozen to enable the class to stop and observe the scene and focus together on how the girl looked and felt and how the crowd was reacting. Then at a signal, the class in a highly ritualised manner drew closer and encircled the TIR as the girl. The teacher narrated that she ran away into the forest and the class then formed a decision alley as if the spirits of the forest were offering her advice. One child in role as the Green girl, walked down the 'alley' between two lines of children as she tried to decide whether to return to face the crowd or run away and never return. She, too, at times voiced her thoughts and inner conflict, sometimes responding to the voices in the trees. The voices included:

'Run as fast as you can; you need to find your true home.'
'Hide in the forest; they'll never find you.'
'Stay here with us; we'll protect you.'
'Don't listen to them; listen to yourself.'
'They are fools; they don't know you.'
'Go to Guy. He is your friend and can help you.'
'Ask Guy; he'll know what to do.'

'Who can I trust? Did Guy know this would happen?'
'There is nowhere to hide.'
'I will always be alone.'
'This isn't fair.'

Many 'advisors' suggested she should go to Guy, back to his family, and so the teacher narrated the children's narrative forwards and described how the green girl ran back to find an empty house; she sat down confused and uncertain and wrote a note. Was she going to stay? This was left open, hanging in the atmosphere which was highly charged. The children, scattered across the room, settled quickly to write. Some wrote from Guy's point of view, others from the girl's; one wrote as the mother of the host family.

Dear Guy,
I am sorry for running away from the fair. I couldn't take the pressure from the people pointing and laughing at me. Thank you for trying to be a friend to me but it didn't work. Please tell the rest of the family thank you for looking after me and my brother. I cannot believe what people said to me – what have I done to them? They just don't know me for who I am and never will.

Dear Guy,
I feel left out. I can't carry on. Thank you for all you've done. Thank you for sticking up for me. I need to know what's going to happen to my brother. I need to go back – I need to tell my family. Their voices haunt me, I am not really so different. I feel like I'm shattered inside, everywhere.

Having shared extracts from their writing, the teacher read to the end of the tale and invited the class to create group sculptures to sum up the message of their work. These were rich and varied: some made their physically shaped sculptures reflect the angst and pain of difference, suggesting their shapes were made of barbed wire or twisted ivy; others depicted more hopeful abstract sculptures with hands of stone to suggest permanence which joined together or reached out. The various titles given to these sculptures were listed on the flipchart and the teacher seized the opportunity to discuss connections and parallels in twenty-first-century Britain. Some of the children also talked about gender differences and the difficulties they encountered with siblings who wanted something else or who, as one child noted, 'come from another planet'. In this session the children had exchanged ideas, experimented with alternative perspectives and interpretations and raised questions and issues; they had not found comfortable closure or easy answers to the challenging personal and moral dilemmas which surfaced. In their final sculptures this was particularly noticeable. In the weeks that followed, they were engaged in a series of drama sessions based upon *The Island* (2007) by Armin Greder, which, in a harder and more graphic manner than *The Green Children*, addresses prejudice. This sustained period of time offered scope for immersion and exploration of the issues.

There are numerous other picture books which explore other PSHE topics, some of which are set within particular periods in history and thus afford the opportunity of combining an exploration of the period and the feelings, motivations and challenges experienced by people at that time. Amongst the many suitable for process drama, recommendations include:

A Bad Case of Stripes (1998, Scholastic) by David Shannon.
The Colour of Home (2002, Frances Lincoln) by Mary Hoffman.
The Bird Man (2000, Andersen) by Melvin Burgess.
Rose Blanche (2004, Red Fox) by Roberto Innocenti and Ian McEwan.
Erika's Story (2004, Random House) by Ruth Vander Zee and Roberto Innocenti.
The Savage (2008, Walker) by David Almond.
The Heart in the Bottle (2007, Harper) by Oliver Jeffers.
The Two Frogs (2003, Jonathon Cape) by Chris Wormell.
I am the Mummy Heb-Nefert (2000, Voyager) by Eve Bunting.
Luba, the Angel of Bergen Belsen (2003, Adams) by Michelle McCann, Luba Tryszynska-Frederick and Ann Marshall.

Developing drama around sustainability: an example

Schools that use a 'creative' or theme based curriculum can also integrate drama. In this next example, drama contributed to a sustainability theme entitled 'It's Rubbish'. The title evoked discussions with the eight and nine year olds about who rubbish belongs to and who is responsible for it. The class explored the amount/types of rubbish being thrown out in their own homes and in school before turning to look at the country as a whole. As part of the work they were introduced to *The Paperbag Prince* (1992) by Colin Thompson, which proved to be an excellent starting point.

The cover was shown on the interactive whiteboard and created considerable discussion. Then using a combination of the text and oral storytelling, the teacher established that the local residents were becoming tired of lorries rumbling through their village, tired of the grime caused by the diesel fumes that clung to their doors and seeped through their windows. The class created freeze frames showing the villagers variously peering out of their curtains, standing at their doors, in a café and out for a walk. Some voiced their thoughts, for example: '*My Grandchildren won't come and see me anymore because of the horrible smell.*' Another child commented: '*When I was young I would play outside all day – I only allow my children out for 20 minutes.*'

Reading on, the class heard that at the dump, a collection of rusty metal drums were oozing poison into the environment. Again the teacher, using his own imaginative additions, explained that the villagers knew that the local councillors were meeting at the town hall. Pausing in the telling, the class discussed what might happen and decided that the villagers would prepare banners to express their views. These were quickly created in groups, some instinctively using rhyme to increase the impact of their objections. These read:

We all have the hump – get rid of this dump!
Don't be a fool – stay away from the poison pool!
Give us our village back!
Pollution is killing us. Show us you care – clean our air!
This is countryside, not a dump!

The drama continued with the villagers, who had been told the council meeting was about to end, waiting for the clock on the interactive whiteboard to reach midday. At this point the classroom transformed into a demonstration, with groups desperately pleading for the dump to close. The TIR, as a councillor, demanded quiet and after some extended and robust discussion agreed to provide the opportunity for villagers to meet members of the council. Almost immediately, small groups of children set about preparing their representations whilst others who were to take the role of councillors met to discuss their position. Desks were arranged to resemble a number of mini meetings and the councillors took their places, checking through their papers. The villagers thought carefully about how to enter the meetings; some chose to be angry and demanding, whilst others were more diplomatic – this was partly determined by the imagined nature of their group, families, friends, young, old and so on. These decisions influenced how the meetings progressed, but all provided a safe context in which the children could explore their views about the dump and wider issues of pollution. However, most remained dissatisfied with the councillor's responses and decided to write to their local MP. Two examples included:

Dear Mr Peters,
I am writing to let you know how disgusted I am that this monstrous dump has been allowed to wreck our lives for so long. Each day I cannot even open my windows because of the smell. People don't want to visit me and I have not seen my grandchildren for over a year! Please find it in your heart to reconsider the location of the dump so we can go back to living in a beautifully valley.

Dear Councillor Matthews,
The dump has to go! I know you did not listen to our demonstration but we will be back. I used to enjoy living in this village but now I just want to move. The lorries wake me up every week when they pass and the fumes are horrible. This used to be a lovely place to live. Please help us get enjoy life again.

Using drama as part of the 'It's Rubbish' topic helped these eight and nine year olds engage with the issues, collaborate and take risks, and use their developing knowledge in an imaginative context. This was built upon by borrowing narrative elements and issues offered in the books *Dear Greenpeace* by Simon James and *One World* by Michael Foreman. Other curriculum themes can also be investigated via layered polysemic texts that offer a narrative context for drama. Literature, combined with TIR, is a potent framing device for developing improvisational process drama and fostering learner creativity.

Creative Touches

Drama involves creation, speculation and reflection and prompts questions to be asked and connections to be made. In contrast to more traditional pedagogic practices, it provides considerable scope to explore language, interpretation and meaning, and fosters children's creativity. Creativity and imagination are not additional elements in drama, but are central to the symbolic and communicative nature of the activity, encouraging empathy and insight. They also contribute to the uncertainty and ambiguity that characterise classroom drama. In order to develop children's creativity though drama, it is suggested that teachers:

■ Develop role play areas based on the 'three Ps of drama' – people, place, predicament.

- Make use of drama conventions in literacy sessions to inhabit texts and foster a creative response.

- Collect rich literature which raises questions and explores issues of significance related to the curriculum and to life.

- Map out process drama lessons using these texts and plan to expand the scope by storytelling additional elements.

- Consider the potential of TIR and take the risk to become 'the meddlers in the middle' (McWilliam, 2007), challenging and extending children's creative learning.

References

Airs, J., et al. (2005). The performing arts, in R. Jones, R. Wyse and D. Wyse (eds), *Creativity in the Primary Curriculum*. London: Routledge, pp. 96–113.

Booth, D. (1994). *Story Drama: Reading, Writing and Role Playing across the Curriculum*. Markham: Pembroke.

Craft, A. (2000). *Creativity Across the Primary Curriculum: Framing and Developing Practice*. London: Routledge Falmer.

Craft, A., McConnon, L. and Matthews, A. (2012). Child-initiated play and professional creativity: enabling four-year-olds' possibility thinking. *Thinking Skills and Creativity*, 7 (1): 48–61.

Cremin, T. (2009). *Teaching English Creatively*. London: Routledge.

Cremin, T., Burnard, P. and Craft, A. (2006). Pedagogy and possibility thinking in the early years. *Thinking Skills and Creativity*, 1 (2): 108–19.

Cremin, T., Goouch, K., Blakemore, L., Goff, E. and McDonald, R. (2006). Connecting Drama and Writing: seizing the moment to write, *Research in Drama in Education*, 11 (3): 273–91.

Cremin, T., McDonald, R., Blakemore, L. and Goff, E. (2009). *Jumpstart Drama!* London: David Fulton.

Grainger, T. (2003) 'Exploring the unknown: ambiguity, interaction and meaning making in classroom drama', in E. Bearne, H. Dombey and T. Grainger (eds), *Classroom Interactions in Literacy*. Maidenhead: Open University Press, pp. 105–14.

Grainger, T. and Cremin, M. (2001). *Resourcing Classroom Drama 5–8*, Sheffield: National Association for the Teaching of English.

Grainger, T. and Kendall-Seatter, S. (2003). Drama and Spirituality: reflective connections. *International Journal of Children's Spirituality*, 8 (1): 25–32

Greenwood, J. (2009). Drama education in New Zealand: a coming of age? A conceptualization of the development and practice of drama in the curriculum as a structured improvisation, with New Zealand's experience as a case study. *Research in Drama Education: The Journal of Applied Theatre and Performance*, 14 (2): 245–60.

Heathcote, D. and Bolton, G. (1995). *Drama for Learning: Dorothy Heathcote's Mantle of the Expert Approach to Education*, Portsmouth, NH: Heinemann.

McWilliam, E. (2008). Unlearning how to teach *Innovations in Education and Teaching International*, 45 (3): 263–9.

Office for Standards in Education (OfSTED) (2002). *The Curriculum in Successful Primary Schools*, HMI 553, October. London: OfSTED.

Pound, L. and Lee, T. (2011). *Teaching Mathematics Creatively*. London and New York: Routledge.

Taylor, P. and Warner, C. D. (2006). *Structure and Spontaneity: the process drama of Cecily O'Neil*. Stoke on Trent: Trentham.

Geography

David Lambert and Paula Owens

Geography translates literally as 'writing the world' or 'earth description': it is the *world* subject according to Alastair Bonnett (2008). The key purpose of geography is that it attempts to comprehend the world *as a whole*. In school, it is helpful to imagine the subject as a resource for helping us respond to questions arising from fundamental human curiosities about the world in which we live – questions that all children ask in some form or other. Such questions are, arguably, ultimately to do with survival in 'our home on planet earth'. The examples that follow below are derived from Howard Gardner's discussion of curiosity and subject knowledge (Gardner and Boix Mansilla, 1994). We have organised these into four groups which roughly speaking align with physical geography, human geography, place-based geography and welfare (or development) geography:

- What is this place made of?
  - Why do things move?
  - What becomes of things?

- Who am I?
  - Where am I from?
  - Who is my 'family'?
  - Who are those people – where are they from?

- Where do I belong?
  - What is this place like?
  - How did it come to be like this?
  - How might it change?

- Who gets what, where and why?
  - What is fair?
  - What is sustainable?

When geography is positioned in this way, it helps guard against its reduction, as so often in the popular imagination, to the transmission (and memorisation) of factual information about the world. Not that the information contained between the metaphorical covers of the atlas is irrelevant, as the Geographical Association (GA) has been at pains to show.[1] But lessons that limit children to the absorption of fragmented and inert information for its own sake fail to grasp the idea of geography. As Horton and Kraftl have pointed out:

> … in any given 'geography', at any given time, there will be loads going on, on all sorts of levels: certainly way more than the rather neutral, even blank, circumscribed term 'geography' suggests … But 'geographies' are always already encountered, and lived in and of particular, everyday moments, in ways which are inherently personal, partial, individual, subjective, embodied and contingent (upon all sorts of things, some of them knowable and sayable, some of them not so knowable and sayable). That is (although one would perhaps never guess from much of what is written about 'geographies') 'geographies' are 'up here' [taps head] and elsewhere, at least as much as they are 'out there'…
> (Horton and Kraftl, 2005: 136)

From the earliest attempts to 'do' geography, therefore, we need more than just data. The imagination is crucial in exploring, representing and understanding a diverse and rapidly changing world. The world is continually being rediscovered, a point that is particularly apt if we think of the minds of young children. Indeed, Kudryavtsev stresses that this act of discovery in childhood is subjective and a distinctive form of creativity, and rather different from forms of creativity shown in adulthood. Whilst the latter is directed to technological, artistic and scientific production, childhood 'is almost the only part of a person's life where creative work is a universal and natural way of existence and where mastering an elementary way of handling a cultural object occurs in the child as a discovery for oneself' (Kudryavtsev, 2011: 46). Thus, what the knower brings to the 'known world' shapes fundamentally what they see and how they respond. Furthermore, it is true that technology brings distant places and the world to our screens, and yet there can be frontiers and *terra incognito* around the next street corner. Doing geography (writing the world) is in this sense a creative act, whether this may involve: synthesising shared and new world-views; making spatial and temporal connections; communicating and modelling ideas we have about the world; thinking through problems; or envisioning solutions.

In this chapter, we make the case that to *do* geography, especially as a young child, is a creative act. Creativity happens when:

- we nourish and develop our geographical imaginations, necessary to better understand the world and the ways that human and physical environments are interrelated;

- we use authentic contexts and direct experiences, such as through fieldwork, as opportunities to make and apply knowledge about the 'real world;

- rigorous subject knowledge underpins, and thus enables or enhances, discovery – this relates to teachers having good subject knowledge and a sense of the subject's overarching purposes (see next section).

The chapter provides examples of these, but of course they are accumulative and add up to an interrelated, cyclical process of 'meaning making'. They draw on the familiar and everyday to encourage children to articulate and communicate what is known and imagined about the world: they explicate their *personal geographies.* Teachers can, crucially, help children move on from this point and to re-evaluate the familiar and the everyday with fresh eyes, seeing what may have been taken for granted in new ways or even seeing what had not been noticed before: children can *develop* their personal geographies. In some circumstances the sharing of personal meanings can help children create new, personal and collaborative understandings – what we may call *collaborative geographies,* perhaps based on visits or fieldwork. On a more sophisticated level still, children imagining and empathising with a range of alternate views and meanings to better understand how different people live in the world may build *empathic geographies.*

These creative geographies build on more static, 'core' geographical knowledge and enable us to explore and discover places in new ways, through personalised, shared and sometimes contested views.

The very idea of geography

Whilst we agree with the thrust of the UK's 2010 Education White Paper (DfE, 2010), that school geography has the important job of introducing children to 'core knowledge' (and this includes geographical knowledge), the effective teaching of geography, particularly in primary schools, needs to acknowledge doing geography as a creative act. Developing so-called core (or essential) geographical knowledge is part of becoming an educated person. Without world knowledge we are limited in our capabilities as citizens in the world (Lambert, 2011). But attempting to communicate and transmit such core knowledge as an end in itself is a relatively useless and futile activity (Catling and Willy, 2009). The development of geographical knowledge takes place in relation to episodes of knowledge production and creation in relevant and purposeful contexts.

And yet, before focusing on exemplars of creativity in primary geography, it is worth acknowledging in a little more detail the development of geography as a field of disciplined thought, or as a source of what Michael Young (2008) calls 'powerful knowledge' (see also Firth, 2011; Catling and Martin, 2011). From the earliest human societies, and especially when human beings began to roam, there has been a need to get to know the land and what we now call the environment: where to find water, food and shelter and how to keep safe from danger. From at least the time of Ptolemy, a Greek who lived in Egypt in the second century AD, there have been attempts to write down and record the known world, thus putting local experience into a 'global' context. For much of history, the task of the geographer-explorer was to extend and deepen this world knowledge and to create an ever more reliable map. Creating and using maps and globes (in paper and electronic forms) may not be the 'be all and end all' of geography, but it remains of central importance. After a slow start (Ptolemy's map was rediscovered and still used over a thousand years after he first published it), remarkable human ingenuity has aided this process, transferring the spherical globe onto a flat piece of paper. Perhaps the most famous is Mercator's projection, which, in 1569, created a world map that for the first time preserved direction entirely accurately (but in so doing distorted the shape of countries and land masses). This map enabled safe global travel and exploration, and astonishingly, Mercator's mathematics are still the industry standard for modern GIS (the 'geographical information science' that underpins today's 'satnav').

Exploration, which arguably reached its peak in nineteenth-century Britain, allowed geographers to gather knowledge from all over our home planet – a task that is still not complete (we know little about the ocean floors, for instance). Exploration – and as we have already stressed, *discovery* – is indeed the essential element of geography's heritage. This is translated in today's classrooms through enquiry questions such as those set out near the beginning of this chapter, in contrast to the stereotype in the popular imagination of geographers mindlessly accumulating vast quantities of descriptive data about the world. Thus, in the middle of the twentieth century the prominent US geographer Edward Ackerman asserted that 'the goal of geography is nothing less than an *understanding* of the vast interacting system comprising all humanity and its natural environment on the surface of the Earth' (Ackerman, 1963: 436; our emphasis). Ackerman was what might have been called an applied geographer: he saw geography as important for informing governments and policy makers. He openly acknowledged that although the goal he identified may ultimately be unobtainable as a human aspiration it is entirely valid.

If we fast-forward to the present day, we can cite Alastair Bonnett (2008), a UK geographer, holding fast to this view, remarking that geography's ambition is indeed 'absurdly vast' (op cit, p. 9) – but that it would be more absurd not to address it. In a sense, this is to remind us that *we now know for sure* that human activity has the potency to destroy life on earth, or at least large swathes of it including its human occupants. Some say (see, for example, Morgan, 2011) that this realisation denotes that we have now entered a new epoch: that of the 'anthropocene'. Human induced climate change is perhaps the single most spectacular evidence of this. This is a mind-boggling fact and in our everyday lives it is hard to grasp, but school geography has the possibility to provide children with some of the means to do so. Note that we are not saying it falls to school teachers to 'save the planet' – we have enough to do! It is, more modestly, our goal to provide children with access to world knowledge and understanding that will prove helpful in facing the practical and moral issues that accompany our times. It is geography's purpose, in the words of the Geographical Association's manifesto,[2] to introduce children to a lifelong conversation about being at home on planet earth.

Geography in school comes alive

> Living geography ... asks young people to think about their life in relation to themselves in the world and what it may become – an impossible undertaking without the deep description of the world offered by geography. (Lambert, 2011: 134)

Creative school teachers do all they can to offset the dead-hand of perceived bureaucratic 'requirements'. Fortunately, geography is a 'living' subject. It focuses on the contemporary world and synthesises a variety of information and perspectives, thus lending itself particularly well to creative knowledge production (Scoffham, 2003; Catling, 2009). For example, places are not static: jobs change and landscapes evolve. Furthermore, the use of scarce space is often contested depending on the perspectives and needs of different user groups which are usually in a constant state of flux. Doing geography can induct children into ways to encounter such dynamism intelligently and productively.

It is worth noting in passing that this may be one reason why geography can be perceived as difficult to teach well (see Ofsted, 2011): the content of the subject can appear to be a little unstable – or at least lacking accessibility or legibility. Fran Martin (2004) has suggested that there might exist two deeply opposing views of school geography, which might be better understood as a continuum. On the one hand, there are facts and statistics that illustrate knowing where places are in the world and what they are like, and on the other hand, there are more personalised and dynamic responses to place that take in an emotional dimension. She argues that it is the latter approach that is more likely to promote creativity: 'If all geography lessons only focused on [pre-packaged] knowledge and skills, rather than moving on to the uncertain, debatable, value-laden elements, promotion of creativity and creative thinking skills would not be possible' (Martin, 2004: 120). Although it is useful to make distinctions such as this, it would be profoundly unhelpful to suggest or conclude that one is superior to the other. In the end, the teacher needs to find ways of merging the two, for there is no doubt that the geographical imagination is fuelled and stimulated by second-hand accounts, mediated images and atlas maps just as much as personalised responses to geographical encounters in 'everyday life'. Indeed, we may argue, following Michael Young's recent writings (Young, 2008), that the fundamental point of geography (or any curriculum subject) is to take children into realms of knowledge that exist beyond everyday personal experience.

However, 'personal geographies', by which we mean the interests, knowledge and the more esoteric consideration of values that children and others hold and which shape the mental geographies inside their heads, are without question of considerable importance. Geography is concerned with the interaction between physical and human worlds, and human activity is influenced by the complex interplay between personal, social and cultural values. Valuing 'personal geographies' helps children comprehend different viewpoints and perspectives. It is a way in for developing degrees of empathy with places and the people who live there. An appreciation of (often conflicting) values can illuminate thinking about how solutions might affect different groups – young people, old people, boys, girls, rich and poor. Think of the everyday, taken for granted, activity of shopping, for example: who wins and who loses when a new supermarket opens on the edge of town (with free car parking)?

Thus, it is useful to consider for one moment what it means to 'know' a bit of geography. This is particularly important because these days, thanks to the internet and Google Earth, satnav and mobile phones, everyone 'knows' or uses some geography. Furthermore, we all have a geographical existence: we live somewhere, shop somewhere, and have relatives and friends possibly dotted around the globe. It makes sense to tune into and exploit the pedagogic potential of such 'everyday geographies' – every teacher knows the strengths of working from the known and what is familiar to children. But in curriculum terms it is a lost opportunity not to move from this point to the unknown and less familiar.

For the teacher, the curriculum, like pedagogy, is about choices. It is part of what we have come to know as 'professional judgement', which itself requires great creativity. We make decisions according to principles we value, hopefully governed by our sense of educational purpose. A curriculum shaped by whim, the topics in the news or themes of contemporary 'relevance' is likely to be incoherent, shallow and, like junk-food, deeply unsatisfying after the initial fat and sugar rush. The rest of this chapter tries to illustrate some creative possibilities in the geography curriculum, fully mindful of the principles and 'warnings' contained in these introductory sections.

Creativity and the promise of geography

Creative teaching takes into account not just what, but how new knowledge is negotiated and connected to other kinds of knowledge that learners bring to the encounter. In geography, fieldwork, exploration and enquiry are key mechanisms for teaching and learning, being expressions of *contemporary educational power* (Lambert, 2011: 129) that invite creative and critical thinking by the children. The teacher's creativity lies in the practical act of 'curriculum making', the process by which she holds in balance the competing priorities of the children as learners and the goals and purposes of the subject. For this to be effective, the teacher certainly needs a range of professional knowledge, including knowledge of the subject in at least two senses. First, we have in mind the nature and significance of geography as an idea as discussed in the earlier parts of this chapter, which if nothing else helps free teachers from what can become the mundane 'delivery' of the official scheme of work. And second, we acknowledge the need for more specific 'content' knowledge without which the planning of geographical experiences can end up somewhat wishy-washy.

Let us refer back to the questions posed earlier in order to illustrate the point. The question *What is this place made of?* can be answered in many different ways. A geographical approach may lead us quickly into looking closely at *material* (rock and soil – or even bricks, tarmac and concrete) and the way in which the *weather* attacks and destroys ('weathering'); and then how (mainly) *water* removes this material, and in so doing *erodes* the land further (the 'work of rivers'). A creative teacher can take this platform in a number of different directions: whether looking at what *other* places are made of (in the UK, or elsewhere in the world, such as in deserts or polar lands) or taking a more 'human' line, such as how builders try to protect materials from weathering and erosion. These examples suggest quite particular topics but in our mind they are absolutely consistent with the overall goal of making sense of ourselves at home on planet earth.

The rest of this section presents three case studies to illustrate in more detail some creative curriculum making outcomes in geography.

The first two case studies arose as part of *Young Geographers*, a 'Living Geography project for Primary Schools' (Catling, 2008). In this project, groups of primary teachers were asked to develop learning sequences focused on geography in the locality. While first-hand experience is a crucial component of geography, it is not always possible – for example, when studying distant places. The third case study examines how Year 4 pupils studied environmental change on St Lucia with the support of the Creativity Action Research Awards (CARA) in ways designed to promote creative thinking skills.

For many of the teachers involved, the departure from tried and tested schemes of work (sometimes perceived to be 'prescribed' or mandatory) presented a degree of risk, not least because of the requirement to build in opportunities for fieldwork. This practical and independent 'curriculum making' activity made demands on their professional judgement and subject knowledge to select content and processes suited to their pupils' needs and interests. It involved a good deal of creative and critical thought. Each of the teachers involved created very different units of work that reflected their pupils' geographical, developmental and cultural contexts.

Developing personal geographies: starting with story

Stories about place are powerful and stimulating influences on the geographical imagination (Rawling, 2011), and can be a means whereby we help pupils to reconnect with, as well as to understand, the world. In this example, partnering story with real first-hand experience and 'messy' real world learning contexts helped provide a fertile ground for creativity when children's innate curiosity was allowed to flourish.

Jane Mulligan, a teacher of Foundation Stage children at Austrey Primary School, used a storybook, *The Journey* (by Neil Griffiths and Scott Mann), which tells the tale of an escaped toy boat and its journey along the river, as a starting point to build on children's inherent curiosity and stimulate discovery and learning about rivers and the locality. The children began by giving a recount of the story: We can see a little red boat. It went past mountains, a water fall, grass, sticky mud, a pond and stones in the river. They then wondered which of the features in the book might be found outside in the locality. Was there a mountain? Where could they find a pond? Was there a river near them? What are rivers really like? These and other questions from the children were then used by the teacher to drive a series of investigations.

Children began their investigation by exploring the school grounds, prompted by their queries about landscape features from the book. They were encouraged to use their senses, take pictures of things that especially interested them and talk about what they noticed. Jane and other supporting adults played a low-key role: helping children with the technical aspects of using digital cameras and recording children's comments and questions. In this child-led activity, pupils were encouraged to say not just what they discovered or noticed but also how they felt about it.

I can hear the wind hushing in the trees.
I can see a greenhouse.
I feel a bit muddy. Squishy mud!
I feel a bit surprised!
We haven't got a mountain, but we have got a hill.

Freedom to explore emotional as well as cognitive responses form a vital dimension of geography education argues Tanner (2010), both shaping and helping us understand our perceptions, meanings and memories of place. The combination of feeling and knowing is an intrinsic part of our personal geographies and has also been shown by research to be a process that deepens learning and memory (Scoffham, 2010) and is an intrinsic part of our personal geographies. The provision of unfettered outdoor exploration, valued responses and personal choice characterised this 'enabling environment' (DCSF, 2008).

The children had been disappointed not to find a river in their school grounds, so a walk was planned to the nearby village to both widen their knowledge of environmental features and, specifically, to experience a stream at first hand. Concepts of rivers, such as 'flow', are not easily portrayed by images or water-play alone, so this fieldtrip gave the children opportunities to pose *what if* questions with the aid of toy boats and sticks and thus explore how rivers and streams *worked*.

It [the boat] floats! Don't let it float away.
We're standing on a bridge!
It's going quite fast.

Mackintosh (2005) stresses that it is of paramount importance for pupils to visit rivers when learning about them and to be encouraged to visualise them (and the processes at work) in lots of different ways to help them develop three-dimensional mental constructs. Without this process (she says), pupils have no cognitive or environmental image on which to locate the terminology and processes they encounter through class-based work and fieldwork.

Back in class, children revisited the story, extending their geographical imaginations by investigating digital maps and aerial imagery. As Jane revealed:

Having discussed what the map might be showing, Katie said that it was 'Here, England'. I then showed the children how we could zoom in and get a closer look at the River Severn. They knew from the story [*The Journey*] where and what the estuary was. Some noticed that the river got narrower. I used the words they had been using to sketch a map of a river.

While the world has opened up through the use of the internet and other virtual media, it is worth remembering that 'no virtual reality can replace real fieldwork and deep curiosity about our world' (Burt, 2003: 59). First-hand experience and fieldwork are considered to be vital aspects of geography, not only in helping children to develop new geographical vocabulary and use it more accurately (Owens, 2005; Ward, 1998) but in providing opportunities for creativity through exploration and investigation (Catling and Willy, 2009). However, as noted by Mackintosh (2005), a combination of approaches, that includes fieldwork, is necessary to enable children to make new connections between their ideas.

The final step in this sequence of learning activities was to let the children build a miniature stream in the school grounds, so that they could apply some of their ideas about rivers to the real world. This entailed imagining how it might be built and planning what needed to be done. Jane explained:

I scribed while the children thought of the materials they would need to make a stream. This led to a lot of discussion about where we would get the water from, and comments that the stream we visited last week was probably too far away (hence we needed a quick map to recap our journey), how we could carry it and which would be better – the suggestion of a cup or a bucket, and why? They decided the bucket. Suzannah thought that we would need teamwork to get the job done.

Having planned their activity with the teacher, the children used their chosen tools – spades, trowels, guttering, stones, sand and buckets – to dig a narrow trench, put in stones, sand and, lastly, water.

I didn't know it was going to be this hard work.

We sprinkled in sand and pebbles – it's like adding chocolate chips!

We've found loads of worms. I've found a really tiny one.

There's a deep bit this end.

It won't soak away because … we put a lot of water in … the clay is stopping it.

Jane reflected on her pupils' responses to this purposeful learning activity as they made a host of new discoveries: The children enjoyed all activities but got most excited when outside, especially stream-building and getting dirty with glee!'

But outdoor experiences are not, on their own, effective guarantors of creative thoughts and actions. Creativity flourished in this example for several additional reasons: opportunities to explore and play; planning driven by pupils' curiosity (thus aiding motivation); essential, basic geographical knowledge (such as specific terminology for environmental features and processes); scaffolded imaginative thought; and authentic contexts, which inclined children more readily to transform learning into problem-solving experiences (Jeffrey and Woods, 2003). These pupils were able to make new meanings and extend their personal geographies as they made links between the story, their imagination and the real world.

Collaborative geography: risks in the local environment

Fieldwork and story were also central to this locality study as the teacher, Jonathan Kersey, asked children, aged six to seven, one key enquiry question: 'How can we keep ourselves safe in our local environment?' The enquiry question provided a clear purpose which could immediately be seen to be of practical value to the children, hence from the start the learning was couched in an authentic context. Jonathon wanted his pupils to work collaboratively, drawing on their personal geographies to create new, shared meanings and communicate them in novel ways, that is, through the medium of film.

The pupils chose to rework *Little Red Riding Hood*, recasting the 'Big Bad Wolf' as the 'Big Good Wolf' who would guide Red Riding Hood to her Grandma's house and help her identify the dangers along the way. Pupils were to be involved in the entire process, from writing the story to film production, taking on the roles of actors, camera operators, musical score production team, narrators, film editors, costume team and props team. Jonathon recalled:

The main benefit of the project was that it encouraged children to look at their local environment for a specific geographical purpose. Locations were chosen not just because the children knew them or liked them but because they suited the purpose of telling the story. This allowed children to evaluate locations and make judgements about their environmental impact on people's lives.

In the resultant 15-minute film, the central characters of Little Red Riding Hood and the Big Good Wolf investigate a variety of dangers in locations that include a wood, a busy main road, an alley, a children's play area and an electric sub-station. Music, setting and appropriate geographical vocabulary were chosen by the pupils to help the film deliver a shared sense of place and event. Here is an extract:

NARRATOR: Little Red Riding Hood continued walking to Granny's, along the main road outside Costcutters. She wanted to go to Granny's house quickly and she wasn't being very careful.

Film shows Little Red Riding Hood walking quickly past the shops and about to cross a busy road. Dramatic music plays.

WOLF: Stop! The road's really dangerous and you've got to use the crossing!

Film shows the wolf helping Little Red Riding Hood to cross on the zebra crossing.

Film switches to a long view of a grass verged alley.

NARRATOR: Little Red Riding Hood walked through an alley. She saw something shiny and she liked shiny things.

Film shows Little Red Riding Hood stopping down to look in the grass where we see some broken glass. Appropriate music changes the mood.

LITTLE RED RIDING HOOD: Mmmm, that's shiny! I'm going to pick it up.

WOLF: Stop! Don't you know you might cut yourself?

Jonathan reflected that this project had fascinated and motivated the children, allowing them to express their own views about places that were special to them. It had also enabled them to 'rediscover' hazards in new contexts.

> Never climb up places where it says 'danger'. The electricity box is very dangerous. There is a yellow danger sign on it. It says danger of death.
>
> Don't pick up glass because you could cut yourself. The alleyway near Prospect Road has lots of dangerous broken glass.

Valuing children's views and places special to them is a strategy advocated by Catling (2003) who urges us to pay special attention to 'children's geographies', a term which, although critiqued as value-laden and contested (Horton and Kraft, 2005), reminds us that children have very different agendas to those of adults (Kelly, 2005; Matthews and Limb, 1999).

Yet different agendas are a powerful reason for the creation of collaborative geographies. If, as we have argued, places are more than static embodiments of facts and figures, but rather dynamic 'sites of multiple identities and histories' (Charlton et al., 2011: 65), then collaborative interpretations have an important role to play in understanding them.

As Ley (2002) has suggested, landscapes are products of actions, layered with meaning, and can be interpreted in many ways: at face value, as an expression of intent and as a reflection of wider societal themes. In this sense, fashioning new, contemporary, shared meanings requires a good deal of creativity because these meanings are never static but fluctuate as individual viewpoints and values change. The creation of collaborative geographies is arguably of great value in understanding common problems and issues and in providing a shared sense of belonging to a landscape. This is part of the enormous sense of purpose and challenge offered through geography.

Empathic geography: environmental conflicts in St Lucia

Over the years, Year 4 class teacher Sarah Lewis had taught about environmental change in St Lucia in a more 'traditional' style, but now wanted to find out how well these pupils could use more complex ideas. More specifically, she was keen to encourage children to think about the conflicting needs between different peoples and to explore some of the tensions between environment and developmental issues on the islands. With support from Creative Action Research Awards (CARA), a programme funded by Creative Partnerships and managed by CapeUK,[3] a research partnership was forged with Dr Emma Mawdsley, a lecturer in geography at Cambridge University. Sarah admits that it took nearly four months to develop their initial ideas and that they were working at the 'experimental end of our experience' (Lewis and Mawdsley, 2007: 19).

The main premise was to ask the pupils to imagine that they were a team of 'geographers' from St Lucia charged with preparing a report in their own choice of media, explaining how the environment was changing, with recommendations for improving the environment and the lives of those who lived and worked there. This was to culminate in a presentation to 'visiting ministers'.

Preparation for this enquiry included developing necessary, background knowledge so that this could be applied to problem-solving. Thus, pupils spent some time learning about geographical contexts to find out: where the island was; what it was like; what people did there; and some of the pressing environmental problems such as conflicting patterns of land use. They were also given use of a specially constructed website where they could find out about characters created for this activity, who represented different and conflicting land uses. Lewis and Mawdsley (2007: 20) explain:

> Each photo was annotated by the 'character', outlining a number of issues that troubled them and which led to tension or conflicts with the interests of one or more of the other characters. For example, Bob was worried about the hotels demanding more of the beach front, and the damage done to the reefs by yachts, but recognised that he sold his fish to the hotels where his wife also worked as a cleaner. Rachel was poor and needed to clear more land for bananas, but she knew this caused soil erosion.

Pupils repeatedly emailed Emma over a four-week period with their questions and suggestions to which Emma replied by suggesting they investigate how other characters might feel (see emails below). While pupils were encouraged to empathise with the characters, it was made intentionally difficult for the children to keep all of them happy at the same time. This was designed to move their thinking away from a narrow response – for example, 'you mustn't cut down trees' – to a more sophisticated level of reasoning that accepted trade-off and compromise.

Dear Dr Emma,
We found out that the coral reef is getting damaged because boats are dropping their anchors onto the coral reef. We want to help the coral reef by recommending that no boats drop their anchors ... (Do you think this is a good idea?)

From the Coral Group

Dear Coral Group,
Protecting the reef is really important, because it is where so many different species live – some for all of their lives and some while they are baby fish growing up.
   But I don't think that you can stop all of the boats anchoring there all of the time. Why not go and find out about Bob the fisherman, and see what he would think? The other people who would be affected are the tourists – the ones that go on yacht and scuba trips want to spend time on the reef.

From Dr Emma

One major problem identified by the pupils was the tensions between tourism, fishing and the environment. After much debate, several groups came up with the idea of zoning and this was a topic of much discussion and excitement during the 'Ministerial feedback':

> Tourist yachts and fishermen could have separate beach areas to stop the damage, caused by anchors to the coral.
>   But what about pollution from the boats? The zoning won't stop that spreading!

The use of 'zoning' is actually in use on St Lucia, having been discovered as a contemporary solution to conflicting land use, yet as children were unaware of this it was a new, breakthrough discovery for them. As Lewis and Mawdsley (2007: 2) report; 'Many groups suggested zoning, particularly of beaches and the coral reef, which is a solution that has been in operation in Soufriere on St Lucia for some years now. [This was not] revealed to the pupils until after the final presentations'.
   Emma and Sarah believe that an important scaffold in this creative learning was that of 'personalising' it through the use of characters. Pupils' creative break-throughs were also fuelled by having the freedom to explore the problems in their own way and having sufficient underpinning knowledge on which to base their

questions and decisions. When this enquiry was completed, Sarah commented on how pupils were able to transfer their learning about complex trade-offs to other class work, confirming a key indicator of creative learning in primary schools (NCSL, 2005).

Getting to 'know' the fictional characters helped pupils to empathise and thus better imagine what their perspectives were. In this sense, this creative act of imagining required pupils to step outside of their own ways of seeing and see afresh with others' eyes. If we accept that places mean different things to different user groups then understanding different perspectives through empathy is a highly relevant aspect of geography as it helps us to consider how and why places change and how change might be influenced in positive ways. This is part of geography's great contribution to 'futures' orientated thinking' which, given the many pressing problems we face, is an arena in which creativity of thought and action is vital.

Conclusion

In this chapter we have tried to open up the idea of geography as a powerful and productive curriculum resource and a sense of it as 'one of humanity's big ideas' (Bonnett, 2008: 7). Geographical imagination, discovery and enquiry are the creative components that thread through each account. We have chosen examples that offer particular insights into the use of media technologies, first-hand experience, critical problem-solving and story as a creative stimulus or enabling narrative.

We have emphasised that the purpose of geography is ambitious and is in itself, like other subject disciplines, the result of great creative human endeavour and at the same time a source of creative inspiration for primary educators. Through the use of three case studies we have tried to illustrate the creative act of curriculum making (rather than delivery). These show:

- some of the main geographical ideas such as interdependence and the inter-action between the physical and human worlds;
- the importance of place specificity in geographical studies, but also of wider locational context (and ultimately the global setting);
- the significance of field work in geography enabling 'exploration' and/or enquiry as a pedagogic strategy;
- the role technology can play in releasing creative learning and communication strategies.

There are possibly many 'conclusions' that we draw from the contents of this chapter. But one issue overrides all others: the question of how primary teachers gain access to, and confidence in dealing with, the geographical knowledge dimensions discussed here. By 'knowledge' we do not just mean the technical aspects to do with particular topics, which in any case is material that can be relatively easily accessed. We mean the conceptual clarity of what geography is about, what it is for and how to 'do it' carefully and well. In this regard it was noticeable during the years of the government funded 'Action Plan for Geography'[4] (2006–11), when primary and secondary teachers worked on curriculum-making projects, often together, it was primary teachers who were more instinctively in tune with a more conceptual curriculum framework (such as that which was introduced for KS3 in 2008). If we want primary teachers to teach geography carefully and well then good guidance, support and exemplars are required, but also a National Curriculum that is not packed with content to be 'delivered' and which gets in the way of effective curriculum making.

Creative touches

- Develop the geographical imagination: inspire pupils to widen their perceptions of the world through a mix of first-hand experience and multimedia encounters. *For example, use story and fieldwork as starting points to investigate places.*

- Explore and investigate the outdoors: use fieldwork to provoke pupils into new ways of seeing and understanding the world. *For example, investigate the school grounds using a multi-sensory approach.*

- Ensure relevance: use resources that are current, real issues and children's own questions as sources of enquiry. *For example, where did the banana in my lunchbox come from? Why has the stream flooded?*

- Communicate without barriers: use a variety of formats such as film, art, maps, talk, poetry, drama, stories, graphs and models to communicate geographically. *For example, make a film about the best places to see in your locality; make a model to show how a stream 'works'.*

- Develop critical thinking: enable pupils to reflect on sources of information and evaluate them; encourage them to consider and compare different views and offer explanations for them. *For example, assume role play to empathise with other views.*

- Ensure subject knowledge underpins geographical enquiry: enable pupils to extend and consolidate their geographical knowledge. *For example, pupils locate places accurately and use appropriate geographical vocabulary.*

References

Ackerman, E. A. (1963). Where is a Research Frontier? *Annals of the Association of American Geographers*, 53: 429–40.

Bonnett, A. (2008). *What is Geography?* London: Sage.

Burt, T. (2003). Realms of gold, wild surmise and wondering about physical geography, in S. Trudgill and A. Roy (eds) (2003), *Contemporary Meanings in Physical Geography From what to why?* London: Arnold, pp. 49–61.

Catling, S. (2003). Curriculum Contested: primary geography and social justice. *Geography*, 88 (3): 164–211.

Catling, S. (2008). *Young Geographers. A Living Geography Project for Primary Schools, 2008 – an Evaluation Report*. Sheffield: Geographical Association.

Catling, S. (2009). Creativity in Primary Geography, in A. Wilson, A. (ed.), *Creativity in Primary Education*. Exeter: Learning Matters, pp. 189–98.

Catling, S. and Martin, F. (2011). Contesting 'powerful knowledge': the primary geography curriculum as an articulation between academic and children's (ethno-) geographies. *Curriculum Journal,* 22 (3): 317–36.

Catling, S. and Willy, T. (2009). *Achieving QTS: Teaching Primary Geography,* Exeter: Learning Matters.

Charlton, E., Wyse, D., Cliff Hodges, G, Nikolajeva, M., Pointon, P. and Taylor, L. (2011): Place-Related Identities Through Texts: From Interdisciplinary Theory to Research Agenda. *British Journal of Educational Studies*, 59 (1): 63–74.

DCSF (2008). *Statutory Framework for the Early Years Foundation Stage May 2008. Setting the Standards for Learning, Development and Care for children from birth to five*. Nottingham: DCSF. https://www.education.gov.uk/publications/eOrderingDownload/eyfs_res_stat_frmwrk.pdf

DfE (2010). *The Importance of Teaching: School White Paper*. London: the Department for Education. http://www.education.gov.uk/schools/toolsandinitiatives/schoolswhitepaper/b0068570/the-importance-of-teaching/ (accessed 29 August 2012).

Firth, R. (2011). Making geography visible as an object of study in the secondary school curriculum. *Curriculum Journal*, 22 (3): 289–316.

GA (Geographical Association) (2009). *A Different View: a manifesto from the Geographical Association,* Sheffield: Geographical Association. www.geography.org.uk/adifferentview.

GA (Geographical Association) (2011). *Curriculum Proposals and Rationale*. Sheffield: Geographical Association. www.geography.org.uk?getinvolved/geographycurriculumconsultation.

Gardner, H. and Boix Mansilla, V. (1994). Teaching for understanding within and across the disciplines. *Educational Leadership*, 51 (5), February: 14–18.

Horton, J. and Kraftl, P. (2005). For more than usefulness: six overlapping points about Children's Geographies. *Children's Geographies*, 3 (2): 131–43.

Jeffrey, B. and Woods, P. (2003). *The Creative School. A framework for success, quality and effectiveness,* London: Routledge Falmer.

Kelly, A. (2005). Exploring Children's Geographies at Key Stage 2. *International Research in Geographical and Environmental Education*, 14 (4): 342–7.

Lambert, D. (2011). Reframing school geography: a capability approach, in G. Butt (ed.), *Geography Education and the Future*. London: Continuum, pp. 127–40.

Lewis and Mawsdley (2007). Geojoes St Lucia Challenge. *Primary Geography,* Autumn 2007, Sheffield: Geographical Association.

Ley, D. (2002). Social Geography and Social Action, in M. J. Dear and S. Flusty (eds), *The Spaces of Postmodernity Readings in Human Geography*. Oxford: Blackwell, pp. 68–76.

Mackintosh, M. (2005). Children's Understanding of Rivers. *International Research in Geographical and Environmental Education*, 14 (4): 316–22.

Martin, F. (2004). Creativity through geography, in R. Fisher and M. Williams, *Unlocking Creativity*. London: David Fulton.

Matthews, H. and Limb, M. (1999). Defining an agenda for the geography of children: review and prospect. *Progress in Human Geography*, 23 (1): 61–90.

Morgan, J. (2011). *Teaching Geography as if the Planet Matters*. London: David Fulton.

NCSL (National College for School Leadership) (2005). *Developing creativity for learning in the primary school – A practical guide for school leaders*. Nottingham: NCSL.

Ofsted (2011). *Making a World of Difference*: http://www.ofsted.gov.uk/Ofsted-home/ Publications-and-research/Browse-all-by/Documents-by-type/Thematic-reports/ Geography-Learning-to-make-a-world-of-difference.

Owens, P. (2005). Children's Environmental Values in the Early School Years. *International Research in Geographical and Environmental Education*, 14 (4): 323–9.

Rawling, E. (2011). Reading and Writing Place, in G. Butt, G. (ed.), *Geography Education and the Future*. London: Continuum, pp. 65–83.

Scoffham, S. (2003). Thinking Creatively. *Primary Geography: Focus on Creativity* 50, Sheffield: Geographical Association, pp. 4–6.

Scoffham, S. (2010). Young Geographers, in S. Scoffham (ed.), *Primary Geography Handbook*. Sheffield: Geographical Association, pp. 15–23.

Tanner, J. (2010). Geography and the Emotions, in S. Scoffham (ed.), *Primary Geography Handbook*. Sheffield: Geographical Association, pp. 35–47.

Kudryavtsev, V. T. (2011). The phenomenon of child creativity, *International Journal of Early Years Education*. 19 (1): 45–53.

Ward, H. (1998). Geographical Vocabulary, in S. Scoffham (ed.), *Primary Sources: Research findings in primary geography*. Sheffield: Geographical Association, pp. 20–1.

Young, M. (2008). *Bringing Knowledge Back In*. London: Routledge.

Useful links

Young Geographers: Austey Primary School: http://www.geography.org.uk/projects/ younggeographers/resources/austrey/

Young Geographers: Southborough Primary School: http://www.geography.org.uk/projects/ younggeographers/resources/southborough

Endnotes

1 In 2011 the GA held a national consultation on a set of curriculum proposals designed to contribute to the National Curriculum Review, leading to new programmes of study for 2014. These proposals can be seen at www.geography.org.uk/getinvolved/geogra phycur- riculumconsultation. They distinguish forms of knowledge in a way that unites the idea of geography across its academic and popular manifestations.

2 The Geographical Association (GA) published a manifesto in 2009 under the title *A Different View*. It is aimed at all teachers of geography, including those in the primary phase. It can be viewed (alongside many teaching ideas and resources) at www.geography.org.uk/adifferentview.

3 CapeUK is a leading independent research and development agency in the field of creativity, learning and development: http://www.capeuk.org.

4 http://www.geography.org.uk/projects/actionplanforgeography/

History

Paul Bowen

Introduction

Perhaps the most important feature of creative teaching in history is that of risk-taking; doing something novel, different and unexpected which has no predetermined outcome. An interesting illustration of this in practice is the work of the notable architect Daniel Libeskind who designed the iconic Imperial War Museum at Manchester which opened in 2002. The story goes that he gained inspiration by taking a teapot, smashing it on the floor and then putting some of the pieces together in a disorganised and disjointed fashion to produce a design for the building. Using a teapot to represent the world and then breaking it showed creativity and imagination but this was equally a purposeful activity which produced a creative response in the form of a building which externally and internally conveyed the chaos and disorientation of war. It is this dynamic style of creativity which should be an aspiration within the primary history classroom.

Good primary history teaching over many years has been associated with features that can stimulate creativity: imaginative thinking, interactive approaches, out of school learning, problem solving, enquiry-based work, independent learning, and integrated approaches that link curriculum areas such as history, art, literacy, geography, drama, music, ICT and design technology. However, in recent years our understanding of creativity has developed, a trend that is reflected in recent literature on primary history. For example, Turner-Bisset (2005) has provided a detailed critical overview of creativity underpinned by pedagogical theory such as the work of Koestler (Turner-Bisset, 2005). The argument is that history teachers who teach creatively 'make creative leaps to connect children with subject knowledge in the broadest selection of ways, drawing on a wide pedagogical repertoire' (Turner-Bisset, 2005: 14). Typically, creative history teaching draws upon a wide variety of resources and approaches whilst also using other curriculum areas such as art and drama. Creative work in history also involves working interactively in novel, unexpected ways, involving risk-taking and open-ended thinking where children need to appreciate that definitive answers to questions are rare because elements of historical understanding are subjective.

What is creativity in the context of history?

The *Excellence and Enjoyment* document (DfES, 2003) did not explicitly refer to history but nevertheless promoted a philosophy of teaching and learning which is highly appropriate for history. Written with the aim of encouraging schools to be more creative, innovative and flexible, it reflected a concern with the rigidity of centralised curriculum structures. The document argued that 'as well as giving them the tools of essential learning, primary education is about children experiencing the joys of discovery, solving problems, being creative in writing, art, music, developing their self-confidence as learners and maturing socially and emotionally' (DfES, 2003: 4). Key themes emphasised included using imagination, enquiry, creativity, e-learning, group problem-solving, play, learning from adults other than teachers, out of school learning, learning in many different ways and rich resources. A very important dimension of creative teaching emphasised by *Excellence and Enjoyment* was the imperative need for personalising learning so that the needs of groups such as the gifted or those from ethnic minorities are suitably catered for.

Another relevant source of guidance for creativity in history is the influential *All Our Futures* report (NACCCE, 1999). Whilst this was an extensive document, four specific criteria are particularly appropriate in relation to creative approaches to history:

- Behaving imaginatively: 'imaginative activity is the process of generating something original'.
- Pursuing purposes: 'creativity carries with it the idea of action and purpose'.
- Being original: 'a person may be original in relation to their own previous work and output or may be original in relation to their peers'.
- Judging value: 'creative work involves judging value, an evaluative mode'.

(NACCCE, 1999: 29–31)

Particularly relevant in this context is the need to recognise the importance of critical questioning on the part of both teacher and pupil in promoting creativity. Evidence continues to suggest that much questioning is of a lower order, focusing on what or how, whereas of greater benefit are more demanding and open ended questions. As Leedham and Murphy highlight, '*Why* questioning also takes us into the realm of speculation and of possible alternatives where knowledge of the culture may be as important as knowledge of the facts' (Hayes (ed.), 2007: 39).

Also central to creative learning in history is the idea of encouraging children to use their imagination. Imagination involves visualising situations from the past, and this skill is important to draw upon when teaching topics such as the Romans, Tudors or Victorians. Typically, teachers need to provide inputs such as television programmes, pictures or a visit to help children construct some idea of what life was like in the past. Trying to understand what life might have been like at a different time or in a different context is a challenging task but it needs to be based on solid historical evidence. As Leedham and Murphy have observed, 'What we are not doing here is giving free reign to fantasy' (Hayes (ed.), 2007: 37).

An important dimension of history is encouraging children to develop human and emotional responses to events and issues. History is about human beings, their everyday lives, experiences and actions, and children need to try to relate to people in the past whether this is an ordinary child in a cold, smelly and overcrowded Victorian classroom or a famous individual such as Guy Fawkes, Henry 8th or Elizabeth 1st. This empathetic understanding is challenging to develop but can be promoted if children are encouraged to ask questions about the motives of individuals. What drove Guy Fawkes, for example, to nearly successfully blow up Parliament? Why did Henry 8th approve the beheading of two of his wives? Exploring the actions of individuals such as Henry can lead to a discussion of moral issues and the alternative choices which could have been made. There is also considerable scope, particularly at Key Stage 2, for children to look at the positive aspects of someone's life such as Elizabeth 1st or Isambard Brunel but also their more unsuccessful activities. Brunel's achievement as engineer to the Great Western Railway, for example, may be contrasted with less successful ventures such as the steamship Great Eastern.

This human and emotional dimension of history is clearly important to explore at both Key Stages 1 and 2. Take the story of Grace Darling who became famous in the Victorian period for helping to rescue shipwrecked passengers on the Farne Islands off the Northumberland coast in violent storm conditions. On a recent boat trip to the scene of the rescue under relatively calm conditions, the exposed nature of the Longstone Lighthouse where she lived and the length she had to row in rescuing survivors off the rock were absolutely evident. A school party on the boat clearly began to gain some appreciation of Grace Darling's courage, physical strength and determination in the face of great personal danger.

History and political debates

A recurring theme in recent years in England has been concern about the status of history as a curriculum area and its perceived marginalisation within schools. The title of a recent Ofsted publication, *History in the balance*, served to reinforce this point (Ofsted, 2007). History, in common with other non-core subjects, often suffers from very limited curriculum time due to the strong focus on numeracy, literacy and the pressures of testing. A common response has been to include history as part of a theme such as toys, seaside holidays, Egypt or World War Two, which provides considerable scope for creative work. After many years of emphasis on subjects in the primary curriculum in England, from 2010 schools began to explore once again planning teaching through themes which link together a range of curriculum areas. This makes good sense because primary aged children think in a holistic way, and a subject-based curriculum can sometimes create barriers to learning. On a recent school visit, a Key Stage 2 class was studying World War Two, and activities encompassed not only history but also art, geography, literacy and science. Geographical skills were developed when using an atlas to identify where countries involved in the war were located, whilst in science the concept of insulation was explored when children made thermos flasks for use at night time in air raid shelters. Nevertheless, this progressive approach does have pitfalls for schools and requires careful overall planning so that the history content is clearly identifiable.

Another interesting and controversial issue revolves around the notion of 'Britishness'. It is often argued that history has an important role to ensure that pupils understand key features of British heritage and values. The popular press and politicians frequently highlight the apparent failure of school history to address this issue, with comments about children's lack of basic historical knowledge about events or famous people such as Winston Churchill, but the frequent marginalisation of history in many schools cannot help the situation. More often, the focus is on English history which is interesting in relation to the concept of 'Britishness'. Defining what this *is* and identifying the sort of history which should support it is clearly contentious and open to interpretation. It can be argued, for example, that the English National Curriculum for history as published in 1999 does not effectively represent the multicultural nature of the United Kingdom today, for, as Ofsted have remarked, 'Too little attention is given to black and multiethnic aspects of UK history. The effect, if inadvertently, is to undervalue the overall contribution of black and minority ethnic people's contribution to the UK's past and to ignore their culture, society and many other achievements' (Ofsted, 2007: 24). The teaching of history in modern Britain needs teachers who have strong subject knowledge but who are also sensitive to the ways in which history can be presented monoculturally, or in ways that 'erase' some children's individual and collective cultural heritage.

How are teachers using history to teach creatively?

Before considering approaches to creative history teaching, some key principles will be outlined which are integral to the process. Whilst history can be taught as a discrete subject, the potential for learning is enhanced by adopting a cross-curricular approach. Some have emphasised how subjects can be a false focus for children and are best viewed as 'mutually independent in an educational sense' (Rowley and Cooper, 2009: 2). What is important, however, is that cross-curricular work is underpinned by a strong subject knowledge and skills base. Teachers need to seek out 'robust links between subjects which take account of the discrete thinking processes at the heart of different subjects and relate them through children's experiences (Rowley and Cooper, 2009: 2). History is central to many activities within society including communication, music, art and human experiences and has rich potential as a starting point for linking work within the primary school. A good example of this approach might be a case study on the theme of *Where do I come from?*, as exemplified by Rowley and Cooper (2009), where history is linked with maths, geography and language.

Another prerequisite of creative history teaching focuses on the role of the child in the learning process. It is essential that children are given opportunities to be active learners, to take some responsibility in the learning process and have some autonomy and choice. This is not a new idea but needs reinforcing. Teachers are generally very good at talking and imparting information, but perhaps more emphasis needs to be placed on listening to children and letting them set the agenda more often by investigating the questions that they would like to explore. Fisher, for example, has identified some initial questions which can promote children's discussion of history and lead to them establishing questions of their own. Examples include: 'Do you have a history? What were the most important events in your life? Could history books be wrong? Do you think your memories of the past are all true? Why?' (Fisher, 2008: 179). An important feature of interactive learning is a strong emphasis on children speaking and listening through activities like drama, and of course historical drama is well-placed to explore children's own historical questions. Drama is potentially one of the most important activities that can support creative work in history, and whilst much classroom interaction is still based on the traditional teacher–pupil relationship, creative teaching requires this to change. Prendiville and Toye, for example, offer 'a way of moving outside this culture, a way that frees children into temporarily breaking with their narrow "pupil" role, into more challenging levels of thinking, talking and attending' (Prendiville and Toye, 2007: 1).

A third ingredient necessary for creative teaching is the need for the teacher to be imaginative. Being imaginative can be reflected in many ways such as teaching style, learning activity or resources. Invariably it involves thinking 'outside the box', risk-taking and changing teaching styles. Fisher has made some interesting observations about the latter, arguing for a 'community of enquiry' approach with greater emphasis on flexible discussion groups rather than whole-class teaching (Fisher, 2008: 40). Whilst recently observing some PGCE presentations which focused on history, I saw some interesting examples of imaginative planning. One group chose to focus on Queen Elizabeth II's coronation to link into a Golden Jubilee theme. The session started with newsreel of the coronation in 1952 whilst the group remained outside the room where the presentations were being held. They then processed into the classroom, imitating the events in Westminster Abbey 60 years ago, a short but highly creative and effective way of capturing the formality and atmosphere of the coronation for the audience. Popular topics such as Ancient Egypt, the Vikings, the Tudors and even World War Two are remote in time and culture, requiring imaginative planning of activities to make them accessible and meaningful to all children. The aim must be to reconstruct a picture of the past which children can engage with through their own imagination and approaches to achieving this will now be explored.

Creative history work requires the teacher to show imagination in designing both teaching approaches and also importantly the learning activities provided for children. As Hoodless observes, 'Creative, innovative practice can involve either creative teaching or creative learning, or a combination of both' (Hoodless, 2008: 122). Creative teaching is often underpinned by the use of a variety of interactive approaches supported by rich resources. Typical examples include use of story, visual sources such as paintings, drama, out of school learning and artefacts. Let us consider some of these in more detail, starting with stories. Our knowledge of distant historical cultures such as the Vikings is often derived from stories and the oral tradition, and some of the best primary history today is where children access the content through historical fiction. At Key Stage 2, for example, novels such as *The Machine Gunners* and *Goodnight Mister Tom* provide an excellent focus for an investigation of the Home Front in World War Two. They convey historical knowledge and empathetic understanding whilst also acting as a focus for reflective discussion (Cooper, 2006: 97). At Key Stage 1, storytelling (as opposed to merely reading a story) is an excellent way to engage children. As Hoodless has emphasised, children are always going to be more excited by someone who can tell an exciting tale face to face, using storytellers' skills such as eye-contact, gesture and 'performed' voices (Hoodless, 2008: 85).

This notion of storytelling rather than reading a story requires considerable creative skill from the teacher who might even use costume and physical artefacts to create more authenticity. This approach has often been used in Key Stage 1 topics focusing on famous people such as Florence Nightingale or Isambard Kingdom Brunel. For children to really imagine the past through the use of story, they need to be active participants through questioning, speaking and listening. Innovative approaches suggested by Bage to achieve this include children presenting voice-overs to archive film, and 'waiting room' scenarios where children imagine themselves in the instant before an historic event (Bage, 2011). In effect, the teacher is 'in role' here and using a drama strategy to engage the children. Other drama conventions can be used such as freeze framing, conscience alley and hot seating. Allowing children to take on roles from another historical period can encourage them to think about how people would have felt or perhaps responded to a situation What is important is that children have a clear awareness of the historical context (Hoodless, 2008: 127).

The power of drama in conveying historical ideas and emotions was demonstrated on a recent visit to the Imperial War Museum at Manchester. The visit took place on 11 November as part of special activities commemorating Armistice Day; two education staff role played a World War One scenario where a soldier left home for the Western Front leaving behind loved ones. Based on surviving letters, the drama was both authentic and moving, providing visiting school parties with a real insight into how war impacts on human relationships.

Oral history, where adult visitors to the classroom talk about life in the past, can also make an important and significant contribution to creative history teaching when exploring historical topics such as seaside holidays or life in the 1960s. The personal reminiscences of a local person can often be a profound experience for children and help bring the historical event or period alive whether it be childhood memories of rationing in the 1940s or excursions to the seaside by steam train in the 1950s. Oral history allows children to reproduce the work of the historian by using first-hand evidence as well as asking questions about reliability. Engagement with adults other than teachers is also a purposeful activity, providing useful links with the local community and encouraging citizenship.

Visual sources such as paintings and photographs are another valuable entry point for creative history. Paintings, for example, can convey emotions, feelings, symbolism and historical information, but to be used effectively they require careful observation, active group discussion and critical thinking to get beneath the surface, to contextualise it historically and to understand its meaning. Leedham and Murphy, for example, provide an interesting example of how one of Holbein's portraits of King Henry VIII can be used as a starter for interesting and creative activities, including children acting as reporters and interviewing Henry, then comparing him with modern day celebrities (Hayes (ed.), 2007: 37). In these activities, children were finding out about the role of Henry as a Tudor monarch but also reflecting upon his actions and putting forward viewpoints about his life. A particularly innovative development in this context is the opportunity for schools to have a video conference facility with the National Portrait Gallery (npg.org.uk), where education officers can lead an interactive session with a focus on a particular painting (see the Visual Arts chapter for further examples of the National Gallery's approach to work with schools).

Justifiable emphasis has also been placed in recent years on the value of using artefacts in the classroom (Turner-Bisset, 2005). The creative use of artefacts is clearly demonstrated in a recent Teachers TV video focusing on a visit by KS 2 children to Brunel's pioneering steamship *Great Britain* at Bristol (*TES*, 2012). Groups of children were given a collection of artefacts associated with a particular passenger about whom they had to make some conclusions, such as their social class and occupation. A great deal of lively debate took place with the children actively involved as 'detectives'. The artefacts were then used by the children to role play their particular character with a strong emphasis on speaking and listening skills.

Most children find artefacts interesting and they can help stimulate challenging discussion which often encourages open ended thinking, listening to other people's ideas and putting forward their own, possibly original, suggestions. Artefacts are particularly useful when contrasting home life in modern times with what it was like in the Victorian period of the nineteenth century. An old flat iron, candle holder, carpet beater, ceramic hot water bottle or chamber pot allow children to investigate the evidence and to interpret it by putting forward their own viewpoints about the objects. The value of artefact-use is evident in the following observations about children working with household objects as part of a homes project:

Pupils had to think, there were many 'what' and 'why' questions, some of which the teacher answered and others which she had directed back to pupils to decide. Pupils also had to date and sequence objects. They were very interested in each others' views and in the fact that it was sometimes difficult to know the truth. Challenge was evident. (Ofsted, 2007: 10)

The emphasis here on extending pupils' thinking is clearly very important and Vella reinforces this point by highlighting the benefits of artefact use in terms of oracy, independent thinking, language, exploratory thought, making inferences, explaining ideas and using imagination (Vella, 2010).

Children should of course be given opportunity to create their own historical models using artistic, design and making skills. A common example of this is for Key Stage 1 children to recreate the timber-framed buildings consumed by the Great Fire of London in 1666, but it is important that this activity is accompanied by a very clear focus on the historical context. Models of these buildings are often displayed in classrooms but there are alternative uses! I recently marked a PGCE assignment which described how the cardboard houses were lined up on the playground as a street scene. The end house was set alight and the class observed how all the other buildings caught fire. The aim was to encourage children to see how the fire could spread but also to appeal to their emotional intelligences and give them a sense of loss at the destruction before them. Although rather suspicious that this burning actually took place, a rather amazing photograph showing a street of model houses furiously ablaze on a playground and the children interested onlookers confirmed what had happened! Here is another example of the teacher having courage and taking a risk, doing something perhaps controversial, maybe unpopular, novel and unexpected – there are similarities between this example and the smashing of a teapot to represent the effect of war, referred to earlier.

A strength of primary history in many schools is the emphasis on out of school learning which offers many benefits and is indeed a long-standing tradition, as this quote from 1937 demonstrates:

Visits, too, where these are possible, to the actual scene of historic events or to the actual remains of times which have passed away are of great value in creating atmosphere and in making history alive. (Board of Education, 1937: 415)

Opportunities to visit historic sites have expanded enormously over the past 20 years, with organisations such as the National Trust and English Heritage placing a strong emphasis on school visits with the support of education officers and workshop sessions. Venues such as Hampton Court Palace near London (Tudors) and Blists Hill Museum in Shropshire (Victorians), through dramatic reconstructions and interactive approaches, provide realistic and interesting ways of engaging with life in a different historical period. Children's imaginations can be stimulated and, with careful observational skills, they can gain considerably from such visits. Out of school learning, however, needs careful organisation, and the planning of follow-up creative work is crucial if the outcomes are to be successful.

Local history is intrinsically linked with out of school learning and provides an opportunity to teach the knowledge, skills and understanding of history in a familiar context for children. Local history has been compulsory at Key Stage 2 (age seven to eleven) in England for many years and investigations such as 'How did life change in our locality in Victorian times?' and 'What was it like to live here in the past?' are particularly useful. Local history can also be especially valuable with younger children at Key Stage 1, for example, using a visit to a Victorian or Tudor house to introduce children to life in a different time. Local history has many dimensions, including focusing on a village, town, industry or famous person, and provides plenty of scope for creative approaches. The Nuffield Primary History Project's Local History Top Ten Features highlights, for example, approaches which include problem solving, investigation and challenge, active learning through simulation, oracy using discussion and debate, open ended thinking, small group work and informed use of the imagination (Nuffield Project, 2010: 15).

Perhaps one of the most important creative activities is facilitating independent project work which has a strong open-ended dimension. Although this is mostly associated with older children in primary schools, it should also be an aspiration with younger children. Independent project work can be undertaken individually or in small groups, the latter being useful in promoting collaborative learning skills and teamwork. The approach can be applied to any history topics such as (for example) *Britain in the 1960s*. The teacher starts by working with the pupils to identify some key questions or areas to investigate such as fashion, women's rights, pop music, politics, immigration, leisure and transport. Independent work needs to be well structured, supported by various resources and carefully monitored. Outcomes can be varied but with plenty of potential for creativity such as a powerpoint presentation, model, an illustrated book, a drama sequence or poster display. Independent group work can be flexible, extending over several weeks or a single lesson. Careful consideration needs to be given to the questions that children investigate because the traditional danger of independent work is that it can soon develop into the regurgitation of information from books or the internet and this has been a feature of some poor history teaching in the past. It is much more productive for children to explore questions that require not only the development of subject knowledge but also encourages their opinions and judge-ments. Effective questions are often in a style that supports problem solving and creative thinking. Take, for example, the topic of the Home Front during World War 2. The challenges and horrors for people living then are clearly apparent but what about asking pupils whether any benefits occurred? Careful consideration reveals that there were positive developments associated with the war including the role of women, technology and medicine. Indeed, with any historical period or famous individual pupils should be asked to critically evaluate the evidence and express some opinions about people's actions or events. Typical examples of questions which can promote this include: What did the Victorian people do for Britain? Did the invading Romans improve Britain? Did Ancient Greeks benefit the world or were they just warlike?

Notice in these examples that children are being asked to critically evaluate evidence and to express some opinions about people's actions or events, which is an important aspect of creativity.

On a recent school visit, a Year 6 class had been studying the Home Front during World War Two using *Goodnight Mister Tom* as a stimulus, and each child produced a beautifully illustrated bound booklet containing a wide range of creative writing. Examples of work included a postcard home from an evacuee, a playscript about a weekend during wartime, instructions on how to build an Anderson shelter and a poem about a child during the Blitz. Some of the most creative responses were complemented by imaginatively produced research-based 'fact files'. These were carefully organised using key questions such as why, when and how did the evacuation of children take place and what effects were there on families and the areas they went to? Bage offers some interesting suggestions for different forms of writing in history such as labelling and captioning, reporting an historical event in a journalistic style, imagining the past through a poem or advert, summarising historical information using diagrams and charts, arguing for and against an historical figure and note-taking using key words (Bage, 1990: 98–9).

A local history case study

This case study is built around work undertaken by a group of student teachers in a school in Alsager, Cheshire. The main theme was to allow Key Stage 2 children to investigate what life was like in their area in the 1900s, using fieldwork, documentary sources and photographs. One of the challenges of local history is that, in contrast to national history topics such as the Tudors or Egyptians, the purchase of commercial, readily available resources is not normally an option. Resources have to be searched for locally and often generated by the teaching team, but this can also be a creative and rewarding process. Local studies with a Victorian or early twentieth-century focus are very common and there are a number of historical records which are readily available but which might need to be simplified and amended to make them suitable for use across the primary age range. Archive centres in county towns or cities have improved considerably in recent years and often have their own education officers, but local libraries will also invariably hold relevant records which are photocopiable.

An interesting range of evidence was assembled for this particular project. Large-scale maps are clearly important and a key resource was a copy of the Ordnance Survey 3rd Edition (1909) for Alsager which provides very detailed coverage, even showing individual buildings and numerous other landscape features. The Alsager extract from *Kelly's Directory of Cheshire* (1902) was also used. Trade directories were very common in the nineteenth and twentieth centuries, and for towns and even small villages there are detailed references to subjects such as schools, religion, shops, transport and industry. This information was also supported by census material from 1901 which provided interesting information about the inhabitants of some of the buildings visited on the fieldtrip. Also essential for this study was a collection of early twentieth-century photographs allowing children to compare locations today with what they were like over 100 years ago. Teachers wishing to plan a local study need to spend time developing a precise and confident working knowledge about the area's history in order to design creative and historically accurate tasks for the children. As preparation for the project, for example, the student teachers used the documents to investigate key aspects of life in Alsager in the 1900s, such as transport, shopping, leisure and schools, so that they had a good knowledge of the area.

The stimulus for the study was a fieldwork activity involving a walk along Crewe Road, Alsager, with documentary sources helping children to understand what the area was like 100 years ago. A route was carefully planned (with risk assessment a priority, which involved crossing only one main road). Children were in groups of four with an adult helper allowing them to talk confidently in a small-group situation. During the walk, stops were made at the following locations for which photographs from the 1900s were available, the aim being for children to identify similarities and differences between then and now:

- Sandbach Road: an old photograph showing horse-drawn carriages was compared with today's busy road scene with cars and lorries. There was interesting small group discussion about similarities and differences. Some children asked how people would have travelled if they could not afford a carriage? Issues such as the rich and the poor and walking were raised. The traffic issue provided useful cross-curricular links with geography.

- Crewe Road: close observation of a surviving wall alongside the road allowed children to locate the scene of an old photograph showing Charles Bennion, the refuse collector, with his horse and cart. Digital cameras were used to record the scene for classroom use, showing the value of ICT use to support the local study.

- St Mary's Church: trade directory information allowed the children to find out when the church was built, how many it seated and that it was made from Alton sandstone. Extracts from the trade directory had been transcribed, enlarged and laminated on card to allow all children to access this primary evidence. A visit inside showed that some of the seating had been removed. Again, small-group work encouraged speaking and listening activity. There were some suggestions about declining church attendance and the reasons for this. One child who had been to the Alton Towers theme park made the link with the church's building material.

- The old police station: students role played outside this building using an authentic scenario to help children identify its purpose. This showed imaginative planning, and imitating this with children in costume and filming the outcome would be good, creative practice. A date stone with the words 'Cheshire Constabulary' was successfully interpreted by more able pupils. Trade directory and census evidence helped the children to find out that Sergeant Henry Thompson and his family lived there in 1901.

- The Mere: using an old photograph, discussion took place about how the Mere had changed from being a lake surrounded by fields to one surrounded largely by houses and difficult to access by the public. Children generally felt it was a shame for Alsager that the Mere was largely surrounded by private land, showing how local studies work draws on a variety of areas including environmental.

- The Chapel, Crewe Road: children looked puzzled at the 1900s photograph of the chapel because the scene had changed so much – and where was the chapel? Then it was observed that there were some new shops called 'Chapel Mews' which marked the site of the demolished chapel. Discussion focused on why the chapel had been replaced by shops. Links were made here with change of land use and redevelopment – important geographical issues.

- Bickerton's shop: the old photograph of the grocer's with its immaculate window display and proud staff contrasted dramatically with the building's current use as a Chinese takeaway. An elderly couple took an interest in our work and talked to the children about what this grocer's shop was like 50 years ago when they shopped there. Children were keen to ask questions. An excellent example of oral history!

Back in the classroom a variety of activities were undertaken. Maps, old photographs and modern digital views were used to review the fieldwork, with a detailed focus on similarities and differences. Group activities included making a model of the church and developing role play scenarios relating to various occupations such as shopkeepers and the police.

A local history project like this one provides considerable potential for creative work. The fieldwork activity and use of evidence like maps involves using first-hand sources, and children can make their own personal observations and conclusions. The inclusion of oral history, for example, allows children to question and evaluate the speaker's evidence, whilst role-play scenarios promote imaginative thinking. The focus on school life using log books provides scope for creative writing and also expressing opinions about what they thought about the harshness of schooling in the 1900s. Modelling activities allow artistic and design skills to be used to produce a purposeful outcome. Independent learning using enquiry-based methods is a theme of the unit, allowing a good balance between finding out about their local area and exploring open-ended questions such as: 'Would it have been enjoyable to live in Alsager in the 1900s?'

Creative touches

- Don't be afraid to work collaboratively even if this sometimes means working outside your comfort zone.
- Choose a topic in collaboration with children if at all possible; try to settle on one they relate to and find stimulating and enjoyable.

- Carefully select activities which encourage children's imagination.
- Allow as many opportunities as possible for open ended thinking and discussion.
- Use rich resources including ICT in the broadest sense.
- Use out of school learning to help 'bring the past alive'.
- Personalise learning to address the needs of varying abilities and interests.
- Create a challenging and risk-taking environment where children can respond creatively.
- Be clear about learning outcomes in terms of subject knowledge, skills and understanding, and have an explicit focus on assessment opportunities.

References

Bage, G. (1990). *Thinking History 4–14: Teaching learning, curricula and communities.* London and New York: Routledge Falmer, Taylor & Francis Group.

Bage, G. (1999). *Narrative Matters, Teaching and Learning History through Story.* London: Falmer Press.

Bage, G. (2002). *Thinking History, 4–14.* London: Routledge.

Bage, G. (2011). Doing History: Storytelling, *Primary History*, 57, Spring: 7.

Board of Education (1937). *Handbook of Suggestions for Teachers.* London: HMSO.

Capita, L., Cooper, H. and Moges, I. (2000). History, Children's Thinking and Creativity in the Classroom: English and Romanian Perspectives. *International Journal of Historical Learning, Teaching and Research*, 1 (1): 14–18.

Cooper, H. (2006). *History 3–11: A Guide for Teachers.* Abingdon: David Fulton.

Craft, A. (2008). *Creativity in Schools: Tensions and Dilemmas.* London: Routledge.

DfEE/QCA (1998). *A Scheme of Work for Key Stages 1 and 2: History.* London. QCA.

DfES (2003). *Excellence and Enjoyment: a Strategy for Primary Schools,* London: DfES.

DfES/QCA (1999) *The National Curriculum: Handbook for Primary Teachers in England.* London: HMSO.

Fisher, R. (2008). *Teaching Thinking, Philosophical Enquiry in the Classroom* (3rd edn). London: Continuum.

Hayes, D. (ed.) (2007). *Joyful Teaching and Learning in the Primary School,* Exeter: Learning Matters.

Hoodless, P. (2008). *Teaching History in Primary Schools.* Exeter: Learning Matters.

Hoodless, P., McCreery, E., Bowen, P. and Bermingham, S. (2009). *Teaching Humanities in Primary Schools.* Exeter: Learning Matters.

Kerry, T. (2011). *Cross-Curricular Teaching in the Primary School.* Abingdon: Routledge.

Leedham, B. and Murphy, M. (2007). Joyful history, in D. Hayes (ed.), *Joyful Teaching and Learning in the Primary School.* Exeter: Learning Matters.

NACCCE (2001). *All our Futures: Creativity, Culture and Education.* London: DfEE.

Nuffield Primary History Project (2010). Local History Fieldwork – Top Ten Pointers for Success. *Primary History*, 55, Summer: 15.

Prendiville, F. and Toye, N. (2007). *Speaking and Listening through Drama 7–11*. London: Paul Chapman.

Ofsted (2007). *History in the balance: History in English schools 2003–2007*. London: Ofsted.

Rowley, C. and Cooper, H. (eds) (2009). *Cross-Curricular Approaches to Teaching and Learning*. London: Sage.

Times Educational Supplement (TES) (2012). www.tes.co.uk/teaching-resource/Investigating-Artefacts-6084006/ (updated 17 January 2012).

Turner-Bisset, R. (2005). *Creative History in the Primary Classroom*. London: Fulton Wood.

Vella, Y. (2010). Extending Primary Children's Thinking through the use of Artefacts. *Primary History*, 54, Spring: 17.

Wallace, B. (ed.) (2003). *Using History to Develop Thinking Skills at Key Stage 2*. London: David Fulton.

Wilson, A. (ed.) (2009). *Creativity in Primary Education* (2nd edn). Exeter: Learning Matters.

Music

Pam Burnard and James Biddulph

Music is a vital part of children's everyday lives. Indeed, *The Importance of Music*, a recent government report, makes it clear that the UK coalition government's view is that music is essential for children as an academic subject but also because it provides important social benefits, contributing to enjoyment and enrichment and improved quality of life (DfE, 2011). Children find immense pleasure in music, whether in creating music or in the multiple forms of children's music-making and play genres that are part of their experience of music in this increasingly digital age. It is easy to see how music permeates their lives; from lullabies at bedtime to the songs that we hear as chants in the playground, from the attraction they feel for innovation and novelty, with their own music notation systems, to the popular phenomena of iPhones, iPads, interactive music video games and mainstream technology that can be found in the lounges of millions of homes worldwide.

In this digital age, children can learn about and understand the musical elements in a variety of ways, including singing (using SingStar and Guitar Hero World Tour), playing (using instrument-shaped controllers), moving (using Wii Music), and making (using Guitar Hero and software that allow players to create their own songs), while developing an appreciation for music (through exposure to a wide repertoire where children's culture and popular culture meet).

Given place, time and resources (in the context of the extensive range of primary core curriculum priorities), children, in the act and process of appreciating, understanding and making music (whether using informal learning practices, such as free experimentation with instruments and imitation of pop tunes, or the traditional music repertoire they share as a group, or formal music-making) can develop skills of collaborative shared working, musical empathy, expressive communication, independence of thought and curiosity. Most importantly, music-making can provide opportunities for children to choose between following and flouting the rules and norms, pushing and breaking boundaries between the old and new, and use music to express something unique. By providing these opportunities, teachers allow children to do what they tend to do naturally – to be creative in music – and themselves become creative teachers.

For example, in Newham, staff at Ranelagh Primary School seek creative ways to develop pupils' creative thinking by advocating a 'structured free-ness', a balance of teacher direction with opportunities for pupils to make choices, and then develop the meaning of a subject together. One such collaborative project was with East London Dance (located in Stratford Circus, London), which brought together choreographers and musicians. The focus was on marking the anniversary of the Abolition of Slavery, a complex and sensitive subject for primary pupils in an ethnically diverse inner-city community. The dancers, musicians and teachers worked together to structure a learning experience that was designed to engage pupils with the complex issues of slavery from an historical and modern perspective through music and movement, drawing on historical evidence, stories, music and dance from several cultures (for example, Nigerian music and British Regency 'Sugar Party' dance). Within this structure (necessary to develop performance and ensure focused learning), pupils were given space to create their own movement, improvise and sing their own text to melodies learnt, ask questions about the subject and make links with modern forms of slavery. Teachers listened, recorded, responded, guided, questioned and raised expectations of what pupils could achieve. At no point did teachers tell or direct pupils what to do. All ideas were welcomed.

Through discussion as a group, pupils quickly appreciated which ideas were more effective. In reflecting on the evolving performance, structured by teachers/ dancers but within a framework which was created by pupils' curiosity and spontaneous ideas, a new understanding was generated by collaborative creative learning, bounded by the inner-city context.

Agency as a theoretical perspective

Christopher Small's coined phrase 'musicking' places relationships at the core of the human activity of music-making and as such we think it an essential task of any teacher engaged in music teaching and learning to reflect on the nature of the relationship between teacher and subject, between teacher and students, the relationship between students and their 'musicking' as well as their school–community context (Small, 1998). We ask how students interact with each other, the role of the music teacher in these interactions and how actively involved they are in their music learning, in the choices, decisions and evaluations made.

Over the last two decades there have been developments in our understanding of 'student or pupil voice', how teachers harness the agency of their students, largely because it is recognised that active students learn better. Agency (the capacity for willed, voluntary action) (Laurence, 2010) is an important concept for creativity in terms of pupils taking active control of their learning activities and in the ways they collaboratively define and work together in ways that are open ended and that encourage pupils to define the questions themselves and engage in agentic behaviour.

From the perspective of social theory, Giddens' (1984) and Bourdieu's (1990) understanding of structure and agency is very useful for our analysis of creativity in the primary music curriculum. Structure is a product of the pattern of practices that social actors engage in. Therefore structure is emergent out of human activity and is produced through norms and values that are played out in classroom activity. Pupils engage in collaborative learning, and acts of initiative are taken by pupils to present their ideas and negotiate a fit between personal knowledge and those of others. Their willingness to see themselves as members of a learning community is seen as mutually constituting the pupils' engagement in community discourse; in this case, the creative emancipatory potential of human agency is seen in the musical activities.

Bandura's (2001) model of agency offers a way to consider and describe agency as a kind of self-regulating activity, involving planning, reasoning, monitoring progress, and reflecting on beliefs about one's capabilities. Viewed in this way, agency can be both a quality of actions produced by an individual as well as the interactions produced by a group of individuals. In other words, when working collaboratively as a group, agency contributes to co-regulation or jointly shared actions or enterprise. The examples below show how careful planning can create opportunities for students to interact collaboratively, evaluating possibilities, thinking about complex issues and using agency to lead their own learning within contexts designed by teachers. The project on the Abolition of the Slave Trade highlights such agency.

According to Holland, et al. (1998), agency is intimately related to (and mediated by) identity. In turn, identity is shaped through activity in social practice and is the principal way in which individuals come to 'care about and care for what is going on around them' (Holland, et al., 1998: 5). Thus, agency and identity are mutually constitutive systems that play out in two forms: (1) acts of improvisation; and (2) acts of self-directed symbolization. Improvisations are actions that are mediated by one's 'sense and sensitivities', what we might also describe as awareness of perceived need to act. Symoblisation refers to the human ability to create imaginary worlds, 'figured worlds'. It allows learners to partic-ipate in activities and use language, signs and symbols, to organise themselves and others in exploratory ways. If we reflect on the Opera Project, questions about how close students are to their learning are raised; to the imagined worlds they create, how the activities were planned to ignite their self-reflection, requiring awareness of their own identity in relation to the characters and storyline that they were exploring.

Taking all these theoretical ideas about agency and structure into consideration, we hope to engage readers with the presentation and analysis of musical activities in an effort to show some of the creative moments of agency and structure that create an opening for teachers and pupils to really open up and think about and practice music in new ways.

In an educational climate dominated by austerity measures, we often overlook the easy learning opportunities that music affords. Knowing that competing primary curriculum priorities and accountability structures can marginalise the place of the arts in tight overcrowded timetables, we overlook possibilities and creative ways to include music-making in children's learning experiences. We forget how children engage in social groups and how most children have experienced music at home with their parents and within the media, and how they understand core music skills from infancy. We forget that music-making is created socially, with the group judging and assessing itself *together*, and that all primary teachers should be aware that they can promote children's creativity and imagination (by providing musical opportunities for exploring, composing new music, improvising together, inventing notations, and so much more) *without needing* much musical knowledge. Leveraging that understanding into the twenty-first-century classroom, where computers and broadband are commonplace, we can leapfrog into vast opportunities to develop children's creativity in music or, as Webster (1990) prefers, 'creative thinking' in music.

Not all children's compositional experience is by definition 'creative'; and, conversely, not all children's 'creative' experiences in music are 'compositional'. Children's interest in novelty fuels creativity within their own musical practices; often they work with spontaneously composed music, creating material within defined formulaic structures, and then pass this on to another child or group of children who receive and assimilate these ideas using other ideas derived from adult and popular culture sources (Marsh, 2008). This kind of composition within genres of children's musical play is easy for teachers to embed in creative approaches to teaching music in their classroom, if they are willing to engage with children within music-making in order to develop music creatively.

All of this implies approaches to listening, talking, singing, playing, composing and improvising which allow room for children's, as well as teachers', creativity to be explored. Composing and improvising are, in any case, a creative process, in which varying levels of creativity can be found, depending on: (i) the extent to which the core elements of creative practice are developed imaginatively; and (ii) how the children are engaged as performers, composers, improvisers, listeners and reflectors.

A number of studies of musical creativity have focused on children making music on instruments. Most of these studies have fallen broadly into two camps: those that have applied experimental task-driven designs (Swanwick and Tillman, 1986), and those that have observed children in naturalistic settings (Barrett, 1996). Findings from these studies suggest that what children do in their own time, and when working from their own starting points, differs markedly. However, the processes of exploring, developing, evaluating, refining, repeating, practising and performing were identified across a range of studies.

A small number of studies of musical creativity have focused on creative song-making processes. Davies (1986) showed how children aged five–seven years were able to achieve their expressive purposes across a range of different song types featuring, in particular, the use of closure devices. Barrett (1996) reported that children aged five–seven were able to develop musical ideas structurally, as a means to realising their musical purposes, using both voice and instruments.

In this chapter we will offer well tested ideas to involve children in music-making creatively, and illustrate the potential of teaching music creatively through the **creative involvement** of the teacher in developing children's musical creativity, knowledge, skills and understanding. We show what it means to teach music creatively to primary school children in ways which promote:

- **Exploring and experimenting** – activities that engage children in exploring sound (made by the voice, instruments, objects, and electronic or digital production).

- **Collaborating** – activities that engage both teachers and children in music-making (creating a purposeful soundscape to relate choices made in composing with choices made by other composers).

- **Risk-taking** – activities which allow children to experiment musically and make sounds without always being assessed or judged. For example, setting an unsupported task involving a problem (*How can you send a baby to sleep with cymbals and maracas? Solve!*); or teachers modelling 'risky learning' by attempting to compose a song with their class.

- **Improvising** – activities that encourage exploration of sounds, both acoustically and technologically derived, within the flow of making sounds together: developing non-verbal communication during improvisations and the sense of play and experimentation; and allowing children to sing new melodies to develop a song.

- **Composing** – activities that focus children to think about structures, purpose and intentions, following improvisation activities. For example, children quickly relate to modern technology. GarageBand (iMac) software offers musical 'soundbites', which can be arranged on a mixing desk, together with the possibility of recording sounds, voice and acoustic instruments to create their own 'soundbites'. (This has been used to create incidental music to accompany class drama and dance performances.)

- **Performing** – activities that engage primary school children in developing their confidence, self-esteem and analytical thinking, helping them to feel the excitement of preparing to perform and the joy of doing so. For example, a Year 3 class's modern version of an opera set in China.

- **Listening** – activities that engage children in listening to a wide variety of music played and made by other artists. Teaching children how to listen effectively is a key feature of primary school teaching. Finding silence spaces in the school day and guided listening activities help to focus children's listening skills. The Year 3 class featured in the next section developed their enjoyment of Puccini's *Turandot* by relating the operatic music with other passionate music with which they were familiar, and then finding the musical attributes that were similar and different.

As shown in the example below, at its best, creative teaching and learning of music in the primary classroom sees children's musical creativity exemplified through composing and improvising. At its richest, learning music is an energising, purposeful and imaginatively vital experience that builds positive attitudes to performing, listening, writing and analysing. At its poorest, music teaching and learning can be a dry, disconnected experience, focused on the instruction of assessable skills, and one that pays little attention to children's affective or creative development as musical learners and music users. Hennessy (2000), writing about teacher confidence, suggests that teachers need to shift from being presenters of content to becoming innovative leaders of explorations. To achieve this, some may need to dispel any lingering myths that creativity is applicable only to the formally trained musician. Researchers of children's composition and improvisation are generally considered as investigating 'musical creativity', because the activity they look into is the 'creation' of 'new' music (which can involve invented notations of children) (Upitis, 1992).

What can the literature tell us about what is 'creativity' and creative learning in music?

In recent years, the perception of creativity as being achievable only by a limited number of talented people has shifted towards a more democratic definition according to which everyone can be creative in some area given the right conditions and support (NACCCE, 1999). The QCA definition puts forward the view that creativity involves five behaviours: asking questions, making connections, imagining what might be, exploring options, and reflecting critically. Another view, as espoused by Boden (2005), is that children's creative endeavours can be differentiated into '**p-creative**' and '**h-creative**' acts, having psychological and historical connotations respectively. Creative Partnerships (2005; para. 2) states that: 'Creative learning is simply any learning that develops the capacity to be creative. It equips young people with the knowledge and skills they need to succeed in today's world, nurturing ways of thinking and working that encourage imagination, independence, tolerance of ambiguity and risk, openness, the raising of aspirations.'

One of the most influential studies of children's musical creativity, which has endeavoured to provide a model that predominantly focuses on children's composition and improvisation, was proposed by Swanwick and Tillman (1986). This well-known model is based on the analysis of compositional exercises, recorded under experimental conditions, of children aged from three to fifteen years. The model postulates that children's compositional processes change as they grow older, with children passing progressively through four compositional stages, demonstrating engagement with Materials, Expression, Form and Value respectively. Each of these stages is seen to correspond with the Piagetian stages of Mastery, Imitation, Imaginative Play and Metacognition (Swanwick and Tillman, 1986).

In the primary music classroom, creativity is about musical imagination, and pupils' ability to compose and improvise. However, music listening and performance are also considered to be forms of creative behaviour, as with children's forms of playground compositions and composition in performance (Marsh, 2008). Whatever definition of creativity and creativity in music you apply, it is very important for primary age children to develop the foundation for creative learning in music at the very start of their formal education (Alexander, 2010; Hennessy, 2009; Jones and Robson, 2008).

Starting points for the musical creative learning journey

In this section, we explore a possible creative learning journey as a starting point for teachers to engage in creative music learning. As a metaphor, the 'journey' encourages teachers and learners to think about the important 'milestones', the upward struggles, the joyful freewheeling, decisions at the 'crossroads' and possible destinations. For UK primary teachers, music teaching is often seen as a daunting task, with concerns about their own abilities to sing in tune, play an instrument, and knowledge of music theory as barriers to successful, enjoyable music teaching and learning. But most people have experience of music in their lives, whether singing in the shower or listening to their favourite band in the car: our suggestion is to start with music you are passionate about because it will instil confidence and connection with the pupils, who will respect your passion even if they don't like your musical choice.

Consulting pupils about their music

A fascinating starting point for creative learning in music comes from consulting pupils. The value of consulting pupils to improve the learning experiences of pupils in school is well documented, because, in eliciting their interests, views and ideas, pupils develop a sense of agency and become more motivated in their learning (Rudduck & Flutter, 2004).

One technique to engage pupils in discussion about their creativity is guided map-making. The question for teachers is: *What musical things do the pupils in my class do after school?* Teachers can guide the pupils through their mapping of their experiences by, for example, asking them to draw/illustrate/sketch/write what they would see in their home if they were 'making', 'solving', 'struggling', 'concentrating', 'using their imaginations', 'being curious or asking questions' and 'playing' in relation to music (and dance). These words are selected because they are all attributes associated with creativity. This technique will provide teachers with information about the types of activity the children are involved in, their level of experience and their interests (e.g., favourite task, hobbies). For example, when Year 3 children were asked when they use their imagination in music at home, children said that they did so when they daydreamed, or while 'humming tunes that I made up', when 'doing film music' or when 'playing a game about castles' or 'thinking about how to get the music right by listening to the internet (iTunes) and imagining what its like on my piano'. It is also useful for teachers to complete the same activity about their own lives, which they can share with the pupils, thus building the sense of collaboration in the creative learning journey: the idea is that the teacher is a *facilitator* of musical learning, also on the creative music journey. This shift in teaching style is important if effective creative learning is to be achieved.

Creative planning – first steps on the musical creative learning journey

Following this elicitation activity, teachers can start to plan the musical creative learning journey. Creative planning can be a very exciting process, and finding ways to engage and think creatively is satisfying and interesting. But, as educators, we know that planning meetings in primary schools can quickly become bureaucratic exercises that are disassociated from the realities of the classroom. Starting a planning session with the generation of questions can engage teachers in finding connections, creating possibilities and discovering learning outcomes (Owen, 2011).

Using *Eccentric Questioning* is an effective strategy. Starting with the theme you wish to explore, create or find an 'Eccentric Question'. For example, how are

Table 9.1 Example of Eccentric Question Planning

How is opera like a roast dinner?
- There are often 3 acts in operas – starter, main and dessert. What is the structure like in the opera we're going to see?
- You feel full after dinner – operas are intense and make you feel full
- Operas can be heavy – so can a roast dinner
- People come together to eat – who goes to operas nowadays? Why?
- Roasts are eaten at home and in restaurants – operas are watched at home and in the theatre – what's the difference?
- Is there music at lunch? What kind? Why? What kind of music is opera? Is there a type?
- Chefs are artists – composers are artists
- Food is a work of art – opera is a work of art
- What does food look like on the plate? What does opera look like on stage?
- Meat and veg – orchestra and singers
- Gravy brings it all together – the storyline links the characters together (the conductor links the stage and the orchestra together)

From this, the teacher then started planning the creative learning journey:

1 Research the history of opera (homework project: children research a scene from an opera and make a 3D design model)
2 What is the structure of the *Turandot* storyline? Is there a natural beginning, middle, end (as in a roast dinner)?
3 How do I engage the children with this music, which is unfamiliar to them? Find current pop songs about love, night time (link with *Nessun Dorma*)? Look at musicals/modern films that use this music.
4 Prepare them for the experience of attending opera (who's who?)
5 How do music, stage design and costumes come together as a whole? Drama, music, visual art?

---

the Tudors like punk music? When were the Beatles like the colour red? When is opera like roast dinner? You can design such questions by choosing random words, linking disassociated images, or using techniques well documented as creative thinking tools, such as Edward de Bono's *Six Thinking Hats*. A Year 3 teacher followed such an approach because his school had arranged for his class to attend a performance at the Royal Opera House in London. Table 9.1 shares his planning journey with an eccentric question starting point.

At this point, aligning pupils' experiences, as discovered in the guided mapping activity and the teacher's *Eccentric Question* planning, and underpinned by knowledge of pupil agency, provides a route map for the creative learning journey. This Year 3 teacher created a large 'working wall' display in his classroom, making explicit the time frame, key learning goals/milestones, possible skills needed during the learning (e.g., questioning, synthesising of information, an open attitude) and making high expectations of their outcomes visible. The display modelled the process of creative learning with music as a focus, identifying problems, successes, failures and linking subjects together. In the next section, we explore how this plan resulted in creative music-making.

Creating and making music

The outcome of this Year 3 project was to create a new version of Puccini's opera *Turandot* and perform it for other children in school. Several techniques were used to develop this creation, but in relation to creative music-making the following three were the most successful: *Active Storytelling* with the use of Learning Journals, *Soundscape* composition and *Songwriting*. They aimed to develop children's ability to write effective text to set to music, as songwriting, and compose incidental music to accompany the action.

Active Storytelling is a technique whereby teachers guide the pupils through the story by engaging them as active participants in acting roles and critically thinking about key events in the storyline. The technique comes from Augusto Boal's *Theatre of the Oppressed* (Boal, 1979), which engages audiences in examining characters and their actions in and during the drama. It is an important technique for musical creativity because, in experiencing the structure of the story through drama and movement, emerging musical choices are generated and evoke real understanding of the intention in creating a specific piece of music. It helps children to build an understanding of the impact and purpose of music in musical theatre, building their critical thinking in relation to emotional effect. Writing out the storyline, illustrating it and creating a one-page version can support teachers, and is a useful resource in the process of teaching. It is best when pupils do not know the story. The process starts with the teacher explaining where the story is set, introducing the characters, asking pupils to suggest what the characters may be like, and building on their imagination of how the story may evolve. This gives the pupils a sense that they are telling the story, making decisions about characters' actions and being fully involved – as one pupil said, 'it's like we're there, living with them'. The pupils' understanding of the story through drama

Table 9.2 Active Storytelling: an approach to engage children in the art of opera

---

Turandot Session 1: structure of the first session

1   I need your help to bring this story alive. I'll need people to help me bring the characters into our classroom. (Sound effects of a city will be played throughout; play traditional Chinese music.)
2   Listen to music: Where do you think the music comes from? The story is set in China. With your learning partner (the person sitting next to you), what do you know about China? Is it hot there?
3   We are in a very rich city. What can you see? Yes, there is a palace. What does the palace look like? Make the palace gardens with your bodies? Who is the fountain? The arched cloisters? Flowering trees? (Take photos of this scene – possibly create garden music/soundscape.)
4   In this story there are several characters; enter the emperor (play Puccini's triumphant music – this is linked with music improvisation where children create triumphant imperialistic music (linked with Star Wars theme by John Williams).

---

and movement supported their learning about the operatic genre because they actively experienced the characters in context by acting and thinking about plot dilemmas and possibilities. Table 9.2 is an example of the initial session.

During this active storytelling, the use of *Learning Journals* supports pupils in thinking creatively about the story. Simple booklets (A4 sheets stapled together to make A5 booklets) allow them to jot notes, illustrate events and capture the sounds that they might hear at different parts of the story. As in visual artists' sketchbooks, the journal emphasises the creative process, building a repertoire of ideas from which they can draw at later stages of the creative music process. The use of a journal helped pupils to develop ideas for creative music learning tasks.

Soundscape is about exploring sounds, using instruments and technology. At the part of the opera where the 'city cannot sleep', the teacher guided the pupils in exploring sounds to create an evocative soundscape. Pupils sat in a circle. The teacher asked them when they find it difficult to sleep (linked with Personal Social *and* Health Education), then what they would see in the city at night, with each child taking a turn to respond. Following this, he asked what sounds they might hear, with pupils responding with sounds created with their voices and/or body. These sounds were 'performed' with pupils making decisions about dynamics and tempo. A question about structure was asked: 'How should we arrange these sounds?' Pupils discussed this in pairs and responded. Following a collaborative decision, there was a rehearsal and a recorded performance (this was further developed and used in the performance to the school). The teacher then made instruments available, inviting pupils to try and recreate their sound using instruments. The pupils listened to Puccini's music and were asked to identify where the music was similar to their own music soundscape, linking listening, composing and appraisal together and building self-assessment and reflective thinking skills. These ideas could take several sessions to develop fully. Table 9.3 shows the overview of the creative learning journey, including drama, music and art (because the genre employs these three arts).

In relation to *Songwriting*, and as suggested earlier, children are natural songwriters. Indeed, using this skill and engaging in songwriting in the classroom

Table 9.3 An example of planning to develop music creativity

Aims:

1 To introduce children to opera
2 To engage children in exploring the themes, story structure and characters of an opera
3 To examine the relationship between drama, music and visual art within the operatic genre

Week	Music	Broadening out from Music
Week 1	Share the qualities of the pentatonic scale.	Introducing stage design.
	Children will explore and play with the pentatonic scale (improvise) using tuned instruments (in pairs chosen at random).	Researching/being curious: show children YouTube clips of stage designs. Discuss what they see.
	Can they create a traditional Chinese sounding improvisation?	Collect images and ideas for class Working Wall (make explicit the creative learning process)
	Half of the children act out market scenes following active story telling activities; the rest play pentatonic music.	(see www.youtube.com/watch?v=XoTa-b7cUw0)
	Sing Mo Li Hua (see www.singup.org).	Teacher models the questioning skills in researching.
Week 2	Listen to the opening music in Act 1.	Where does the story take place? (Peking Palace)
	What do the children feel when they hear this music? Draw what they hear. Build bank of language for Working Wall.	Research images of traditional Chinese architecture. Look at the shapes of roofs, colours, designs, and patterns.
	Now watch the opening scene on YouTube (www.youtube.com/watch?v=NXDfLVy1gRg)	Collect images in an art book or Learning Journal.
	Improvise in groups of three: the purpose is to create the effect of grand, imperial music.	Children sketch their own patterns, designs, and palace drawings on ideas collected.
	Task for 5 mins:	Teacher models curiosity in researching.
	Perform, listen and respond: How did the music create the effect intended? What did the group do? Which instruments did they choose? Why? To what effect?	
	Build on the previous session so that a musical composition emerges with following structure: Grand Opening leading to children singing Mo Li Hua song.	
Week 3	Create a musical arrangement of a text.	Research Chinese traditional dress.
	Warm up with tongue twisters, limericks and raps.	What would the characters wear? Who is rich? Royal? Poor? Commoner? Servant? (Refer to Learning Journal.)
	Then show different riddles and riddles created in the drama session.	Design costumes/headdresses.
	Play clapping games, stimulated by text.	
	Children use voice and instruments in groups of four.	
	Create a rhythmic performance of riddle texts.	

Week	Music	Broadening out from Music
Week 4	Listen to Nessun Dorma (which has been used in sports coverage and adverts): What is the piece about? Listen again. What instruments do you hear? Soundscape: improvise, leading to composition. How can we remember the piece? How could you record it? Explore different ways of noting the music.	Create stage design and costumes using fabric, paint, and model building. Teacher works with one group to create a stage set. Other children work independently on either character models or costume design.
Weeks 5 & 6	Songwriting (see below): learn and practice the song for performance.	Continue from previous session.

is an effective way to deepen knowledge about a topic (e.g., characters and plots) as well a way to engage in complex music-creating skills. As in the example above, songwriting can be a highly effective pedagogic tool in developing pupil agency. Generalist primary teachers with little experience of positive creative music-making may feel that songwriting is unattainable because of the reasons suggested above. The technique described below has been used by so-called 'non-specialists' in challenging inner-city primary schools to great effect. A good starting point is

Table 9.4 Example of Songwriting Session

Songwriting Session 1:
1   Identify the theme/event in the story.
2   What kind of feel do we want to create? Will it be fast, slow, walking pace? Relaxed, tense, energetic?
3   Ask pupils to write a sentence that a character might say or think (use their Learning Journals for ideas). They should work together to write their sentence/phrase on a strip of paper.
4   Blu-tack strips of paper onto the board and read through each. Which sentences sound effective when spoken out loud? Why? Are there words to change?
5   Think about the 'hook'. Which phrase/couple of words/word is 'catchy' and can be used in the chorus? Think of other songs. Why do they keep the listener's attention? (Rhythmic quality? Alliteration? Emotive?)
6   Re-arrange strips so that the 'flow' of the phrases makes sense.
7   Edit strips. Agree final verses and chorus.
8   What does this mean about the structure? Verse-chorus-verse-chorus-chorus?
9   Use backing track (created on software, downloaded, played on piano/guitar). Ask children in small groups to sing their line. All pupils singing at once (warning: this can be noisy, but pupils always seem focused). Teacher must listen carefully for possible emerging melody.
10 Sing and share. Each group sings their line. Celebrate and discuss. Call and response arranged so that everyone sings each group's musical contribution. A musical idea may emerge. Teacher may need to lead on deciding the melody.
11 Record each melody. (End of session.)

Post writing:
1   Teachers to listen to the recordings and learn the melody so that they can teach it to the class in the next session.
2   Type up agreed song words.

by drawing on teachers' own enthusiasm for a style of music as well as their skills in teaching writing in literacy.

Learning Journals were used to collect musical ideas, for recording the structure of an improvisation and drawing a visual representation of a piece of music (guided listening activity). It is also valuable to draw on the vast and varied resources provided by technological advances: for example, YouTube, downloadable backing tracks, creative music-making software and GarageBand (available only on Macs), are some of the possibilities on offer. Table 9.4 shows an example of a songwriting session (which can be adapted for subsequent sessions to revise and refine).

The creative learning environment for teaching music creatively

The environment that the teacher creates influences the nature of learning. Likewise, a music 'champion' in the school is important in raising the value and profile of the subject, galvanising staff, bringing the school together in significant events (e.g., assemblies) and providing extended musical learning opportunities in and after school (Hennessy, 2009). The environment and the ethos this creates are especially relevant when thinking about developing spaces for creative learning and creative music-making. Each teacher will have challenges related to the physical space of their classroom but there are other subtle influences on children, which teachers could consider, in order to engage children's creative learning skills. Creating a musical school environment and classroom creates a sense of creative potential and playfulness. In Wellington College, Berkshire, pianos are found along corridors with signs saying 'Please play me' and 'Make beautiful music'; pupils stop, improvise or play a piece and then continue on their way. How different this is to some schools where the piano is locked and only played by the singing teacher! What message does this send to children? Reflection on these issues prompts teachers to review their practice and learning classroom environments because they come to understand that these have a huge effect on music creativity. Questions to engage teachers' reflection on this include:

1   Is there regular teacher modelling of creative attributes (e.g., does the teacher model 'getting stuck' and their thinking about possible solutions)?

2   Is the class environment cluttered and overstimulating? Is there 'blank space' for quiet reflective thinking? Are there instruments and listening stations available for children? (Early Years' settings provide musical instruments for children to use throughout their learning day.)

3   Does the teacher engage in dialogue about creative learning? Does the teacher talk about music?

4   Are pupils encouraged to ask questions? (For example, dedicate a space for pupils to write interesting, deep and 'powerful' questions.) Can they ask questions about music?

5   What behaviours does the teacher expect? What strategies for managing behaviour are employed? How do teachers manage the challenges of children using instruments? Have teachers taught children how to respect and use instruments?

6   Are risky learning tasks planned for pupils? Are they challenging? Do they expect a lot from pupils? Is 'risk in learning' celebrated?

7   Is music used throughout the learning day? (For example, the Year 3 teacher played *John Williams' Indiana Jones theme* to indicate time to tidy up. Music was played to welcome pupils to class. A class song was created using a well-known pop melody.)

8   What values and ethos do teachers create in their classroom that inhibit or encourage creative learning? Is your school like Wellington College, passionate about children engaging imaginatively and creatively throughout their experience of the school day?

Teaching for creative learning in music

As shown in the example above, the possibilities of creative music-making are many and can be developed by any primary generalist 'non-specialist'. One of the biggest challenges teachers face is in documenting moments of significant creativity in music, and understanding how these evolve, develop and change among children. What do we take to be creativity in music and what constitutes creative learning spaces which open up the possibilities of thinking differently around a musical issue? How should creativity in music be taught to achieve progression? And if progression is an outcome of what and how we teach, what are the aspects of teaching that will enable progress in musical creativity to occur and be assessed?

Spaces that enable children to work creatively in music entail being open to the unforeseen and the unforeseeable. As the Year 3 teacher attempted it, this will entail:

- Creating an environment of musical possibility (**Questioning and challenging**).

- Using time and creating opportunity for children to contribute their ideas in performing and discussion contexts, as well as in composing (**Making connections and seeing relationships**). Making time and creating opportunities for teachers to engage with the pupils in music-making activities.

- Enabling children to work imaginatively with sound itself (**Envisaging what might be**). Giving children plenty of experience of seeing and hearing how other people work creatively in music, and a range of models to consider, including teacher-led modelling of creative processes.

- Giving children plenty of time and opportunity to pose questions and contribute their ideas through play (**Playing with ideas and keeping options open**).

■ Making opportunities for children to represent musical ideas in a variety of ways and reflect on processes as well as outcomes.

■ Ensuring the creative involvement of the teacher (as music leader, champion and learner) in music-making with the children (**Intentionality and risk-taking**).

In this digital age, where learners create music learning contexts within and across settings, fostering musical creativity and the possibilities of teaching music with a commitment to reimaging pedagogical spaces for a creative approach to teaching music, brings many challenges; but, equally, it brings responsibilities. Consider an environment of possibility in which individual musical agency and self-determination are fostered and children's musical ideas and interests are valued, discussed and celebrated. To bring this about requires us to think deeply about how we understand, articulate and hope to answer questions such as: 'What do pedagogies that enable creativity look like? When is a pedagogy innovative?' We know that pedagogies that enable creativity include allowing children choice and ownership of their learning, time for reflection, creating a stimulating environment, and modelling creative action within a genuine partnership. Not all spaces in a school can or should always allow for all of these possibilities, but the school should work towards design solutions that contain as many of these as possible. Posing questions and play can be implemented in ways that include possibilities for one-to-one musical conversation, collaborative group dialogue, and communication and musical interaction (in real time or asynchronous time – for example, through email or interactive blogs).

The pedagogies that relate to flexibility of space and time and engage the imagination are often those in which the teachers position themselves off centre-stage and promote learning through the children's own chosen activities and interests. Whilst not afraid to use direct instruction and teacher-led work where necessary, music teachers who seek to balance teacher-led and child-led activities create the time and space for children to explore their environment and the materials provided, encouraging both actual and mental play. The features of this distinct pedagogic practice appear to promote and foster the children's full engagement in problem-finding and problem-solving activities and thus support their development as young possibility thinkers.

Underpinning the pedagogic practices of standing back, profiling learner agency and creating time and space are the teachers' conceptions of children as young musical thinkers and creators and of learning as a process of discovery. These pedagogues often lead by following, creating flexible maps en route with the class, and enabling the children to experience a high degree of ownership of, and immersion in, their musical learning. Creative pedagogies involve being co-participative and combining in action as the music teachers encourage the children to direct more of their learning journeys.

FIGURE 9.1 Representation of a creative approach to teaching music (adapted from Craft, Cremin, Burnard and Chappell, 2008; Cremin, Burnard and Craft, 2006)

Inspirational spaces are not simply rooms for the teaching and performance of music. The whole curriculum can be approached through creativity. Bringing together more than one curriculum area into a single space can promote creativity in musical teaching and learning. Spaces that suggest creativity should signal a respectful and trusting relationship between learner and teacher in the physical setting because the required acceptance of risk, trial and error and freedom to experiment and feel immersion in the activities is supported by such a setting. In such spaces, it is important that teachers respect the knowledge and inventiveness that young people can bring with them to school and that can become a resource for others, including the teachers themselves.

Creative spaces are more likely to be found at the edges of rooms than in the middle because these are the sites where we might find nooks and crannies, meeting corners and softer, less exposed, areas for dreaming and thinking, immersion and being imaginative. The same might be said of the outdoor school environment, where it is often around the edges of buildings that pupils gather to socialise and where imagination and meaning flourish in relation to the natural and built environments.

The amount of time available on the timetable for supporting meetings and the sustainability of dialogue, networking and talking about pedagogic practice is crucial for the development of pedagogic innovation. Building in adequate amounts of time for reflection on practice and for supporting partnerships, peer mentoring collaborations and collegiality is essential if teachers are to search and research practice and question one another on their pedagogic practices – and, in so doing, intervene. Teachers who choose to work collaboratively with other teachers (including visiting professional artists) have the potential to co-construct new pedagogic practices and change practice in teaching music. In order to develop, transform and improve their teaching of music (whether as a beginning teacher or as an experienced practitioner) in the formal setting of a primary school, teachers need to foster play and engagement, risk-taking and collaboration, integrating reflection, review, feedback and celebration into their practice.

This representation identifies various ways of utilising children's and teachers' engagement with creative learning, both being valued and nurtured in the broader context of a playful enabling environment. This engagement includes posing questions (as the driving process), alongside self-determination, play, immersion, innovation, being imaginative and risk-taking. One of the operational elements of pedagogy associated with nurturing creativity in music is that of standing back, placing a high value on learner agency, and making time and space for creativity, as shown in Figure 9.1.

Creative Touches

Start simply, build progressively:

- Find easy ways into creative musical learning. Start with the classroom environment and the ethos you create. Move on to how pupils and staff use and engage with music in their lives. Show and share tangible changes.
- Be a creative advocate for music. Create a presentation or materials that you can use both within your school to convince colleagues and out of school. This will help to build a whole-school ethos around creativity in music.
- Focus on one area at a time (for example, in developing more creative learning in music), and use this to raise awareness and encourage staff to think about applications in other spaces in the school.
- Organise a 'Musical Enquiring Minds'-type project where pupils have an opportunity to negotiate the aim of the project and are instrumental in designing how it is carried out (see www.enquiringminds.org.uk).
- Set up a 'music inventors' or 'music creators' club after school.
- Transform one small area in the school into a space designed for creativity in music and imagination. Make sure that the pupils have some ownership of the project.
- Learn from the pupils by engaging in research to understand their musicking, their relationships and interactions and in speaking with them.

If music educators are to successfully develop pupils' creativity in music, further attention will need to be paid to what it might mean to develop creativity in a way which progresses, for all children. The approaches described above seek to explore the potential for mapping progression in children's music-making creatively (Burnard, 2006). We need to place more reliance on empirical research to fully comprehend how children's understanding changes over time, and focus on developing theoretical explanations.

References

Alexander, R. (ed.) (2010). *Children, their World, their Education:* Final Report and Recommendations of the Cambridge Primary Review. London: Routledge.

Bandura, A. (2001). Social-cognitive theory: An agentic persepctive. *Annual Review of Psychology*, 52: 1–26.

Barrett, M. (1996). Children's aesthetic decision-making: An analysis of children's musical discourse as composers. *International Journal of Music Education*, 28: 37–62.

Boal, A. (1979). *Theatre of the Oppressed*. London: Pluto Press.

Boden, M. (2005). *The Creative Mind: Myths and Mechanisms*. London: Routledge.

Bourdieu, P. (1990). *The logic of practice*. Translated by Richard Nice. Standford, CA: Stanford University Press.

Burnard, P. (2006). The individual and social worlds of children's musical creativity, in G. McPherson (ed), *The Child as Musician: A Handbook of Musical Development*. Oxford: Oxford University Press, pp. 353–74.

Craft, A., Cremin, T., Burnard, P. and Chappell, K. (2008). Possibility thinking with children in England aged 3–7, in A. Craft, T. Cremin and B. Burnard (eds), *Creative Learning 3–11 and How We Document It*. Stoke-on-Trent: Trentham, pp. 65–75.

Creative Partnerships (2005). *The Rhetorics of Creativity: a review of the literature*. London: Arts Council.

Cremin, T., Burnard, P. and Craft, A. (2006), Pedagogy and possibility thinking in the early years. *Journal of Thinking Skills and Creativity*, 1 (2): 108–119.

Davies, C. (1986). Say it till a song comes (reflections on songs invented by children 3–13). *British Journal of Music Education*, 3 (3): 270–93.

De Bono, E (2000). *Six Thinking Hats*. London: Penguin.

DfE (2011). *The Importance of Music: A National Plan*. London: DfE.

Giddens, A. (1984). The Constitution of Society. Outline of the Theory of Structuration. Cambridge: Polity Press.

Hennessy, S. (2000). Overcoming the red-feeling: The development of confidence to teach music in primary school amongst student teachers. *British Journal of Music Education*, 17 (2): 183–96.

Hennessy, S. (2009). Creativity in the music curriculum, in A. Wilson (ed.), *Creativity in Primary Education*. Exeter: Learning Matters, pp. 134–47.

Holland, D., Lachiocotte, W., Skinner, D. and Cain, C. (1998). *Identity and agency in cultural worlds*. Cambridge, MA: Harvard University Press.

Jones, P. and Robson, C. (2008). *Teaching Music in Primary Schools*. Exeter: Learning Matters.

Laurence, F. (2010). Listening to Children: Voice, Agency and Ownership in School Musicking, in R. Wright (ed.), *Sociology of and Music Education*. Farnham: SEMPRE, pp. 243–62.

Marsh, K. (2008). *The Musical Playground: Global Tradition and Change in Children's Songs and Games*. Oxford: OUP.

NACCCE (1999). *All our Futures*. London: DfEE.

Owen, N. (2011). *Placing Students at the Heart of Creative Learning*. London: David Fulton.

Rudduck, J. and Flutter, J. (2004). *How to Improve Your School: Giving Pupils a Voice*. London: Continuum.

Small, C. (1998). Musicking: The Meanings of Performing and Listening. Hanover, NH: Wesleyan University Press.

Swanwick, K. and Tillman, J. (1986). The sequence of musical development: A study of children's composition. *British Journal of Music Education*, 3 (3): 305–39.

Upitis, R. (1992). *The Compositions and Invented Notations of Children*. Portsmouth, NH: Heinemann Educational Books.

Webster, P. (1990). Creativity as creative thinking. *Music Educators Journal*, 76 (9): 22–8.

The Visual Arts

Alison Mawle

The subject of art when represented in national curricula is often accompanied by the claim that it stimulates creativity and imagination. Although the notion of creativity refers to a range of capabilities that are relevant to the whole curriculum, creativity is particularly associated with the subject of art and design and particularly with the making of art. Art is seen as a 'creative art' and is often referred to as 'a creative subject' through which children get a chance to 'be' or 'do something' creative.

Why are the visual arts so full of potential for developing pupils' creativity? What are the significant challenges in the primary classroom and some of the ways that individual teachers or whole-school communities rise to them, so that pupils experience the 'joyful exercise of creativity … [where they] become most fully alive' (Jones, 1996)? What values, experiences and relationships can we cultivate in order to facilitate the notoriously slippery concept?

Creativity in the visual arts

While this chapter is concerned solely with the relationship between creativity and the visual arts, art is about more than just creativity. In fact, it was not until the late nineteenth century that the two became linked. Until this time, the study of art was concerned with the acquisition of drawing skills which were taught by experts in discreet steps for a social utilitarian purpose. Around the turn of the twentieth century, art education developed so that the skills of learning **in** art were accompanied by learning **about** art and the societies that produced it. To this can be added the notion of a child's personal response which was advanced most fervently by the Child Art Movement in the 1910s and 1920s. Proponents such as Franz Cizek, Roger Fry, Marion Richardson and Bill Viola championed the fostering of personal expression and what they believed to be children's innate creativity. Intervention was offered but only on an individual basis when requested.

These changes coincided with a burgeoning body of research and debate into notions of childhood, developmental psychology and the broader purpose of education which continues to the present day. Children were no longer considered, for example, as little adults to be filled up with the necessary knowledge and skills. Instead, they were recognised as individuals with distinct personalities and talents, the development of which was inextricably linked with their relationships to the people and communities around them.

So education, and specifically art education, no longer served solely a functional, subject-specific remit; rather, a democratic theory of education evolved which came to be seen as central to the healthy development of every individual (Lowenfeld, 1947) and of society as a whole. Herbert Read presented this case most strongly in his influential book, *Education Through Art (1963)*. In it he stated that aesthetic education (defined as those forms that enabled self-expression: art, craft, design, music, dance, poetry and drama) is fundamental in developing individuality, specifically in determining one's thoughts and choices. He reasoned that since people exist in relationship to the society around them, developing children's aesthetic sensibilities was the key to social consciousness.

Elliot Eisner picked up the baton in articulating what is distinctive about art. He encapsulated the theories of such influential thinkers as John Dewey, Suzanne Langer and Richard Fry and summarised the justification for arts education as: a means of self-expression; as academic study; and to produce practising artists. Like Herbert, he believed that the study of art enables people to experience and understand the world around them. However, he went further in advocating that art is distinct from the other arts in that it alone concerns 'the aesthetic contemplation of visual form' (Eisner, 1972: 9). By stopping to look and reflect, one sees more; one's awareness is heightened; and one's capacity to respond is increased. Since artists throughout history have responded to the world in which they live, engaging with art either as a viewer or a maker, provides the opportunity to consider and reconsider both one's own and others' opinions and beliefs.

It is this that enables us to see the clear link between art and creativity. The key is in the room that it gives to one's own responses, understandings and expressions. Creativity is concerned with the making of new and personal connections. Experiencing art opens the doors to a host of personal reflections and expressions, both mental and physical.

Not all art-making is creative, but art-making has the potential more than many other activities to facilitate creativity. More helpful than arguing the merits of particular art activities, is considering the conditions that foster such behaviour. The phrasing of the English National Curriculum for art and design (2000) implies that creativity is an innate quality in all children that can be brought out through exploration of, and increasing control over, materials and techniques. This suggests that creativity and creative ability is part of what it means to be human and raises the question of whether it can also be taught. While this forms the focus of contemporary debate, what is certain is the leading role of the teacher in the demonstration and development of their pupils' creativity.

To produce a mental or physical product that is new and of value requires the making of meaningful connections which did not previously exist (Fawcett and Hay, 2004). It requires someone bringing themselves – their experience, their knowledge and understanding, their beliefs and opinions, their imagination and intuition – to a situation and having the opportunity to express a personal response within it. Sometimes this happens instantaneously but in the main, it requires a process: an initial stimulus or 'encounter' (Witkin, 1974) with which one engages followed by a period of exploration and investigation in which one's own personal response or responses are developed. Or, seen another way: it is about children finding their own solutions to the problem at hand.

For children to exhibit creativity in their art-making according to the definition of this book, they must make something that is deemed original and of value by appropriately qualified people. In the classroom context, these judgements fall to the pupils themselves – which in turn implies that there is some intention involved – and to the teacher.

It is easy to confuse the ability of a child to be creative with their ability to reproduce reality as closely as possible. While the two certainly are not synonymous, they are linked because, as Eisner (1972) articulated, it is impossible to innovate until one has mastery over a particular material, technique or process, a view that was later echoed by Howard Gardner (1999). The confusion arises when one equates confidence in using a particular material with the goal of realism. In stark contrast to the proponents of the Child Art Movement, who believed that instruction inhibited children's creative development, it is widely agreed that the teaching of skills at appropriate moments (Piaget and Inhelder, 1958; Lowenfeld, 1947; Witkin, 1974) alleviates the frustration that children experience when they cannot express their ideas as they wish to. This frustration, which reaches its zenith by the end of the primary years, partly explains why so many children give up on art as a subject around this time (Watts, 2005). In doing so, they deny themselves that opportunity for their creativity to be expressed through future art-making. The skill of a teacher is in balancing instruction and the subsequent practice of the new skill, with opportunities for exploration, experimentation and the development of individual preferences and choices.

Another useful addition to the debate are the findings of two studies carried out by Kerry Thomas in Sydney and Illinois into the relationship between teacher–pupil exchanges and creativity in art-making. She concluded that 'the realization of creative outcomes was dependent on the capacities of the teachers and pupils to engage in highly inferential forms of social reasoning that were reliant on tactful exchanges' (Thomas, 2010). Thomas goes on to characterise 'tactful exchanges' as those cautions or suggestions that help the pupils to reflect and rethink. In this way the pupils retain the ownership over their work and the control, which directly relates to their self-esteem and identity. This approach implies a shift in the role of the teacher from that of instructor, or expert to facilitator (Hallam, Lee and Gupta, 2007). How easy it is to offer one's own opinion instead of phrasing a prompt in such a way as to give the power back to the child – especially when time is short.

Grafton Primary School: a case study

There are no simple answers to the challenges inherent in the ideas outlined above. Moreover, there are as many approaches to the visual arts as there are schools. Grafton School in Holloway, north London, is just one of many schools which continue to acknowledge and find ways of rising to some of these challenges. The observations outlined below are gleaned from visiting the school, talking with pupils and staff, and seeing the pupils' outcomes over a period of three years. The school is led by Nitsa Sergides, who has been honoured for her services to education. Justin Ward (quoted below) is the creative arts coordinator and art and design subject leader. He is also an Advanced Skills Teacher for art and design.

As soon as one enters the building you are aware of the high value given to the visual arts. The colour and vibrancy of the artwork which fills the entrance hall and continues as far as the eye can see are in stark contrast to the noise and pollution of the adjacent Holloway Road. Large-scale sculptures, which have long since outgrown display boards, combine with two-dimensional work to create an enticing welcome. Immediately the visitor is drawn into and beyond what they see to wondering about the experiences, stories and thinking that surround the making of these pieces. The message is clear that the visual arts are important and integral to the children's education.

Simultaneously one senses the value given to each individual child within the making process. Grafton School serves an ethnically and culturally-diverse community, the richness of which is reflected through the visual expression of a number of cultural heritages, specifically Somali and Turkish. Sometimes children work individually and the work bears the stamp of the child's individuality, while at other times collaboration is facilitated. The result is a dynamic learning environment with which every child can identify.

A sense of belonging is something that the staff foster through the experiences they provide as well as the environment in which they work. As Justin explains, 'Children don't make progress unless they are valued, they have got self-esteem, they feel part of something.'

Commitment to the arts, and specifically the visual arts, is demonstrated by the headteacher's investment in the resources to make it a reality. As well as a generous budget, time and money is given to ensuring that staff have the necessary expertise and related confidence to lead art and design in their own classrooms. Staff workshops are held that focus on working with different materials, for example. In this way the expertise, knowledge and skills that exist among the staff are shared. 'I offer my skills and knowledge but it has snowballed because there is a willingness. Nitsa has employed ambitious and competitive people who want to continually improve and offer the children better and better provision.' Ongoing support is also given by the subject leader through lesson observations and subsequent collaboration. 'Once we have developed something together, then we make it policy, so it's followed through.'

The school employ an artist and a writer in residence who work alongside teachers for half a term at a time. The artist (or writer) plan together with the teacher so that each other's expertise is utilised without compromising continuity. Teachers describe the buzz and energy that this collaborative way of working encourages, together with the positive impact on the children's experiences and subsequent learning.

The pressure to reduce the time given to art and design within the timetable is acknowledged, and fiercely protected. However, art and design is also threaded through the whole curriculum. 'It's a vehicle through which to learn. We're using certain materials and resources … we make things as a way of finding out. This way of thinking changes the way you teach. Science is a way of looking at the world, RE is another. Art and design is just one of many different lenses.'

Grafton School has participated in the National Gallery's Take One Picture programme for a number of years. Schools across the United Kingdom are invited to respond to a focus painting from the Collection, and to submit the pupils' cross-curricular responses to the annual Take One Picture display at the National Gallery. Grafton cite a number of reasons for their experience of the programme being a significant stimulus for initiating art and design in the school: connecting with the Gallery established the message within the school that art is important; it is easy to introduce to the staff, and the flexibility in approach means that they retain ownership; and the children now know that the National Gallery paintings, being the nation's collection, belong to them.

They introduced the programme through an annual arts week but now use the picture for a half-term focus, feeding a number of subjects. 'Rather than a dollop of art and design, it is healthy for children to have it regularly and frequently throughout the year. However, some art is better than no art. We had to start off like that. Another example is black history week. It started off as a week, but we were quick to embed it into our already culturally diverse curriculum.'

Regarding teaching for creativity, staff embed the teaching of skills within bigger projects so that pupils are able to use their newly-acquired skills to express their own ideas which are developed through a given project, over a number of lessons. The shape of these units vary: some start with philosophical enquiry or making and then narrow, while others start off with, for example, observation and drawing and then develop according to the children's responses, for example into writing or painting. Drawing and observation are part of each unit, as is the development of visual literacy. 'Visual literacy is equally important to reading and writing. It helps them to see the world in a different way and to appreciate it. Then they can even look at a piece of chewing gum on the floor and notice things about it – for example, the contrasts in colour. So the world doesn't become dreary any more.'

Medium-term plans ensure that children encounter a range of experiences, tools and media during their time in the school. Progression is considered too. For example, pupils return to some of the same materials in Year 2 as Year 1, but they use them in a more sophisticated way or in response to a more challenging stimulus. Progression is also a key feature in the systems for assessment. At the end of each unit, pupils' reflections are sought about each stage of the process they have experienced. Most of the teachers' judgements are made during lessons. Attainment targets have been broken down into different aspects (e.g., observation, experimentation) and also into steps which the most confident staff are able to hold in their heads. Rather than an onerous burden, the teachers look and listen while the children are in process and note any significant comment or action. It is seen as a way of getting to know the children, which makes future planning easier.

While structures are in place that support planning, there is also a general agreement that flexibility within and between lessons is very important. 'If you say, "that's interesting, but I need to stick to my plan", then you are going to miss something amazing. If you go with the children, they take ownership, they value it, their self-esteem builds and then they learn more. It's about being prepared but not planning everything. It takes confidence.'

Teachers identify the danger of this approach as the potential fracturing of focus and a subsequent lack of quality in the outcomes. To avoid this, certain limitations are imposed. For example, if the focus is colour mixing, the palette is limited or alternatively the size of paper. If the focus is on line drawing and where things are in relation to each other, colour is not introduced. By focusing on certain components, space is left for children's individuality.

Following the lead set by teachers, pupils also take risks. Pupils in one class have even coined a term for those unexpected things that happen when you are exploring materials. They described it as a 'happy accident' when the colour ran when they applied glue to tissue paper, and the term stuck.

Children experience a wide range of sources of inspiration. For example, when designing and making costumes inspired by the Ditchley portrait,★ the pupils used the following as their frames of reference: Tudor portraiture; the costumes in Veronese's *The Family of Darius before Alexander*;★★ and the work of Alexander McQueen. Through discussion, pupils compared and contrasted the different materials and designs, and offered up their own personal responses. They noticed the protective appearance of the padding in the Tudor portraits, which progressed to a wider exploration of protective clothing. The project coincided with Lady Gaga's meat dress which the children were particularly fascinated by. This led on to further inspiration from the designs of Andrew Logan and Zandra Rhodes, including the crushing up of old CDs. A number of elements were brought together in the pupils' final, highly original designs which involved unexpected components, for example the use of metal mesh and a vacuum hose.

Implications for the primary classroom

Having explored why the visual arts are ripe for developing pupils' creativity and gained an insight into how one particular school manages the inherent challenges within the primary school, what conclusions can we draw as to the values, experiences and relationships that foster creativity in the visual arts?

Values

In any school a broad and balanced curriculum does not happen by accident; it is a considered decision driven by the senior leadership team and, ultimately, the headteacher. The disproportionate emphasis on attainment in English and mathematics by politicians, inspection bodies and the press means that unless one is certain of the value of art education for its own sake, and the powerful relationship between attainment in the visual arts and that in other subjects, then it will almost certainly become a casualty of the overburdened timetable.

Conversely, it becomes a tangible trademark in schools where the headteacher champions art education as an opportunity for the fostering of pupils' creativity; as a valuable skill-set and potential career option; as an intellectual pursuit; and for the development of pupils' understanding of themselves within the society in which they live. Teachers with similar values are attracted to these schools and the core belief infuses every area of school life. There is a vibrancy and energy that is expressed tangibly in the learning environment but also in the attitudes of the staff and pupils.

Valuing art education has a number of practical implications, most notably staff professional development and planning for experience. Lack of confidence around art-making is something that many people take into adulthood, and into teaching. It is perhaps the only subject where one believes from an early age that one either 'can' or 'cannot'. This insecurity can also distort the significance of teaching art skills in relation to the other aspects such as looking at art, learning about artists, and the development of a personal response. This can be another reason why the subject may not be prioritised or why pupils are left to their own devices. Some schools address this lack of confidence by investing in professional development led by a confident practitioner within the school (if they are fortunate enough to have one), or otherwise by sharing expertise across schools through joint training. These opportunities not only build a skills-base that the pupils can benefit from, but also enable staff, if enough time is given, to experience the joy of the creative process for themselves, and so renew their commitment to creating the opportunity for their pupils to do the same.

Schools may also invest in freelance artists to lead specific projects, working over a period of time with class (or classes) to provide both specialist skills and the important opportunity for pupils to engage with people who make art for a living. The presence of an artist does not guarantee a creative experience for pupils, however. Indeed, planning for creativity is easier when one knows the children well. It is only when pupils are empowered to make their own creative decisions that they make their own personal connections and expressions. The benefit of working with an artist is increased when an opportunity for staff training is built into their residency. Then staff experience the learning process for themselves while also deepening their understanding and pre-empting some of the issues that will arise when working with pupils.

Art and design is one of a number of vulnerable curriculum subjects in a timetable dominated by the giants of English and mathematics. This is true of both pupil time within the school day but also, and importantly, the amount of time that the average teacher is able to devote to planning and resourcing the subject. As a result, it is easy to focus on activities and outcomes in art and design, particularly if one is planning for single lessons often at short notice, or when one has a particular display in mind and an idea of how one wants it to look. While these lessons may be enjoyable, this reductionist approach may subliminally reinforce both the teachers' and the pupils' view that art and design does not have any particular value or purpose.

The emphasis on product over process is symptomatic of a system which prizes measurable outcomes that are conducive to an assessment-driven curriculum. It is easier to assess demonstrable knowledge, understanding and skills; it is far harder to quantify originality of thought or vibrancy of imagination. These messages are communicated to children in all sorts of ways both explicitly and implicitly; for example, through what we say and perhaps more importantly through what is not said or acknowledged. Encouraging creativity involves noticing and praising children's originality of thought and action. And of course children need the opportunity to demonstrate these before this is possible. Capturing these moments, either through annotated photographs or the noting of a child's verbal contribution, creates a holistic picture of a child's attainment and achievement. When this approach is shared across the school and becomes part of the ethos, the confidence to take risks increases dramatically.

Some schools acknowledge the pressure on time by devoting specific weeks of the school year to art and design, as one might for science or design technology. This helps to raise the profile of the subject and provides the opportunity to build in longer blocks of time for independent and collaborative working. Pressure on the timetable and on time for teachers to plan is also eased when art and design is embedded within the broader context of the focus of the term or half-term, rather than being kept as a separate, often marginalised entity. In this way the knowledge, skills and understanding of different subjects support each other and coherence is brought to a potentially fragmented curriculum. So too, when a context is shared across subjects, a greater depth of exploration is enabled because of the time saved in establishing each new context. In turn, learning becomes more meaningful and ultimately more satisfying.

In the majority of schools there is a perception that art education is important but it is not sufficiently understood and articulated to withstand or, more realistically, to support the more immediate demands of the core subjects. Fortunately every teacher has the power at their disposal to eschew these values within their own classroom. The values one holds either individually or corporately determine the experiences that one provides.

Experiences

For children to engage in a creative process requires continuity both within and between lessons. It requires enough time for children to bring themselves to the situation, to make those meaningful connections with their personal knowledge, ideas and experiences. The teacher plays the pivotal role in enabling the children to engage their own memories, critical thinking and imagination. It does not often happen automatically, particularly if it is not embedded or expected across the school. The teacher is the gatekeeper; they hold the key to unlocking the pupils' potential. The challenge (and joy) is that the key for every child is different. Dwelling on this is both exciting and overwhelming. Fortunately there are certain things the teacher can do which are helpful in unlocking the creativity of all children.

The first are the decisions the teacher makes in advance of each unit of work: for example, in deciding on the overarching focus; the selection of artists for investigation and related opportunities for experiencing art work in situ; the strategies and key questions for guiding the looking experience; the skills that will be taught; the opportunities for pupils to make their own choices, both considered and intuitive; the limitations that will maintain a supportive focus; and the media that will be used. Outcomes are also important to consider at this point, although these may evolve as the unit progresses. There may be one but are more likely to be a variety over the course of the unit. These may also be physical or sensory; analogue or digital; permanent or temporary. One may also give prior thought to how the unit will be displayed in such a way that creativity is celebrated. For example, very simply, can children's individual choices be demonstrated by showcasing parts of the process as well as the final outcomes?

Linked to the emphasis on process is the importance of keeping the bigger picture in mind at all times when planning. Parallels can be made with the teaching of English in this regard. Instruction on the use of a full stop or comma is meaningless until it is considered in the context of writing, with the reader in mind. Then it becomes a tool that one can use with power – and the writer feels powerful. In the same way, the syntax of art and design (for example colour, tone, composition) are helpful in both the discussion and the making of art. One may focus on one or another, or instruct on the use of a particular tool or technique, but an art work is more than the sum of its parts. When a pupil can use the elements to express themselves, rather than as an end in itself, then creativity can flourish.

Second are the decisions that are made within and between lessons. These rely on observing pupils and listening to them with a critical eye and ear. One can be organised and resourced – indeed it is essential that one is – but the focus has shifted to planning for an experience and the children play a significant part in determining the future direction of the project. Things might be added, omitted or changed from the original plans according to what pupils say or do; for example, the selection of other artists' work for consideration or extra instruction on the use of a particular material. This is also where it can come down to the individual child – enabling them to follow their own particular areas of interest. The better one knows the children, the more subtle the necessary changes will be.

While opportunities for creative thinking are provided by the asking of genuinely open, key questions identified beforehand in relation to particular sources of inspiration, the responses to children's answers are of equal if not more importance. Responses can be verbal or non-verbal – both are equally powerful to the child. By valuing pupils' opinions, withholding one's own judgement and rather enabling other pupils to respond and build upon them, an atmosphere of trust is established and an environment is created where personal connections are not only permitted but expected. It is into this atmosphere that challenge can be introduced as an important means of testing and exploring different ideas and opinions.

As well as the teacher's subject knowledge, the success of both the planning and leading discussion relies on the teacher knowing their pupils – their strengths, weaknesses, fears and interests – and on the way that they perceive the pupil. This takes us back to the teacher's values and relates directly to the relationships that are established in the classroom.

Relationships

The most significant relationship in developing pupils' creativity is that of the teacher and pupil.

One of the challenges with the visual arts specific to the primary context is managing the shift in role of the teacher at different stages of a unit of work, most critically from that of instructor to facilitator. In a secondary school the students move to the art room which looks and feels different to the more formal set-up of the regular classroom. Pupils arrive ready for a different kind of experience and a different relationship with their teacher. In the primary school, both teachers and pupils are required to make that shift without any physical or personal distinction, which can be difficult to manage for both the teacher and the pupil. Being aware of this tension enables the teacher to manage it more effectively by, for example, changing the way they use the space or in the communication of their expectations.

Another tension that exists in the teacher–pupil relationship within art and design education in particular is in the nature of the teacher's intervention while the children are exploring ideas or making. At the two extremes are no intervention at all, for fear of inhibiting the child's creative flow, and explicit direction at each stage. This applies to the behaviour of every adult, not just the teacher. Both approaches may be driven by a number of factors other than one's beliefs about a child's creativity; for example, personality or the pressure of time.

Clearly there is a place for both types of intervention, but it is helpful to refer back to the values that one holds with regard to children's creativity in order to determine the timing and nature of each. When children are equipped with the relevant skills, inspiration and level of challenge, they require and relish the time to explore the possibilities for themselves. However, intervention of a supportive and expansive nature can be helpful and is sometimes necessary to assist pupils within this process. On occasion it may require direct instruction or the offering of an 'expert' opinion, preferably invited by the child, but usually a carefully-phrased prompt is much more effective. Adults often have to consciously rein in a tendency to jump in, often unsolicited, and instead take that moment longer to watch and identify the appropriate question or observation which supports the pupil in working something out for themselves. In this way the control remains with the child and their confidence remains intact. It is by overcoming challenges for themselves that pupils develop the stamina and perseverance needed to learn independently.

In the context of the primary classroom, high-quality, individual exchanges with all pupils on a regular basis are not a realistic proposition. There are, however, more opportunities for pupils to reflect independently or in pairs. It is worth modeling and supporting this process – the rewards are enormous.

The importance of expecting and enabling pupils to find their own solutions to the challenge set cannot be underestimated. By providing the opportunity to do so and by encouraging pupils' to work through their ideas, an intangible transaction takes place. The child moves from being at best a compliant bystander to an active decision-maker. The subsequent motivation that they experience as a result of this sense of ownership enables them to exert some control over the direction in which the process is going. They develop the confidence to communicate their ideas because they are now 'within' the process, rather than simply a willing onlooker. Children who experience this will want to talk about their work. They can explain their decisions and speak with pride about the difficulties they encountered and the steps they took to overcome them.

As well as the mutually supportive relationships between staff within schools mentioned above, there are also significant relationships with other teaching communities. Although they are thin on the ground, seeking out professional development and networking opportunities are significant in building, invigorating and sharing expertise.

Creative touches

Suggestions for developing opportunities for creativity in the visual arts:

- Reflect on your own art education: your confidences and fears. What advantages do they bring? What would be the first step in overcoming any barriers?
- Find stimuli that will enable children to engage with 'big' ideas.
- Expose pupils to a range of cultural heritages.
- Look for relevant links across the curriculum.
- Raise questions that prompt reflection and encourage the pupils to do the same.
- Enable children to experience original artworks as often as possible.
- Plan sequences of lessons where skills are taught and practised, but with a view to the children using them to explore and express their own ideas.
- Empower children with the language to talk about art.

- Build in opportunities for extended blocks of time for children to explore and create, so that the momentum that has built up can be capitalised upon.

- Make time to watch and listen to pupils.

- Respond to the children during and between lessons and be prepared to be flexible with your plans.

- Demonstrate the value of the process as well as the end product.

- Plan for experiences that will engage all of the senses.

- Praise children's thinking and encourage originality.

- Look out for local arts events and training opportunities for your own inspiration and learning.

References

Addison, N. and Burgess, L. (eds) (2003). *Issues in Art and Design Teaching*. Oxford: Routledge Falmer.

Dewey, J. (1934). *Art as Experience*. New York: Minton, Balch & Co.

Dewey, J. (1938). *Experience and Education*. New York: Simon & Schuster.

Eisner, E. W. (1972). *Educating Artistic Vision*. New York: Macmillan.

Fawcett, M. and Hay, P. (2004). 5x5x5 Creativity in the Early Years. *The International Journal of Art and Design Education (iJADE)*, Vol. 23, No. 3.

Fisher, R. (2009). *Creative Dialogue. Talk for Thinking in the Classroom*. London: Routledge.

Fryer, M. (1996). *Creative Teaching and Learning*. London: Paul Chapman.

Gardner, H., (1999). *Intelligence Reframed. Multiple intelligences for the 21st century*. New York: Basic Books.

Hallam, J., Lee, H. and Gupta, M. D. (eds) (2007). An Analysis of the Presentation of Art in the National Primary School Curriculum and its Implications for Teaching. *iJADE*, Vol. 26, No. 2.

Herne, S., Cox, S. and Watts, R. (eds) (2009). *Readings in Primary Art Education*. Bristol: Intellect.

Hickman, R. (2005). *Why we Make Art and why it is Taught*. Bristol: Intellect.

Lowenfeld, V. (1947). *Creative and Mental Growth*. New York: Macmillan.

Jones, L. (1996). 1,000 Teachers Can't be Wrong. *RSA Journal*, Vol. CXLIV, No. 5472, August/September.

Piaget. J. and Inhelder, B. (1958). *The Growth of Logical Thinking from Childhood to Adolescence*. London: Routledge.

Read, H. (1963). *Education Through Art*. London: Faber and Faber.

Robinson, K. (ed.) (1989). *The Arts in Schools. Principles, Practice and Provision*. London: Calouste Gulbenkian Foundation.

Steers, J. (2009). Creativity: Delusions, Realities, Opportunities and Challenges. *iJADE,* Vol. 28, No. 2.

Taylor, R. (1986). *Educating for Art*. London: Longman.

Thomas, K. (2010). What is the Relationship between Social Tact in the Teacher–Pupil Exchanges and Creativity? Reconceptualising Functional Causes of Creativity in Artmaking. *iJADE*, Vol. 29. No. 2.

Watts, R. (2005). Attitudes to Making Art in the Primary School. *iJADE*, Vol. 24, No. 3.

Witkin, R. (1974). *The Intelligence of Feeling*. London: Heinemann.

Queen Elizabeth 1 (The Ditchley portrait), Marcus Gheerhaerts the Younger, c. 1592, National Portrait Gallery.

**The Family of Darius before Alexander*, Paolo Veronese, 1565–7, National Gallery.

11

Creativity Across the Curriculum

Russell Jones and Dominic Wyse

As we write these final words the National Curriculum in England is still under review:

> Instead of new curricula for English, mathematics, science and PE being introduced from 2013 – and any other subjects in 2014 – the new curriculum for all subjects will now be introduced in 2014. (Department for Education, 2012, online)

The most positive aspect of the Conservative–Liberal Democrat coalition government's ideology is that there appears to be some genuine commitment to 'allowing' schools to have more freedom in their curriculum development, although this is given most freely to schools who sign up to other government agendas such as becoming academies. But the rhetoric of more control being given to teachers is contradicted by parallel initiatives such as the phonics test for six-year-olds, or the decision to only have grammar, punctuation and spelling as part of the externally marked statutory assessments of writing for Year 6 pupils. The result of this contradiction is likely be narrowing of the curriculum, as a result of inspection pressures, comparisons of school and teacher scores, payment by results (if carried out) and other accountability measures that will bolster the changes.

The decision to ignore (and remove) the new primary curriculum, developed as a result of the New Labour review of the National Curriculum, smacks of political ideology rather than balanced consideration of evidence. Two things in particular were welcome in the New Labour curriculum: the replacement of curriculum subjects with areas of learning, enabling a sensible match with the Early Years Foundation Stage, and, as we mentioned in our introduction, the greater emphasis on more active forms of creativity. The central rationale for the new (new) coalition curriculum is the perceived need to compete in international league tables of pupil attainment. This seems a rather barren rationale and vision for what society might want for its nation's children.

Consistent with the development of the National Curriculum since its inception from 1988, the core subjects of maths, English and science are the first to have draft programmes of study. The detail (and in some cases their place in the curriculum at all) of all other subjects in the curriculum (apart from PE) remain unclear. But the decision to have a subject-based curriculum rather than one based on themes and pupil–teacher choice, or broader areas of learning, or competencies (like the RSA curriculum), or transdisciplinary themes (like the international baccalaureate), or other models such as those in Northern Ireland, Scotland and Wales (Wyse et. al., 2012), carries with it many risks that have been documented in relation to the previous National Curriculum in England.

In view of these constraints that teachers work under, building genuinely creative classrooms is not going to happen without commitment, determination, idealism and energy. But what the contributors to this book have shown us are the many possibilities for starting and building creative classrooms and schools. To conclude the book we offer some of the ideas that cut across most of the chapters.

First and foremost, our approach requires some adjustments in ways of thinking. There are many benefits from becoming a 'creative advocate' in your setting. This applies not only to experienced teachers but equally to beginning teachers or to those seeking to work differently. Look for opportunities to lead creative thinking in planning meetings, and seek opportunities to counteract bureaucratic processes. Plan spaces for learners and teachers – a 'creativity week' or a 'cross-curricular week' might be the starting point that could bring together creative energies. There will be other colleagues who are waiting for someone to open doors; you could be the catalyst for those first creative steps in the school. We want to reconceptualise the role of the teacher as not just an organiser and presenter of content but as an innovative leader or an 'explorer' within the curriculum. Schools need to be places of investigation for learners and teacher alike. Always seek to locate those 'What if …?' questions in the classroom and in the staffroom. Even when questioning takes a walk to a dead end, the process of exploring questions is itself a creative one and establishes the principle that 'norms' and 'traditions' are to be explored and challenged.

We need to continue to explore the idea that creativity is not unique to arts-based subjects. The guiding principles and creative challenges that all authors promote here are applicable across the curriculum. We have seen that some headteachers have art as a curriculum priority, and seek a vibrancy, energy and colour that are highly visible in learning environments. As experienced teachers, we are familiar with these settings and we recognise those tangible features, but there are no reasons why this should be ascribed only to arts-based subjects. We would advocate this same vibrancy and energy across the entire curriculum and not just the visual arts. There are settings that burst with scientific or historical energy that are equally exciting and creative environments.

For some children (and for some educators), those first few creative steps are likely to be tentative. If these steps are met with criticism, resistance and dismissal, they are unlikely to progress. Many children are used to a diet of instruction, strict guidance and formal assessment; they will need to be supported and encouraged when the 'rules' begin to change.

After considering the ideas and evidence presented in this book, the role and value of talk in the creative process is paramount. Regardless of the curriculum area, talk is a key component of creativity, and teachers can begin to examine their own practices to seek out opportunities for talk to be foregrounded. Talk allows learners to communicate their ideas and gives teachers the opportunity to evaluate, reflect, discuss and facilitate creative outcomes. Talk also allows learners to share ideas and develop collaborative, democratic strategies to test hypotheses, solve problems and raise more questions. All this begins with the teacher who understands and plans for productive talk in the classroom.

For us, one of the most damning elements of contemporary education is that far too often, children will say that they never seem to have time to finish their work. Clearly, there are times when lessons are self-contained or when they exist in small, interrelated sequences of lessons, but there is a need for children to push beyond those boundaries and to follow lines of their own interest. Teachers need to seek out the necessary space in their planning so that pupils can follow lines of inquiry through to completion. In maths, in science, in creative writing, across the complete curriculum, there needs to be opportunity built in for children to follow at least some of their ideas through to completion and this needs to be decided at the curriculum planning stage. If this is not carefully managed by teachers then some children will experience a steady diet of short, self-contained, closed tasks that are completed as a matter of course, and spaces for more creative engagement will be left abandoned and never reach completion. This happens too frequently in the name of curriculum coverage. Teachers need to develop the (collective and collaborative) courage to defend and protect the space that children need to complete their creative lines of inquiry.

We are very taken by the idea of generosity. Creativity requires generosity as it encourages teachers to step away from what *they* want from a lesson and instead accept that there are other outcomes, other possibilities and other objectives that can all be achieved outside the original lesson plan. This is not easily done and it by no means suggests that teachers merely abandon their planning; it simply establishes the case that unless teachers demonstrate some generosity in the pedagogical ethos in their classrooms they are extremely unlikely to ever achieve creative outcomes.

Do not be overwhelmed by formal documentation or by the objectives set for lessons. We have seen several examples here of work that has been carried out within National Curriculum frameworks and with specific objectives planned, but which have evolved into highly creative endeavours. Your lessons should have shape and purpose, typically guided by clear ideas about what you want children to learn, but inquiry should never be limited to objectives. Learners and teachers should be equally aware that sometimes there are other avenues of exploration, other possibilities and other outcomes which do not mean that pre-planned objectives have failed, but may mean that better learning is taking place.

Welcome the unexpected, the unpredictable and the unconventional. Whilst planning, be prepared for contributions and suggestions that you will not have predicted. This is not a failure on your part; it is always going to happen if your classrooms become more creative places. Look for connections. In your discussions with pupils there will be opportunities for you to make new connections or to encourage children to make new connections for themselves. Demonstrating the ways that new connections lead to unexpected outcomes means you visibly value and support that process. If you are proactive, and passionate about notions of possibility, then you will encourage others to follow your lead.

Above all, be courageous. Creative classrooms are not easy places to build; they do not happen because you followed a set of 'tips' that resulted in work that looks impressive on the wall. There will be times when you will be frustrated, exhausted and under pressure to take simpler routes through the day, but these are also the times when you need to be courageous. Risk-taking may not come easily at first, but the more it becomes part of your professional being, the more it will yield creative results in your classroom. The ethos and atmosphere that saturates every chapter in this book takes considerable courage and commitment – creativity comes at a price. It is not a casual, 'do as you like' approach; we have seen that it is based on highly skilled, professional interactions in the hands of teachers who understand learning processes, who understand the needs and abilities of their pupils, and who are prepared to be industrious and resourceful with that knowledge to establish creative climates in schools.

References

Department for Education (2012). *National Curriculum Review Update*. Accessed 1 May 2012. Available from: http://www.education.gov.uk/schools/teachingandlearning/curriculum/nationalcurriculum/a0075667/national-curriculum-review-update.

Wyse, D., Baumfield, V., Egan, D., Gallagher, C., Hayward, L., Hulme, M., Leitch, R., Livingston, K., Menter, I. and Lingard, B. (2012). *Creating the Curriculum*. London: Routledge.

Index

academies 162
accent 19
accountability 4
   structures 133
achievement 58, 75, 77
Ackerman, Edward 101
Action Plan for Geography 112
active learning 57
active storytelling 138–9
activities 55, 57, 69, 120, 124, 127, 132, 134,
     156
   child-led 105
   classroom 132
   Design and Technology 68, 77
   group 127
   learning 106, 107, 131
   musical 132, 143
   problem-finding 144
   problem-solving 144
adulthood 34
aerial imagery 106
affective development 135
after-school clubs 146
agency 85, 131–5, 136
   learner 144
   musical 144
   pupil 141
All Our Futures: Creativity, Culture and
   Education 5, 117
Almond, David 9
ambiguity 89
American Psychological Association 2
analytical thinking 134

Angel of the North 1–2
anthropocene 101
archive centres 125
art 116, 117, 119, 149
art and design 149
art education 150
   value 155
art materials 151, 152
artefacts 122–3
artist in residence 153
artists 3, 155
assemblies 84
assessment 7, 20, 37, 75, 153, 156, 164
   procedure 42
   psychometric 2
   self-assessment 139
   summative 7
   writing 162
attainment 155, 163
   targets 154
authentic contexts 107
authentic learning 51
authenticity 72, 121
autonomy 120

baccalaureate, international 163
backing tracks 142
Be a Mathematician (BEAM) 46
BEAM *see* Be a Mathematician
beginning teachers 1, 145, 163
Big Book of Brain Games, The 47
bilingualism 19–20
Blists Hill Museum 123

Boal, Augusto 138
body language 85
Bono, Edward de 4, 138
brainstorming 4
Britishness 119
broadband 133
Brunel, Isambard Kingdom 121, 122
bullying 89

cameras, digital 105, 126
CapeUK 109
CARA *see* Creativity Action Research
    Awards
case studies 36
celebration 146
Child Art Movement 149, 151
child development 89
childhood 150
child-led activity 105
children's geographies 108
choice 27, 105, 120
    pedagogical 76
Churchill, Winston 78, 119
Cizek, Franz 149
class-based work 106
classical music 3
classroom
    social setting 59
classroom activity 56, 132
classroom drama 84
classroom ethos 59
Clegg, Alec 21
climate change 101
cognition 70
cognitive learning 57
cognitive limitations 70
cognitive responses 105
collaboration 57, 145–6, 152
collaborative classroom ethos 51
collaborative creativity 57
collaborative engagement 85
collaborative exploration 83
collaborative geography 107–9
collaborative learning 124, 132
collage 23–6
collegiality 145
commercial practice 71

common sense 73
communication 119
    expressive 130
community discourse 132
Compare bears 39
competence, emotional 79
competencies 163
composing 133, 134, 135
compromise 110
computers 133
conceptual knowledge 55
conferences, writing 22, 28
confidence 134, 159
conflict, value 14
connections 42, 44
    creative 83
conscience alley 121
Conservative–Liberal Democrat coalition 162
constructivism 55–8, 68
content approach 68
content knowledge 35
contextual knowledge 68
contextualised learning 74
contingency 36
Continuing Professional Development (CPD)
    34
    mathematics 34
conversations, creative 61
core subjects 163
costing 77
CP *see* Creative Partnerships
CPD *see* Continuing Professional
    Development
'creative conjecture' 11, 58
creative connections 83
creative conversations 61
creative development 135
creative engagement 83, 87
creative exploration model 56
creative learning 52–3, 138
Creative Partnerships (CP) 5–6, 7, 54, 109,
    135
creative planning 137
creative process 1, 13, 17, 73, 74, 78, 139
creative reasoning 60
creative responses 54, 62
creative teaching 52–3

creative thinking 131, 157
    leading 163
creative writing 21–2, 125
Creativity Action Research Awards (CARA)
    104, 109
creativity research 2
Creativity Wheel 54, 59
Cresswell, Helen 17–18
critical questioning 117
critical thinking 112, 122, 157
criticism 29
cross-curricular teaching 77, 119
Crossley-Holland, Kevin 90
Csikszentmihályi, Mihaly 2–3, 17
cultural diversity 153
cultural heritage 119
curiosity 85, 105, 107, 130, 131
curriculum *see also* National Curriculum 13,
    21, 69, 77, 78, 83, 86, 89, 94, 103
    assessment driven 156
    development 162
    framework 112
    language 19–20
    literacy 19–20
    music 132
    planners 67
    provision 63
    RSA 163
    structures 117
    subject-based 119, 163

D&T *see* Design and Technology
Darling, Grace 118
Dear Greenpeace 95
decision making 46, 70
Design and Technology (D&T)
    activities 68, 77
    teachers 66
design technology 54, 116
development
    affective 135
    creative 135
development geography 98
developmental interdependence hypothesis 20
developmental psychology 150
Dewey, John 150
DfES *see* Education and Skills, Department for

dialect 19
dialogic classroom 51
dialogic enquiry 55
dialogic space 58
dialogue 54, 71, 145
    group 144
difference 90
digital cameras 105, 126
digital maps 106
discomfort, emotional 72
discovery 99, 111, 117
    geographic 101
discussion 53, 158
    groups 120, 122, 131
Ditchley portrait (Elizabeth I) 154
diversity 90
documentation 164
domain knowledge 68
drama 13, 14, 116, 120
    classroom 84
    improvisational 83
    process 84, 85, 86, 89, 95
    story 84
    techniques 34
dramatic tension 86
drawing 153
    skills 149

Early Years Foundation Stage 42, 86, 162
East London Dance 131
Eccentric Questioning 137–8
Edison, Thomas 56
Education and Skills, Department for (DfES)
    6
Education Select Committee 7
Education Through Art 150
Education White Paper, 2010, 100
Einstein, Albert 4
Eisner, Elliot 150, 151
e-learning 117
electronics 68
Elephant in the Classroom, The 33–4
emotion 72–3
    negative 72–3
emotional competence 79
emotional discomfort 72
emotional engagement 73, 74

emotional intelligences 123
emotional investment 72
emotional literacy 74, 118
emotional response 23, 105
empathic geography 109–11
empathy 85, 89, 95, 103, 110
    musical 130
engagement 53, 145
    creative 87
    imaginative 87, 91
English (as second language) 20
English Heritage 123
    events 84
enquiry 103, 111, 117
enquiry-based work 116
enterprise 71
Entertaining Mathematical Puzzles 47
environment 101
    St Lucia 104, 109–11
ethical principles 89
ethnic minorities 117
European Union 7
evolutionary development 70
examination, public 71
Excellence and Enjoyment 6, 117
Excitement of Writing, The 21
expectation 72, 131, 138, 158
experience
    first-hand 104
    imagined 88, 89
experienced teachers 163
experimentation 29, 45, 145
exploration 151
    geographic 101, 103, 106
exploratory talk 62
exploratory thought 123
expressive communication 130
extrinsic motivation 4, 10, 21

facial expression 85
factors 36
facts 102
factual information 99
failure 34, 78
Family of Darius before Alexander, The 154
fear of failure 34
feedback 29, 40, 146

Feldman, David 17
fieldwork 100, 103, 104, 106, 107, 126–7
film 107
first-hand experience 104
Foreman, Michael 95
Foundation Stage 105
fractions 40
freeze framing 85, 87, 90, 94, 121
Fridaskolan 11
Fry, Richard 150
Fry, Roger 149

GA *see* Geographical Association
Gaiman, Neil 28–9
games, video 130
GarageBand 134, 142
García Márquez, Gabriel 18
Gardener, Howard 17
gender differences 93
Geographical Association (GA) 99
    manifesto 102
geography 116
    children's 108
    collaborative 107–9
    empathic 109–11
gesture 85
gifted children 117
globes 101
Goodnight Mister Tom 121, 125
Google Earth 103
Gormley, Anthony 1–2
    Angel of the North 1–2
grammar 22
Graves, Donald 27
Great Britain (steamship) 122
Greder, Armin 93
Green Children, The 90, 93
Griffiths, Neil 105
group sculptures 87, 93
group work 52, 84, 124
groups 45
    discussion 120, 122, 131
    mixed ability 57
    problem solving 117
guided map-making 136
Guildford, J. P. 2
Guitar World Hero Tour 130

Gulf of Mexico
  oil spill 61

Hampton Court Palace 123
handwriting 22
Harry Potter (character) 22
'h-creative' acts 135
headteachers 163
His Dark Materials 17
historic sites 123
history 13
  local 124, 125–7
  oral 121–2, 127
History in the Balance 118
hot seating 85, 88, 121
human experiences 119
human geography 98

ICT 116, 126
identity 132, 151
imagination 99, 111, 112, 116, 117, 123,
    133, 136, 144, 157
imaginative engagement 87, 91
Imaginative Play (Piaget) 135
imaginative thinking 107, 116
imaginativeness 146
imagined experience 88, 89
Imitation (Piaget) 135
immersion 146
Imperial War Museum, Manchester 116,
    121
Importance of Music, The 130
improvisation 83, 84, 88, 95, 132, 133, 134,
    135, 142
  structured 84
independence 70
independence of thought 130
independent learning 116, 127
independent thinking 123, 130
Indiana Jones 143
individuality 150, 152
industrial practice 71
industry, leaders 67
inference squares 59
inferences 123
information
  accessing 68

factual 99
  sharing 61
information technology 30
initiative 70
Inner London Education Authority 27
innovation 72, 85, 146
  pedagogic 145
insight 95
inspection 162
inspirational spaces 145
Institute for Prospective Technological
    Studies (IPTS) 7
instruments, musical 133, 139
intellectual development 58
interactive approaches 116
interactive whiteboard 75, 94
interior monologues 87
international baccalaureate 163
internet 103, 106, 124, 137
interpretation 95
interthinking 62
intonation 85
intrinsic motivation 4, 10, 21
investigation 53, 106, 151
IPTS *see* Institute for Prospective
    Technological Studies
Island, The 93

James, Simon 95
Journey, The 105
judgement 13

KAL *see* knowledge about language
Kelly's Directory of Cheshire 125
Key Stage 1 121, 123, 124
Key Stage 2 6, 69, 86, 119, 121, 124, 125
Key Stage 3 6, 69
Key Stage 4 6
King, Stephen 18
knowledge 70, 119
  base 68
  conceptual 55
  contextual 68
  domain 68
  personal 132
  process 68
  professional 103

subject 112, 124
knowledge about language (KAL) 19–20

Lady Gaga 154
landscapes 108–9
Langer, Suzanne 150
language 17, 29, 57, 85, 95, 123
    acquisition 19
    curriculum 19–20
    development 19
    planning 28
    teaching 28
lateral thinking 91
leaders of industry 67
league tables 163
learner agency 85
    profiling 144
learning 105, 117, 142
    active 57
    activities 106, 107, 120, 131
    authentic 51
    cognitive 57
    collaborative 124, 132
    contextualised 74
    creative 52–3, 138
    experiences 45, 48, 69, 133, 136
    independent 116, 127
    opportunities 90, 133, 142
    out of school 116, 121, 123
    outcomes 137
    personalised 117
    process 12, 73, 74, 120
    spaces 143
    trajectory 55
Learning Journals 138–9, 142
lesson planning 11
lesson plans 11
Libeskind, Daniel 116
libraries 125
life experience 85
linguistic responses 27
listening 134
    skills 122
literacy 86, 116, 118
    curriculum 19–20
    emotional 74
    sessions 87–9

skills 75
    visual 153
literature 17
Little Red Riding Hood 107
local history 124, 125–7
Local History Top Ten Features 124
Logan, Andrew 154

Machine Gunners, The 121
Manchester, Imperial War Museum 116, 121
Mann, Scott 105
map-making, guided 136
mapping 146
maps 101, 125
    digital 106
Mastery (Piaget) 135
mathematical thinking 35
mathematical vocabulary 41
mathematics 12, 86, 89
    learning 42–7
    negative attitudes 33
    teaching 42–7
Mathematics Counts 33
McQueen, Alexander 154
meaning 95
'meaning making' 100
media 77, 133
media technologies 111
memories 157
memory 105
mentoring, peer 145
Mercator's projection 101
metacognition 8
Metacognition (Piaget) 135
metacognitive processes 70
meta-menus 59
mime 85
mind-maps 4
mixed ability 39
    groups 57
mobile phones 103
models 123
moral codes 89
motivation 12, 21, 27, 28, 69, 71, 76, 107, 108
    extrinsic 4, 10, 21
    intrinsic 4, 10, 21

Mozart, Wolfgang Amadeus 4
multi-culturalism 119
multi-lingualism 19
multi-literacy 22
multiples 36
music 116, 117, 119
   activities 132
   classical 3
   curriculum 132
   listening 136
   software 130, 134, 142
   theory 136
musical agency 144
musical empathy 130
musical instruments 133, 139
music-making 133, 143
   activities 143

NACCCE 5–6
National Curriculum *see also* curriculum 6,
   7–8, 10, 11, 29, 112, 119, 150, 162, 163
   frameworks 164
   New Labour review 162
   online version 7
   Wales 8
   website 8
National Gallery
   Take One Picture programme 153
National Literacy Strategy 9
National Portrait Gallery 122
   website 122
National Trust 123
NCETM (website) 47
negative emotions 72–3
networking 145, 159
neuroscience 20
New Labour 162
   National Curriculum review 162
new technologies 66
Nightingale, Florence 121
Northern Ireland 7, 8, 10, 163
novice teachers 44
NRICH (website) 46–7
Nuffield Primary History Project
   Local History Top Ten Features 124
number patterns 36
numeracy 37, 118

objectives 164
observation 61, 87, 152, 153, 157, 159
Ofsted 63, 86, 118, 119
oil spill, Gulf of Mexico 61
Okri, Ben 9
One Hundred Years of Solitude 18
One World 95
open-ended exploration 83
open-ended thinking 117
Opera Project 132
oracy 123
oral history 121–2, 127
originality 1, 2, 13
out of school learning 116, 121, 123
outcomes 74, 77, 78, 123, 124, 138, 143,
   144, 151, 152, 154, 156, 157, 164
outdoors 112

paint 23
paintings 122
Paperbag Prince, The 94
participation structures 57
partnerships 145
'p-creative' acts 135
pedagogic innovation 145
pedagogical choices 76
peer mentoring 57, 145
percentages 40
performing 134
person domain 72–3
personal choice 105
personal experience 102
personal expression 149
personal geographies 100, 103, 105, 107
personal knowledge 132
personal preference 68
personal reminiscences 121
personal values 89
Personal, Social and Health Education
   (PSHE) 83, 89–93, 139
   topics 93
personalised learning 110, 117
personalised responses 102
personality 2
PGCE 123
phonics test 162
photographs 122, 126

physical geography 98
Piaget, Jean 135
pianos 142
Picasso, Pablo 4
place-based geography 98
planning 11, 12, 35, 36, 38, 41, 47, 50, 52, 58, 76, 106, 118, 119, 120, 132, 154, 155, 156, 157, 158, 163, 164, 165
  creative 137
  curriculum 67
  language 28
play 84, 117, 144, 145, 146
playfulness 78, 85
pneumatics 68
poetic writing 23
poetry performances 84
political debates 118–19
popular culture 84, 130
possibility thinking 58, 85
PowerPoint 124
practice continuum 84
practising teachers 34
prejudice 89, 90
primes 36
problem-finding
  activities 144
problem-solving 36, 37, 85, 111, 116, 117
  activities 144
  group 117
  skills 67
process approach 22, 68
process domain 73
process drama 84, 85, 86, 89
  improvisational 95
process knowledge 68
processes 69, 144
product domain 73–4
professional development 155, 159
professional knowledge 103
profit margins 38
progress, monitoring 132
project work, independent 124
prompts 46
PSHE see Personal, Social and Health Education
psychological research 2
psychology

developmental 150
psychometric assessment 2
public examination 71
Puccini, Giacomo 134, 138
Pullman, Philip 9, 17–18
pupil achievement 77
pupil agency 141
pupil consultation 136
pupil development 77
pupil progress 11
puppet plays 84

QCA 135
quality of life 130
questioning 40

racism 89
ratios 40
Read, Herbert 150
reading 20–21
  processes 21
realism 151
Realistic Mathematics Education (RME) 36
reasoning 37, 38, 132
reflection 85, 89, 146, 154, 159
reflective thinking 139
reminiscences 121
research 53, 88
resources 39, 43, 45, 50, 54, 78, 84, 86, 120, 121, 125, 142, 152
response 110, 151, 153, 158
  cognitive 105
  emotional 105
  personalised 102
review 146
Rhodes, Zandra 154
Richardson, Marion 149
risks 71, 104, 107–9, 123, 145
risk-taking 13–14, 29, 53, 56, 72, 73, 74, 78, 85, 116, 120, 134, 145, 146, 154, 165
rivers 106
RME see Realistic Mathematics Education
role adoption 91
role play 83
role play areas 86–7
RSA curriculum 163

satnav 103
SCAMPER 3–4
schemes of work 104
school productions 84
science 86
    applications 61
    learners 50
Scotland 7, 8, 10, 163
SEAL *see* Social and Emotional Aspects of
    Learning
self-assessment 139
self-awareness 79
self-confidence 117
self-control 89
self-determination 144, 146
self-esteem 73, 134, 151, 154
self-expression 34, 42, 72, 150, 157
self-reflection 132
Shakespeare, William 17
shared thinking 60
singing 130
SingStar 130
situated learning experience 45
Six Thinking Hats 138
skills 35, 69, 86, 119, 157
    literacy 75
    problem-solving 67
Small, Christopher 131
Social and Emotional Aspects of Learning
    (SEAL) 89
social deprivation 52
social groups 133
social practice 132
social theory 132
software
    music 130, 134, 142
Songwriting 138, 139
songwriting 141
Soundscape 138, 139
speaking skills 122
spelling 22
spiritual development 89
spontaneity 85
St Lucia
    environment 104, 109–11
staff training 155
staff workshops 152

starter activity 60
statistics 102
stimulus 22, 23, 151
story 107, 121
story drama 84
storytelling 94, 121
    active 138–9
strategies, writing 22
structure 132
'stuckness' 44, 142
subject knowledge 112, 124
subject narrative 55
subject-based curriculum 163
summative assessment 7
sustainability 83, 94–5
Sweden 11
    Fridaskolan 11
symbolisation 132

Take One Picture programme 153
talk 11, 43, 50, 57, 58–62, 164
    exploratory 62
    tools 59
teacher in role (TIR) 84, 85, 87, 89, 90, 92,
    94, 95
teacher modelling 73
teacher–pupil relationship 158
teachers 1
    beginning 1, 163
    experienced 163
    practising 34
teaching 117
    creative 52–3
    cross-curricular 119
    instrumentalist approaches 67
    programmes 79
    style 120
    traditional 70
teamwork 75, 124
team-working 77
technology 30, 139
    design 54
    media 111
    new technologies 66
tension 87
    dramatic 86
testing 118

tests 4
textbooks 43
Theatre of the Oppressed 138
theatre trips 84
thinking 70
   aloud 60
   analytical 134
   creative 131, 157, 163
   critical 112, 122, 157
   imaginative 116
   independent 130
   lateral 91
   possibility 85
   reflective 139
   skills 2
Thinking Together project 63
   website 63
Thompson, Colin 94
thought
   imaginative 107
Times Educational Supplement 9
timetable 133, 145, 155, 156
TIR *see* teacher in role
Torrance tests 2
toys 87
trade directories 125
trade-off 110
trainee teachers 45
training
   staff 155
trial and error 145
trust 13
Turandot 134, 138

UAM *see* Using and Applying Mathematics
uncertainty 71–2, 73, 74, 89
understanding 55, 60, 62
unpredictability 12
Using and Applying Mathematics (UAM) 37

values 103, 155–6
Veronese, Paulo 154

video conferencing 122
video games 130
Viola, Bill 149
virtual media 106
visual literacy 153
vocabulary
   mathematical 41
Vygotskian principles 73

Wales 8, 10, 163
   Foundation Phase Framework 8
   National Curriculum 8
websites 46–7, 63, 109, 122
welfare geography 98
Where do I come from?
   case study 120
whole-class discussion 50
whole-class projects 38
whole-class teaching 27
Wii Music 130
Williams, John 143
work
   class-based 106
   fieldwork 106
worksheets 43
workshops
   staff 152
   writing 22, 27–8
writer in residence 153
writing 21–3, 117
   assessment 162
   conferences 22, 28
   creative 21–2
   poetic 23
   process approach 22
   processes 22
   strategies 22
   workshops 22, 27–8

Young Geographers
   case studies 104
YouTube 142